MW00569707

TOUR GUIDE
AUSTRIA

Produced by AA Publishing

Written by Adi Kraus

Original photography by Adrian Baker

Edited, designed and produced by AA Publishing.

© The Automobile Association 1995.

Maps © The Automobile Association 1995.

Distributed in the United Kingdom by AA Publishing, Norfolk House, Priestley Road, Basingstoke, Hampshire RG24 9NY.

A CIP catalogue record for this book is available from the British Library.

ISBN 0 7495 0962 7

The contents of this publication are believed correct at the time of printing. Nevertheless, the publishers cannot accept responsibility for errors or omissions, or for changes in details given in this guide or for the consequences of any reliance on the information provided by the same. Assessments of attractions and so forth are based upon the author's own experience and, therefore, descriptions given in this guide necessarily contain an element of subjective opinion which may not reflect the publishers' opinion or dictate a reader's own experiences on another occasion.

We have tried to ensure accuracy in this guide, but things do change and we would be grateful if readers would advise us of any inaccuracies they may encounter.

Published by AA Publishing (a trading name of Automobile Association Developments Limited, whose registered office is Norfolk House, Priestley Road, Basingstoke, Hampshire RG24 9NY. Registered number 1878835).

Colour separation: Daylight Colour Art Pte, Singapore

Printed and bound in Italy by Printers SRL, Trento

Front cover: *Telfes, Tirol*

Title page: *Hallstatt, Oberösterreich*

Above: *Stephansdom, Vienna*

Opposite: *Seefeld, Tirol*

CONTENTS

INTRODUCTION

This book is not only a practical guide for the independent traveller, but is also invaluable for those who would like to know more about Austria.

The book is divided into four regions, each containing between five and eight tours. The tours start and finish in major towns and cities which we consider to be the best centres for exploration. Each tour has details of the most interesting places to visit *en route*. Side panels cater for special interests and requirements and cover a range of categories – for those whose interest is in history, wildlife or walking, and those who have children. There are also panels which highlight scenic stretches of road along the route and which give details of special events, crafts and customs. These are cross-referred back to the main text.

The simple route directions are accompanied by an easy-to-use map of the tour and there are addresses of local tourist information centres in the towns *en route* as well as in most start towns.

Simple charts show how far it is from one town to the next in kilometres and miles. These can help you to decide where to take a break and stop overnight, for example. (All distances quoted are approximate.)

Before setting off it is advisable to check with the information centre at the start of the tour for recommendations on where to break your journey and for additional information on what to see and do, and when best to visit.

The lakeside town of Zell am See was visited by D H Lawrence

Traditional Austrian costume

ENTRY REGULATIONS

EU nationals need a valid passport or identity card; British visitors' passports are accepted. Nationals of Australia, Canada, the US and New Zealand need only a valid passport.

CUSTOMS REGULATIONS

Visitors can bring in cameras, video recorders and other items for their own use. Visitors over 18 years of age from EU countries may bring an unlimited amount of smoking materials and alcohol for personal consumption into Austria. Visitors resident outside Europe can bring 400 cigarettes (or 100 cigars or 500g of tobacco).

EMERGENCY TELEPHONE NUMBERS

Fire 122
Police 133
Ambulance 144
Car breakdown 120 or 123

CREDIT CARDS

Major credit cards are accepted in banks, good hotels, shops, restaurants and garages; cash dispensers only when displaying a card sign.

HEALTH

No inoculations are needed to enter Austria. Citizens of the UK should obtain form E111 from their post office for free medical treatment, but additional insurance is recommended.

CURRENCY

There are 100 *Groschen* in 1 *Schilling*. Coins are in 2, 5, 10 and 50 *Groschen*, and 1, 5, 10 and 20 *Schillings*. Notes are in 20, 50, 100, 500, 1,000 and 5,000 *Schillings*.

BANKS

Banks are open Monday to Friday 8am–12.30pm; 1.30–3.30pm Monday to Wednesday and Friday; Thursday 8am–12.30pm, 1.30–5pm.

TIME

Austria is one hour ahead of Greenwich Mean Time (GMT) in winter and two hours in summer.

POST OFFICES

Post offices are open Monday to Friday 8am–noon and 2–6pm. On Saturday many open from 8am to 10am. In larger towns main post offices open 24 hours a day, also Sundays and holidays. Letter boxes are bright yellow.

TELEPHONES

There are separate phone booths for coins and phone cards. Cards can be obtained from post offices and tobacco kiosks (*Tabak-Trafik*). International codes are: Australia 0061, Canada and USA 001, UK 0044, Ireland 00353. Cheap rates apply from 6pm–8am (from 6pm Friday through to 8am on Monday, and public holidays). Calls from hotels are expensive.

ELECTRICITY

220 volts AC on a continental 2-pin plug.

USEFUL WORDS

The following is a list of useful words and phrases.
English German
yes ja
no nein
please bitte
good morning/day guten Morgen/Tag
goodbye Auf Wiedersehen
excuse me entschuldigen Sie bitte
how are you? wie geht es Ihnen?
very well, thanks; and you? danke, gut; und Ihnen?
do you speak English? sprechen Sie Englisch?
I don't understand Ich verstehe nicht
my name is. . . Ich heisse. . .
where? wo?
when? wann?
today heute
yesterday gestern
where is. . .? wo ist. . .?
open offen
closed geschlossen
good gut
bad schlecht
big gross
small klein
expensive teuer
cheap billig
how much does it cost? wieviel kostet es?
Monday, Tuesday, Wednesday, Thursday, Friday, Saturday, Sunday Montag, Dienstag, Mittwoch, Donnerstag, Freitag, Samstag, Sonntag
1 to 10 eins, zwei, drei, vier, fünf, sechs, sieben, acht, neun, zehn

PUBLIC HOLIDAYS

1 January – New Year's Day
6 January – Epiphany
Easter Monday
1 May – Labour Day
Ascension Day
Whit Monday
Corpus Christi
15 August – Assumption Day
26 October – National Holiday
1 November – All Saints' Day
8 December – Immaculate
    Conception
25 December – Christmas
    Day
26 December – St Stephen's
    Day

EMBASSIES AND CONSULATES

Australia: Mattiellistrasse
2–4, A-1040 Wien. Tel: (01)
512 85800, outside office
hours 512 73710.
Canada: Dr Karl Lueger Ring
10, A-1010 Wien. Tel: (01) 533
3691.
Ireland: Landstrasser
Hauptstrasse 2, Hilton
Centre, A-1030 Wien. Tel: (01)
7154246.
UK: Jauresgasse 3, A-1030
Wien. Tel: (01) 713 1575–79.
Consular section: Tel: (01) 714
6117.
USA: Boltzmanngasse 16,
A-1091 Wien. Tel: (01) 31339.

TOURIST OFFICES

Australia: 3rd Floor, 36
Carrington Street, Sydney,
NSW 2000. Tel: (02) 229
3621.
UK: 30 St George Street,
London W1R 0AL. Tel: (0171)
629 0461.
US: 11601 Wilshire
Boulevard, Suite 2480, Los
Angeles, California 90025.
Tel: (310) 477 3332; 500 Fifth
Avenue, Suite 2009–2022,
New York, NY 10110. Tel:
(212) 944 6880.

For enquiries in Vienna tel:
(01) 315511.

AUSTRIAN TELEPHONE NUMBERS

At present, when dialling
Vienna from abroad use the
prefix 01. When dialling
Vienna from places in Austria
the code is 0222. All Vienna
numbers will be changed to 7
digits, some still have only 6
digits.

COUNTRY DISTINGUISHING SIGNS

On the maps, the following
international distinguishing
signs indicate the location of
countries around Austria:

(CH) = Switzerland
(CZ) = Czech Republic
(D) = Germany
(H) = Hungary
(I) = Italy
(SK) = Slovakia
(SLO) = Slovenia

MOTORING

Accidents

As a general rule you are required
to call the police when individuals
have been injured or considerable
damage has been caused. Failure
to give aid to anyone injured will
render you liable to a fine.

Documents

You must have a valid driving
licence, passport, third-party
insurance and vehicle registration
document. A green insurance card
is strongly recommended.

Car hire

Car hire is available at most
airports, railway stations and in
larger towns. Drivers must be
over 21 and have driven for at
least a year.

Breakdowns

If your car breaks down, try to
move it to the side of the road so
it does not obstruct traffic flow. A
warning triangle is obligatory and
hazard lights, if fitted, must be
used.
    The motoring club ÖAMTC
(Österreichischer Automobil-,
Motorrad- und Touring Club –
Schubertring 1–3, A-1010 Vienna
(tel: 0222 711 99-1231), operates a
24-hour breakdown service. Call
120 for *Pannenhilfe* (breakdown
service).
    On motorways a patrol can be
summoned from an emergency
telephone. A small arrow on
marker posts on the verges indi-
cates the direction of the nearest
one. When calling, ask for
Pannenhilfe.

Driving conditions

Drive on the right, pass on the left.
There are on-the-spot fines for
speeding and other offences.
    Many mountain roads require
payment of tolls (*Maut*), and some
are closed in winter or barred for
cars with trailers. Refer to the
maps.

Speed limits

On motorways 130kph (81mph);
outside built-up areas 100kph
(62mph); built-up areas 50kph
(31mph).
    Traffic regulations are strictly
enforced, particularly in relation
to speeding and the use of alcohol.

Route directions

Throughout the book the following abbreviations are used for
Austrian roads:

A – Autobahnen (motorways)
SS – Schnellstrassen
Bundesstrassen are indicated by
their number only.
Landstrassen are not numbered
on the maps.

The Brenner motorway

TIROL & VORARLBERG

High mountains form the central part of this area, often extending above the snow and ice barrier. The foothills are covered with meadows and pastures which provide a livelihood for the inhabitants – tourism also contributes to the economy. On a wider scale, large hydroelectric schemes not only supply the energy for local needs, but a substantial amount is also exported to the power-hungry industrial areas of Western Europe.

The south of the high central mountain range is influenced by the warm and mild air from the Mediterranean. Vines could not survive the harsh winters of North Tirol, but they grow quite readily on the slopes in South Tirol, which, as well as being one of the most picturesque regions of the country, also has a thriving fruit-growing industry.

Two topographically different rock formations extend over the three mountain ranges. Calcareous limestone rocks form the mountains in the north, then a line of crystalline rock, which includes the highest peaks and the bizarre shapes of the limestone-based Dolomites, extends to the northern Italian plain. Early rock formations are exceptions to the overall pattern, like the Kalkkögel, an old conglomerate of limestone rocks southwest of Innsbruck.

North Tirol has long valleys and many alpine passes are only open from May to late autumn, when the first snow sets in. The most important link between north and south, the Brennerpass, is open all year round.

When travelling from north to south Tirol remember that the currency in Südtirol is the Italian *lire* and passports are still necessary. The enormous volume of traffic between the north and south causes serious problems for the inhabitants of the Tirol and its ecology, who reap little benefit from it.

The other important link from east to west through Tirol and Vorarlberg is also open for the whole year. Here the problem with snow has been solved by blasting a tunnel through the mountain, thus preventing traffic jams.

Tourism is important to the region, supplementing the sparse income which is gleaned from the land, and it is fortunate that a natural balance has been maintained, in contrast to artificial developments.

Due to its importance as a link across the Alps between the north and southwest of Europe, history has left its mark on the region and many churches, abbeys and castles are proof of an eventful past with frequently changing fortunes of war. Arbitrarily created borders will gradually lose their significance in a united Europe.

Tour 1

This tour starts from the shores of the Bodensee (Lake Constance) and continues through the gentle hills of the Bregenzer Wald. It gradually reaches heights of 1,500m (4,920 feet) and leads through famous resorts, perhaps better known for their winter sports, up to the top of the Arlbergpass. After a quick descent into Tirol the first turning is taken and the Silvretta Hochalpenstrasse, a well laid-out road across the Alps, leads to the top of a pass, where a stunning panorama unfolds. The way down winds round bends and serpentines, through attractive pastures and villages, and ends up on a stretch along the upper Rhine valley.

Tour 2

After an attractive side trip the tour leaves the province of Vorarlberg and the way leads east into Tirol, over or under the Arlbergpass. The route then turns south into the southern part of Tirol, where the climate becomes milder. Further down the valleys, vineyards cover the foothills of the mountains. The tour continues through the Tirol and passes the Inn at St Leonhard, where a dedicated Tirolean freedom fighter was born, later to become the province's most celebrated hero. The return to the northern part of Tirol leads over a high mountain pass and a good road into the Ötztal (Ötz valley), popular with mountaineers and skiers. A left turn at the end of the valley leads back to Landeck.

Tour 3

The starting point for this tour is the well-known summer and winter resort of Seefeld. At first, the tour turns into the Leutasch valley, which lies off the main tourist routes and appeals because of its remoteness and the imposing scenery created by the Wetterstein range. The route then continues into a region naturally fenced in by mountains, including the Zugspitze, a peak which forms part of the border with Bavaria. Turning south along the River Lech you'll enter another remote Tirolean valley, the Namloser Tal ('Valley without a Name'). A pass provides a connection with the main Inn valley and a trip through the Sellrain valley avoids the main road and leads to Zirl with a short but steep ascent back to Seefeld.

Tour 4

From the capital of Tirol, a small undulating side road runs through villages, the main traffic at a distance further down the valley. After deviating into some lesser-known valleys the main Brennerpass is reached. Südtirol starts immediately after the pass; its first village, Gossensass, exudes a more southern appearance. The capital of the region, Bozen (Bolzano in Italian) has acquired a strong Italian presence due to Italian immigration after Südtirol was annexed in 1919. The

The traffic-free centre of Innsbruck is perfect for strolling around

Dolomites now come into view and the drive continues through what is one of the most scenic routes in Europe. Many passes have to be negotiated until the return route enters East Tirol and a tunnel linking up with the province of Salzburg. After a stop at the famous waterfalls, a pass leads back into Tirol and the Ziller valley, at the end of which a left turn leads back to Innsbruck.

Tour 5
The tour from Kufstein takes in the northeast of the Inn valley, then turns briefly south to the village of Alpbach. The route continues through the Tirolean lowlands and some of the well-established village resorts *en route* to Kitzbühel, past the jagged peaks of the Wilder Kaiser mountains and encircles the area bordered by the province of Salzburg and Bavaria. The last leg passes along the Bavarian border returning to Kufstein.

Tour 6
The Kaunertal is one of the Tirol's lesser-known valleys. Having passed through a series of little villages, the route soon leaves

these settlements behind. The large Gepatsch reservoir is passed and a few bends later the road terminates at the Weisssee glacier.

The drive along the Pitz valley, in contrast to its neighbouring valley, leads through many small hamlets and villages towards the end of the road at Mittelberg, the starting point for many mountaineers.

Because of its close proximity to Innsbruck, the Stubai valley has many villages that have become tourist resorts for summer and winter holidays. At the end of the valley a cableway takes visitors up into the snow region.

The Axamer Lizum is only a short distance from Innsbruck: it once hosted the Olympic Games. The rugged peaks of the Kalkkögel mountains are also near by.

The trip to the Zillertal offers a great variety of interest and this valley is perhaps the most traditionally Tirolean of all.

Hall in Tirol, 9km (5 miles) east of Innsbruck, is an old salt-mining town which played an important part in the economy of the country.

3 days – 272km (169 miles)

GREEN PASTURES & GLACIERS

Bregenz • Dornbirn • Schwarzenberg • Bezau Lech • Bielerhöhe • St Gallenkirch • Bludenz Hohenems • Bregenz

Bregenz, on the Austrian shores of the Bodensee (Lake Constance) is the capital of the westernmost province of Austria, the Vorarlberg. A cablecar takes you up the 1,063m (3,488-foot) high Pfänder mountain, from where you can watch the lake steamers plying between neighbouring Switzerland and Germany. Originally a Celtic settlement called *Brigantion*, the Romans captured it in 15BC and changed its name to *Brigantium*. The flourishing settlement was destroyed in AD200 by the Alemannians, but it later became an important lakeside trading centre. Old houses in the Oberstadt (Upper Town) are still surrounded by remnants of the former town wall. The onion-domed Martinsturm was originally part of the town fortifications around the 13th century, but it received its present shape around 1600. The tower's windows offer fine views across the roofs of the old town.

Beautiful Austrian alpine flowers

i Anton Schneider Strasse 4a

> *From Bregenz take the 190 south to Dornbirn.*

Dornbirn, Vorarlberg

1 Dornbirn, the largest town in the province, dates back to around AD500. Called *Thorinpuiron*, it was renamed Tornbüren in AD825, and when the Habsburgs took power in 1380, its name was changed to Dornbirn. After a rebellion against Napoleonic and Bavarian intruders in 1832, the foundations of the first textile factories were laid and this industry still provides the bulk of the town's income and wealth. An annual textile fair enjoys inter-national repute. The **Rotes Haus** (Red House) next to the **parish church of St Martin** was erected in 1639 by the Rhomberg family and still plays an important part in the fortunes of the area. It was restored in 1954 to its original design and the craftsmanship of this style of build-ing is remarkable.

A short stop in **Bödele**, about 10km (6 miles) from Dornbirn, is recommended. The resort area of the Bregenzer Wald starts here. Set among alpine meadows, forests and moorland lakes it offers rewarding panoramic views over neighbouring Switzerland, Bodensee (Lake Constance) and the gentle Allgäu Alps of southern Germany, as well as the Bregenzer Wald itself.

i Altes Rathaus

> *From Bödele take the secondary road east to Schwarzenberg.*

Schwarzenberg, Vorarlberg

2 The road to the village of Schwarzenberg leads through the enchanting region of the **Bregenzer Wald** (Forest of Bregenz). The painter Angelika Kauffmann was born here, and in 1780 became a founder member of the Royal

Bregenz's lower town sits comfortably on its lake shore

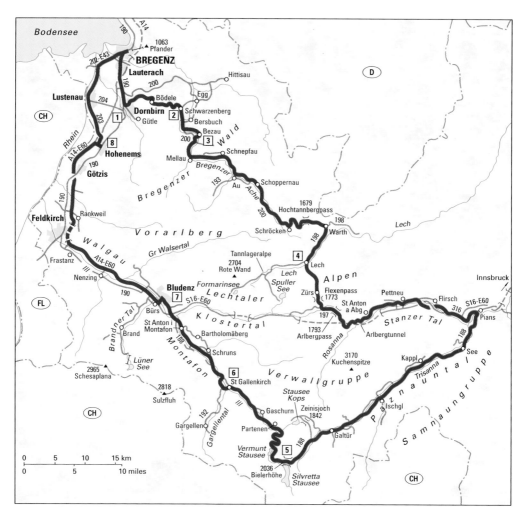

Academy in London. One of her paintings, *The Crowning of Our Lady*, adorns the high altar of the local **parish church**.

Before leaving the village a short trip north to **Egg** and **Hittisau** offers more insight into the local economy of the Bregenzer Wald. Hittisau has a **museum** dedicated to the workings of alpine dairy farming and Egg takes pride in the **parish church of St Nicholas**, recently restored to its former glory. Both resorts offer walks through delightful countryside.

[i] Verkehrsamt

From Schwarzenberg drive south to Bezau.

Bezau, Vorarlberg

3 Bezau is considered to be the main village of the Bregenzer Wald region and used to be the terminus for the Wälderbahn, a narrow-gauge railway line from Bregenz. The service was suspended in 1982 and one of its lovely old engines stands forlornly by the former station as a reminder of a bygone era. A 6km (4-mile) stretch of track still operates in summer and offers the delightful experience of travelling at a slow pace through pleasant country to nearby **Bersbuch** and **Klausberg**.

[i] Verkehrsamt

Take the 200 southeast via the Hochtannbergpass to Warth, then turn right for the 198 to Lech.

Lech, Vorarlberg

4 Probably better known as a major winter sports centre, Lech also offers an extensive summer programme. High alpine walking courses, rock climbing, tennis tournaments and hiking tours are only some of the activities featured. The **parish church of St Nicholas** was founded by settlers from the Wallis region, which now lies in Switzerland. Like many other church buildings, it was built over many centuries. The nave and spire were begun in the 14th century, the choir was added later, and the altars were only finished in 1790. Recent restoration has uncovered frescos dating back to the Romanesque period.

Before leaving Lech, a short drive of 13km (8 miles) is recommended along the Lech river, upstream to the **Tannlageralpe**. From here you can turn off either south to the larger **Stausee Spuller See** (Spuller See reservoir), or west to the **Formarinsee**, smaller and more remote. Numerous hikes can be undertaken from either lake, following mountain paths from hut to hut.

[i] Verkehrsamt

From Lech continue south on the 198 via the Flexenpass to the 197. Turn left towards the Arlbergpass, then down to St Anton am Arlberg and on to the S16/316 to Pians. A sharp right turn southwest on the 188, the Silvretta Hochalpenstrasse, leads to Bielerhöhe.

FOR HISTORY BUFFS

6 Between St Gallenkirch and Bludenz lies the town of **Schruns**. From here a steep, narrow road leads up to the village of **Bartholomäberg**, the oldest settlement in the Montafon valley. Founded in the 9th century it spreads out over a sunny hill from a height of 700–1,200m (2,300–3,950 feet) and contains many of its original old farmhouses. From the 14th to the 18th century silver and copper were mined here and relics from this activity can still be found in the parish church. The church's historic organ dates from 1792, while the sacristy contains a Romanesque/Byzantine 12th-century enamelled cross from Limoges in the south of France.

BACK TO NATURE

1 From Dornbirn a short 6km (4-mile) drive southeast leads to the village of Gütle, from where a 10-minute walk takes you to the entrance of the **Rappenlochschlucht** (gorge). A well-secured path runs through the gorge past the gushing waters of the Ache river to the **Stausee Staufensee** (Staufensee reservoir). A little further on lies the **Alplochschlucht**, another gorge with an imposing waterfall.

FOR CHILDREN

5 At the Bielerhöhe you can take the children for a boat ride on the **Silvretta Stausee** (Silvretta reservoir) which also offers exciting views over the lake and the snow-clad mountains beyond.

7 A stop at Bludenz gives the opportunity of travelling on a vintage steam train to Schruns and back. You can even enjoy a ride on the footplate.

RECOMMENDED WALKS

6 Branch off from St Gallenkirch into the Gargellental and the village at the end of the road. The absence of through traffic in **Gargellen** makes it an ideal centre for walking and hiking tours.

Bielerhöhe, Vorarlberg

5 An interesting detour is possible just after leaving the main road from Galtür. A steep mountain road turns off to your right via Kleinzeinis to the 1,842m (6,043-foot) high **Zeinisjoch** and the **Stausee Kaps** (Kaps reservoir). Near the Zeinisjochhaus, the road does a U-turn and then descends to a path parallel to the upward route. This round trip offers magnificent scenery on the way. The main Silvretta road is rejoined a short stretch further up from the point where it was left.

The 2,036m (6,679-foot) high pass on the Bielerhöhe not only forms the border between the provinces of Tirol and Vorarlberg, but also divides the flow of the rivers which originate there. The Trisanna on the Tirolean side joins the Inn and later the Donau (Danube), which flows to the Black Sea. The Ill, however, flows northwestwards to the Rhein (Rhine), which heads into the North Sea. The Bielerhöhe offers fine views over the large **Silvretta Stausee** (Silvretta reservoir) and the 3,000m (9,800-foot) high snow-clad mountains behind.

i Restaurant Silvrettasee, Bielerhöhe

Continue northwest on the 188 to St Gallenkirch.

St Gallenkirch, Vorarlberg

6 Descending via many twists and turns, a final straight drive leads to the village of St Gallenkirch, with its remarkable late-Gothic **parish church**. It was originally built in the late 15th century, but was reconstructed in 1669, and still maintains its early stone arches in the nave. The painted ceiling depicts motifs from the Old Testament, added in 1775. The main attention, however, is focused on the richly decorated altars in rococo style, a rare feature in this area.

i Verkehrsamt

Continue on the 188 northwest via Schruns to Bludenz.

Bludenz, Vorarlberg

7 Bludenz lies at the crossroads of five valleys, the Montafon, Brandner, Kloster, Walser and Wallgau. Bronze Age finds indicate there was an early settlement here. In AD830 the name *Villa Pludeno* appears for the first time, and in 940 King Otto I donated a church to Bishop Waldo. In 1228 Bludenz belonged to the Counts of Montfort, and Count Rudolph, first of the line, built a castle. When the Montfort dynasty came to an end, the last count, Albrecht III, abolished serfdom and in 1394 sold the castle to the Habsburgs. Three fires in 1491, 1638 and 1682 devastated the town and only the **church** and the **castle** were saved owing to their elevated positions. An interesting engraving from 1643 shows that Bludenz was once surrounded by a wall. Two of its former gates, the lower or **Mühletor**, and the upper or **Feldkirchertor**, together with the **Pulverturm** (Gunpowder Tower) still stand. The Feldkirchertor now houses the local **museum**.

The **Altstadt** (Old Town), with its picturesque arcades and narrow streets, invites relaxing strolls. The steeple of **St Laurentius'** parish church dates back to 1514.

A 12km (7½-mile) drive south, via Bürs, leads to the village of **Brand,** one of the area's favourite mountain resorts. A further 6km (4 miles) on lies the lower terminus of the Lüner See cableway, which takes you up to the **Douglasshütte** (1,979m/ 6,408 feet). Here you can enjoy the magnificent scenery on a 1½-hour walk around the lake or, if you are feeling energetic, you can try a climb up the 2,965m (9,728-foot) high **Schesaplana mountain**, which forms part of the border with Switzerland. The climb takes about 3½ hours.

Back in Bludenz, don't miss a trip on the **Muttersberg cableway**, which reaches the top in five minutes and offers very rewarding views over the town and surrounding countryside.

i Verkehrsamt der Stadt Bludenz, Werdenbergerstrasse 42

From Bludenz take the A14 northwest to the exit Hohenems.

Hohenems, Vorarlberg

8 The town of Hohenems derives its name from the Ems family, who held high office at the Imperial Court in the late 12th century. Papal

connections were established when Wolf Dietrich von Ems married the sister of Pope Pius IV, both members of the influential Medici family. The ruins above **Schloss Hohenems** date back to 1170, when an imperial decree ordered the conversion of Alt-Ems into a fortress. The present Schloss Hohenems is a rectangular Renaissance building designed by Martino Longo of Milan and built between 1562 and 1567. In 1755 and 1779 two handwritten manuscripts of the *Nibelungen* saga were discoverd here and later formed the basis of Wagner's *Ring Cycle* operas. Near by, the **parish church of St Karl Borromäus** contains an interesting altarpiece from Flanders, ordered by Hannibal von Ems in 1575. An **open-air museum** demonstrates the workings of an ancient saw mill.

ⓘ Verkehrsamt

From Hohenems take the 203 north, via Lustenau, back to Bregenz.

Bregenz – Dornbirn 12 (7½)
Dornbirn – Schwarzenberg 14 (8½)
Schwarzenberg – Bezau 7 (4½)
Bezau – Lech 43 (27)
Lech – Bielerhöhe 89 (55)
Bielerhöhe – St Gallenkirch 25 (15½)
St Gallenkirch – Bludenz 20 (12½)
Bludenz – Hohenems 40 (25)
Hohenems – Bregenz 22 (13½)

Above: the resort town of Lech is well provided with sports facilities of all kinds, including angling

---

Below: sunset over Bregenz

6 days – 457km (283 miles)

OVER THE ARLBERGPASS TO TIROL

**Feldkirch • Rankweil • Damüls • Ludesch
Arlbergpass • St Anton am Arlberg • Landeck
Ladis • Serfaus • Nauders • Reschenpass
Mals • Schlanders • Unserfrau in Schnals
Karthaus • Meran • Schloss Tirol • St Leonhard
im Passeiertal • Obergurgl • Sölden • Oetz
Feldkirch**

Feldkirch, on the Swiss/Austrian border, is dominated by the mighty Schattenburg castle which rises above the town. The Counts of Montfort ruled here in the 13th and 14th centuries. The former living quarters in the tower have walls 4m (13-feet) deep. These rooms now house the Heimatmuseum (Town Museum) and display collections of Gothic furniture, an armoury and old coins. Of the town's old fortifications, three gates still stand; the Cat's Tower acquired its name from the lion heads which decorate its cannon – it also contains a bell weighing 7.5 tonnes. The Marktplatz is surrounded by houses with ground-level arcades. Of note is the Wellsperghaus, with its Gothic oriel and high roof.

[i] Verkehrsverein Feldkirch, Herrengasse 12

From Feldkirch take the local road northeast to Rankweil.

Schattenburg castle, set above the town of Feldkirch

Rankweil, Vorarlberg

1 A pilgrims' church stands on top of the Burgberg, in the grounds of a former castle, surrounded by a wooden rampart which offers extensive views right across the Rhine valley to the Alps. Notable inside the church are the intricate wood-carvings of the Rankweiler Madonna (Our Lady of Rankweil) and a Romanesque crucifix of 1233, which was covered in 1728 by a layer of silver for protection.

[i] Verkehrsverein

Continue east through the Laternser Tal, over the Furkajoch, to Damüls.

Damüls, Vorarlberg

2 Damüls lies within a sunny alpine pasture nearly 1,500m (4,920 feet) above sea level. A small church with an onion-shaped steeple can be seen from a distance – the interior displays late-Gothic frescos. Also notable is a woodcarving of St Theodul, and the carved wood and stone altars. The wooden ceiling was added and painted in the 17th century, in local style.

A chairlift takes you up to the Ilga-Alpe, 1,810m (5,938 feet). The energetic will be rewarded after an hour's walk to the top of the Mittagspitze by fine views.

[i] Verkehrsamt

From Damüls, take the 193 south to Ludesch.

Ludesch, Vorarlberg

3 The village of Ludesch, together with Thüringen on the opposite side of the Lutz river, forms the entrance or exit of the Grosses Walsertal, one of the five valleys leading to Bludenz. The parish church is dedicated to St Sebastian, and was erected as a thanksgiving for the ending of the plague in 1637. The old parish church of St Martin stands higher up and dates back to the 12th century.

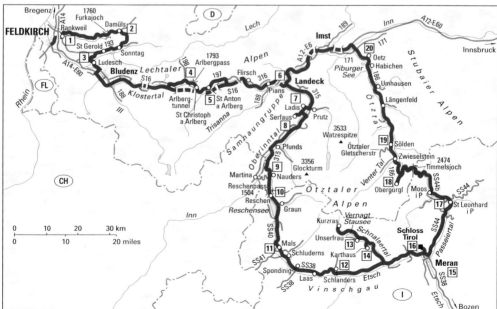

The inner courtyard of Feldkirch's Schattenburg castle, now a pretty setting for the restaurant

ⓘ Verkehrsamt

Continue south to join the A14 at Bludenz. Drive east to Langen, then either take the tunnel road 14km (9 miles) or drive over the Arlbergpass to St Anton.

Arlbergpass, Vorarlberg/Tirol

4 The weather will probably determine whether you drive over the pass or through the tunnel. Unless you are in a hurry or it rains, the drive over the pass should not be missed for the thrill it provides – first through pastures and then past impressive rock formations.

ⓘ St Christoph am Arlberg, Tirol

From the top of the pass descend via St Christoph to St Anton.

St Anton am Arlberg, Tirol

5 St Anton is one of the most famous winter sports centres in the world. This is, of course, less obvious in summer, but even a short stop in one of the hotels will confirm the high standard of this resort. St Anton lies in the foothills of the surrounding mountains – don't leave before experiencing the excitement of going up the **Galzig mountain** by cablecar, then further to the **Valluga peak**, 2,809m (9,216 feet). The views over the snow-clad mountains are magnificent.

ⓘ Verkehrsamt, Postfach 40

Drive east on the S16/316 to Landeck.

Landeck, Tirol

6 The first view you will probably have of Landeck is the massive castle keep, which stands high up on a crag. Built in 1200 and extended in the 15th century, most of the original castle was destroyed by a fire 300 years later. Partially restored in 1949, it now houses the **Heimatmuseum** (Town Museum), which exhibits Tirolean art treasures. It is open in summer only, but from the tower there are fine views over the town and the Inn valley. The **parish church** is dedicated to the Assumption of Our Lady, and it is one of the rare Gothic church buildings in northern Tirol. The winged altar is called the Schrofensteinaltar, and is dated 1520.

Two kilometres north of Landeck lies **Stanz** and the imposing ruins of the **Burg Schrofenstein**, which dates back to the 12th century. A short distance west of Landeck is the village of **Pians**. Of special interest is the 14th-century **chapel of St Margaretha**. Beautiful Gothic frescos provide a feeling of intimacy.

ⓘ Fremdenverkehrsverband Landeck und Umgebung, Malser Strasse 10, Landeck

From Landeck continue on the 315 for 13km (8 miles) to Prutz, then over the bridge to Ladis.

Ladis, Tirol

7 About 7km (4½ miles) out of Landeck, on the road to **Prutz**, stands the Pontlatzer bridge, which

SCENIC ROUTES

1 The stretch from Rankweil through the picturesque **Laternser Tal** and up to **Furkajoch** leads through very attractive countryside.

10 The drive from Reschen along the large reservoir winds partly through beautiful larch forests and the views over the lake towards the mountains are rewarding.

bears a plaque in memory of Tirolean victories over invaders in 1703 and 1809. Before reaching the village of Prutz, look out for the ruin of the **castle of Laudegg**, on a crag on the opposite side of the Inn river. It commands a splendid position overlooking the valley below, an important defence consideration in the Middle Ages. A chairlift provides an alternative link to the road to **Obladis**, a health resort with sulphur springs.

i Verkehrsamt

From Ladis drive via Fiss to Serfaus.

Serfaus, Tirol

8 Serfaus is well known as a winter sports resort and claims to have an extra helping of sunshine per year (an average of 2,016 hours), a claim apparently backed up by meteorological data. A legend dates the pilgrims' church back to AD804. Old frescos were uncovered during restoration work in 1962, but its main treasure is a small 12th-century picture of *Our Lady on a Throne*. A subterranean rail link leads to the terminus of the **Komperdellalm cableway**, which claims a record speed by taking only seven minutes to travel 2.6km (1.6 miles) to the 1,976m (6,483-foot) high top.

i Verkehrsamt

From Serfaus return via Fiss to Ried, then turn right on the 315 to Nauders.

Nauders, Tirol

9 Emperor Maximilian I ordered **Schloss Naudersberg** to be fortified: it used to be a checkpoint for cross-Alpine traffic. The castle stands on a hill and offers a wide view over the area. Originally built in 1330, the 15th and 16th centuries saw additions including an enclosed compound, the Zwinger, towers and the castle's ceiling arches. It now houses a worthwhile **museum**. The Romanesque **chapel of St Leonhard** has late Gothic frescos, revealed during restoration in 1951.

i Verkehrsamt

Continue south for 6km (4 miles) to the Reschenpass.

Reschenpass, Reschen, Provinz Bozen

10 The Reschenpass (1,504m/4,934 feet) leads into the province of Südtirol, and also constitutes the watershed between rivers flowing north and south. Even in the Bronze Age the pass was used as a crossing point over the Alps, and the Romans later built a connection to the *Via Claudia Augusta*, which led to Augsburg in Germany. In 1950 a large reservoir was opened, and two villages, Graun and Reschen, were drowned. They were rebuilt on the shores of the new lake, but the church steeple of the former **parish church of Graun** still rises defiantly from the water. In clear weather you can see the highest mountain in South Tirol, the **Ortler**, at 3,905m (12,812 feet) above sea level.

i Verkehrsamt, Reschen

SPECIAL TO...

18 Between Obergurgl and Sölden lies **Zwieselstein**, from where you can enter the **Venter Tal** (valley). From here an easy climb leads up to the **Similaunhütte (Similaun hut)**. This is near the location where, in the autumn of 1991, the 4,000-year-old body of a man was discovered. It was taken to Innsbruck University and is now being studied together with other relics found on the same spot. The find is now referred to as the 'Ötzi', the man from the Ötz valley.

15 Meran's town museum possesses a model of the first typewriter by Peter Mitterhofer, from the village of **Partschins**, west of Meran. A joiner by profession, he made his invention in 1864 out of wood and created a real masterpiece. Two years later he walked all the way to Vienna to have his work recognised.

Serfaus, a winter resort, stands on a plateau above the Inn valley below the Silvretta mountains

Continue for 22km (14 miles) on the SS40 to Mals.

Mals, Südtirol

11 Mals has its origins as a stopping place on the Roman *Via Augusta*. The village now prides itself on a skyline of five towers, three of which are Romanesque, another crowns the Gothic **parish church** and the fifth – 33m (108 feet) – is part of the 12th-century **Fröhlichsburg**, in the centre of the village. The former **church of St Benedikt** houses 9th-century frescos, considered to be the oldest in the German-speaking culture. Mals is now a popular tourist spot in winter and summer.

i Fremdenverkehrsverband

From Mals drive southeast on the SS40 to Spondinig and continue east to Schlanders on the SS38.

Schlanders, Südtirol

12 Schlanders lies at the beginning of the Schlandraun Tal (valley) and is considered to be the economic and cultural centre of the Vintschgau valley. The 90m (295-foot) spire of the **parish church** comes into view some distance away – supposed to be the highest church tower in South Tirol, it dates from 1505, although documentary evidence dates the church to 1170. The **Schlandersburg** is considered to be one of the finest examples of

Renaissance architecture in the area and notable is the Loggienhof inside the castle, with arcades on each floor.

ⓘ Verkehrsverband, Kirchplatz

Continue east on the SS38 and turn left into Schnalsertal, just before Kompatsch.

Unserfrau in Schnals, Südtirol

13 Unserfrau is a delightful little village and old pilgrim's centre. Records of church activities here are noted since the 14th century. The church commands an imposing position on a rocky hill and the original building of 1307 was rebuilt in 1750. A carving dated 1300 and dedicated to Our Lady graces the church and also gave the village its name.

The adjoining area is typical of the South Tirol: steep slopes covered in luscious vegetation descending into deep river valleys, and old farmhouses mainly constructed of wood. The road through the Schnalsertal (Schnals valley) continues in a climb past the large **Stausee Vernagt** (reservoir), and a last steep gradient to Kurzras. A cableway leads up to 3,251m (10,666 feet), high enough for summer skiing.

ⓘ Verkehrsverein, Unserfrau in Schnals

From Kurzras drive back to Unserfrau and on to Karthaus.

Karthaus, Südtirol

14 The history of Karthaus is closely connected with the **monastery** of **Allerengelberg**, secularised in 1782 by order of Emperor Josef II. Originally a timber construction, records from the peasant uprising in 1525 mention the 'ravaging of a stone building'. The cloistered monks were unpopular with the villagers, and after the dissolution ordered by the Emperor, the buildings were sold to locals. The monks' cells within the walls of the monastery have, over the years, become large farmhouses and the only remaining buildings from the monastery are the priory, the kitchen and remnants of the cloister. The latter still reveals grilles in the walls, through which the monks were handed food and drink, thus preventing any contact with the outside world.

ⓘ Verkehrsverein

From Karthaus, turn southeast to the main SS38 at Kompatsch, and then east to Meran.

Meran, Südtirol

15 The southern slopes at the confluence of the Etsch and Passeier rivers were settled in prehistoric times, long before the Romans erected a military station here, the *Castrum Maiense*. The growing importance of the Counts of Tirol made Meran the capital of Tirol, which in the 14th century extended over a greater area than today. The administration of Tirol was moved to Innsbruck in 1420, after which the importance of Meran declined. There are records which show that the **Lauben** (arcades) in the old town were used as cowsheds in 1702, having previ-

FOR HISTORY BUFFS

2 Between Damüls and Ludesch, in the Grosses Walsertal, the road passes through the small village of **St Gerold**. Here the hermit Gerold settled in 941. A dispute with the German rulers broke out and poor Gerold was charged with treason and had to flee into the forests. On the intervention of the Abbot of Einsiedeln, he was pardoned. Later the abbey of Einsiedeln erected a small monastery on his burial site to protect future settlers.

2 A simple herdsman named Heinrich Findelkind founded a hospice in **St Christoph** on the Arlberg, east of the top of the pass. He intended to save travellers who lost their way or had an accident. In his first year of operation he saved seven lives. A Christian fraternity developed from his modest beginnings and today there are still 3,000 members.

ously been a playground of the ruling aristrocracy. A sudden change in the fortunes of the town came by chance in 1836, when the personal physician of the Princess of Schwarzenberg praised the healing powers of the climate and grapes of Meran. Only two years later Emperor Ferdinand I came with his entourage to Meran and many European kings followed his example – since then the town has never been short of visitors. There are many remarkable buildings in Meran, including remnants of the old **city wall**, and it's worth a walk to enjoy them. The **castle** was built in 1470 to provide accommodation for visiting dukes, and is well preserved in its original Gothic design. Wooden floorboards and arches over the doors take you back to the Middle Ages. Closed on Sundays and holidays, it has an interesting exhibition of historic furniture and a collection of musical instruments. The **Städtische Museum**, at Gallileistrasse 43, also closed on Sundays and holidays, exhibits objects from prehistoric times, along with Gothic sculptures.

i Kurverwaltung, Freiheitsstrasse 45

From Meran continue north to Dorf Tirol.

Schloss Tirol, Meran, Südtirol

16 Suitably positioned on a rocky hill stands an impressive **castle**, the former seat of the Counts of Tirol. Significantly, one of the first Tirolean eagles can be seen at the entrance door to the great hall, and it is not surprising that this castle became a symbol for the whole of Tirol and now houses a **museum** of Tirolean history and art. Built between 1140 and 1160 and besieged by the King of Bohemia in 1347, the castle started to decay when, the Counts of Tirol moved their residence to Meran in the 16th century, partly because of the unstable foundations. Restoration work at the end of the last century altered the original designs substantially and only the portals of the *palas* (living quarters) and the castle's chapel still remain from the old Romanesque buildings.

i Verkehrsamt, Dorf Tirol

From Dorf Tirol return east to the SS44, then north to St Leonhard.

St Leonhard im Passeiertal, Südtirol

17 St Leonhard is known to all Austrians as the birthplace of Andreas Hofer, the hero who fought – and lost – against the superior forces of Napoleon and his Bavarian allies. The son of an innkeeper, Hofer rallied the Tirolese to defend their country against the invaders. He enjoyed initial successes against the Bavarian and French forces near Innsbruck, but on 14 August 1809, the defeated Austrian Emperor was forced to sign a peace treaty with Napoleon. Hofer was now alone and went into hiding. When a ransom was offered he was betrayed, and shot on 20 February 1810 at Mantua

The internationally renowned resort of Sölden offers skiing in summer as well as winter

in Italy. The **Sandwirt Inn** in St Leonhard houses a small **museum** dedicated to its famous son.

ⓘ Verkehrsverband

From St Leonhard turn left on the SS44b to Timmelsjoch and down to Obergurgl.

Obergurgl, Tirol

18 The fine view over the mountains from the Timmelsjoch warrants a stop here. A good road then leads down to Obergurgl, one of the highest Austrian winter sports resorts and also a centre for mountain hikes. The glacier near Obergurgl became famous when Professor Auguste Piccard landed here in his balloon on 27 May 1931. It had taken him up to a height of 15,781m (51,772 feet), making him the first human to reach the stratosphere.

ⓘ Fremdenverkehrsverband

From Obergurgl drive down to Zwieselstein and Sölden.

Sölden, Tirol

19 Sölden is the main centre for mountaineering and winter sports in the upper Ötztal (Ötz valley). A road tunnel links two glaciers, the **Rettenbach** and **Tiefenbachferners**, where skiers can enjoy their sport even in summer, with further assistance provided by ski-lifts. The Ötz valley is one of the longest in Tirol, a total of 48km (30 miles) from Obergurgl to the main Inn valley. Enough time should be allowed for the drive downwards, as many bends and oncoming traffic, especially on narrow stretches, can cause delays.

ⓘ Fremdenverkehrsverband Innerötzal

Take the 186 to Oetz.

Oetz, Tirol

20 The village of Oetz was known in the 12th century and some of its houses are beautifully decorated

Oetz, with its beautiful backdrop

with frescos dating from the 16th century. The **parish church** enjoys a picturesque setting on top of a crag and the spot also affords visitors fine panoramic views over the Inn valley.

The **Piburger See**, a lake fairly warm by mountain lake standards, lies about 3km (2 miles) west of Oetz. A short distance south lies the village of **Habichen**, which has an old bell foundry dating back to 1632. A chairlift is also available to take you up into the 2,000m (6,562-foot) high pastures on the slopes of the **Acherkogel mountain.** Between Habichen and Oetz the main river, the Ötztaler Ache, pushes its way through a gorge – a spectacle worth seeing.

ⓘ Fremdenverkehrsverband Oetz, Postfach 2

From Oetz continue on the 186 north to the Ötztal entrance to the A12 and drive west to the Zams exit and Landeck. From here you can return to Feldkirch.

Feldkirch – Rankweil 6 (4)
Rankweil – Damüls 27 (17)
Damüls – Ludesch 24 (15)
Ludesch – Arlbergpass 36 (22)
Arlbergpass – St Anton am Arlberg 7 (4½)
St Anton am Arlberg – Landeck 29 (18)
Landeck – Ladis 14 (8½)
Ladis – Serfaus 6 (4)
Serfaus – Nauders 37 (23)
Nauders – Reschenpass 6 (4)
Reschenpass – Mals 22 (13½)
Mals – Schlanders 23 (14)
Schlanders – Unserfrau in Schnals 31 (19)
Unserfrau in Schnals – Karthaus 23 (14)
Karthaus – Meran 24 (15)
Meran – Schloss Tirol 5 (3)
Schloss Tirol – St Leonhard im Passeiertal 20 (12½)
St Leonhard im Passeiertal – Obergurgl 42 (26)
Obergurgl – Sölden 13 (8)
Sölden – Oetz 31 (19)
Oetz – Landeck 31 (19)

RECOMMENDED WALKS

15 When in Meran, take a relaxing stroll along the Kurpromenade. Going upriver you reach the Steinerner Steg, a 16th-century bridge across the Passeier river. The choice is now whether to continue along the Gilfpromenade to the Gilfklamm, where the water rushes through a narrow stretch of the river bed, or turn towards the slopes of the Küchelberg, where the Tappeinerweg, flanked by luscious southerly vegetation, leads to the terminus of the Küchelberg chairlift. The latter promenade was named after a physician from Meran, called Tappeiner.

2/3 days – 252km (156 miles)

THE OUTER REGION OF TIROL

Seefeld in Tirol • Leutasch • Nassereith
Ehrwald • Reutte • Imst • Zirl • Seefeld

Seefeld is 1,200m (3,937 feet) above sea level. There is evidence of human settlement in prehistoric times, but the area became important when the Romans built a military road here to cross the Alps to connect with their outposts further north. Later, in the Middle Ages, the town gained importance again as a trading route. It became the centre for pilgrimages to the parish church of St Oswald and many legends are connected with Seefeld and the saint. The church is notable for its well-preserved Gothic portal, adorned by a delicate stone relief. Inside, the beautifully decorated Gothic font is worth seeing. Seefeld is also a well-known winter sports centre and hosted several events during the Olympic games of 1964 and 1976.

The chapel of Seekirchl at Seefeld stands at the start of a valley which climbs above the Inn

ⓘ Fremdenverkehrsverband, Rathausplatz

From Seefeld take the 177 north to Scharnitz. Continue on the same road, now the 2, for 3km (2 miles) and then take a left fork before Mittenwald. Follow the signpost for Leutasch with a sharp left turn back to Austria on the L14.

Leutasch, Tirol

1 When you have passed through the narrow valley at the border, the landscape suddenly widens into the Leutaschtal (Leutasch valley), which is flanked by the imposing limestone mountains of the Wetterstein-gebirge (Wetterstein range) on one side, with the 2,196m (7,205-foot) high Arnspitze on the other. Although there is a village of Leutasch, divided into Unter and Oberleutasch, the whole valley really belongs to one community. It consists of about 20 little hamlets spread around the valley for 16km (10 miles). The great advantage for the visitor lies in the valley's position off the main tourist routes. That, and the scenic beauty of its surroundings, makes it an ideal place to relax in, well away from it all.

At **Moos**, about 4km (2½ miles) south of Leutasch, is a chairlift up to the Rauthhütte, a mountain hut, starting point for many excellent walks. A favourite walk is the one to the top of the **Hohe Munde**, which takes about 3½ hours, with the reward of breathtaking views.

ⓘ Fremdenverkehrsverband, Leutasch

From Leutasch drive on the L35 south to Bairbach and then turn sharp right to Telfs and the 189 west to Nassereith.

The sparsely populated valley of Leutasch, flanked on one side by the Wetterstein range

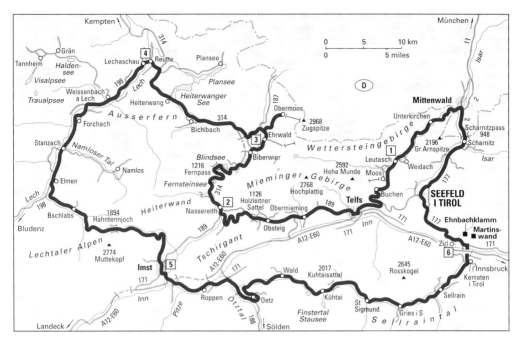

Nassereith, Tirol

2 Nassereith is a small, sleepy village, but an important staging point on the way to the Ausserfern region from the capital, Innsbruck. The village is known for its annual event, the *Schellenlaufen*, which takes place at the end of the carnival season, just before Easter. Villagers parade the streets wearing masks and ornate costumes and the noise created by small bells is supposed to drive out the winter. The **Heimatmuseum** (Local Museum) has a display on this ancient Ash Wednesday custom, and exhibits the masks worn by the participants. Five kilometres (3 miles) up the road to the Fernpass lies a small alpine lake, the **Fernsteinsee**. By hiring a rowing boat you can visit the ruin of the former hunting lodge of **Sigmundsburg**, which was erected on the island in about 1460. The crystal clear waters of the lake will tempt many to spend a little time here and anglers might also like to try their luck.

i Fremdenverkehrsamt

From Nassereith take the 314 over the Fernpass and turn off to Ehrwald.

Ehrwald, Tirol

3 Crossing the Fernpass over a well-made road you reach the village of Ehrwald, passing through Biberwier. Ehrwald offers a true alpine panorama, dominated by the 2,968m (9,738-foot) high, impressive **Zugspitze mountain**, which also forms the border between Tirol and Bavaria. It is no coincidence that both countries have developed excellent facilities to get to the top. The **Tiroler Zugspitzbahn** starts 5km (3 miles) north of Ehrwald in the village of **Obermoos**. The construction of the Tirolese cableway is hailed as one of the most impressive in the Alps. The original plans were realised between 1924 and 1926. Large cabins can ferry 100 people and the journey takes only seven minutes. From the top, it is possible to get to the German side

and the peak of the Zugspitze, but the ride up from Obermoos alone provides an abundance of magnificent views, which are quite unforgettable.

i Fremdenverkehrsverband Ehrwald-Zugspitze, Kirchplatz 1

From Ehrwald take the 314 via Bichlbach to Reutte.

Reutte, Tirol

4 The town of Reutte is noted for its tastefully painted houses, a feat accredited to members of the local Zeiller family, fresco artists who lived here in the 17th and 18th centuries.

Outside the town stand the ruins of **Schloss Ehrenburg**, which withstood 30 years of religious wars but was abandoned to decay in 1800. The floodlit ruins create an impressive picture at night. The small **Urisee** and **Frauensee** lakes offer bathing facilities near the centre, but a short trip to the nearby **Plansee** is strongly recommended. The Plansee lies sheltered from any through traffic about 6km (3½ miles) east of Reutte and its position is a delight for every nature lover. The road runs on only one side of the lake; on the other steep mountains descend sharply to the lake and do not allow room for a road. There are also very few buildings, but there are plenty of stopping places to enjoy this beautiful part of unspoilt nature.

i Fremdenverkehrsverband, Untermarkt 34

From Reutte continue on the 198 southwest to Weissenbach am Lech, Stanzach and Elmen and then take a left turn over the Hahntenjoch Pass to Imst.

Imst, Tirol

5 When leaving Reutte two detours are suggested before the final stage to Imst. The first starts at **Weissenbach** and takes a right turn to **Grän**. No one will fail to admire the beauty of the **Haldensee**, just

SCENIC ROUTES

1 The drive through the Leutasch valley is scenic and highly enjoyable. The mountains on either side of the valley provide a very impressive background.

FOR CHILDREN

1 Children will enjoy rides on the **Sommerrodelbahn**, a summer toboggan run near Weidach, close to Leutasch.

BACK TO NATURE

3 When in Ehrwald take a stroll through the surrounding larch forests which are inhabited by red squirrels. They are quite used to visitors and readily accept a few hazelnuts.

RECOMMENDED WALKS

3 A cableway 4km (2½ miles) southeast from Ehrwald provides easy access to the **Ehrwalder Alm**, an alpine pasture and a good starting point for many hikes in the area.

Standing at 854m (2,802 feet), Reutte appeals to both winter skiers and summer hikers

SPECIAL TO…

The **Seekirchl**, the circular chapel near Seefeld, is the town's landmark. It was originally built on an island in a man-made lake, the Kreuzsee. The chapel is of a design quite unusual for Tirol and was completed in 1666. The surrounding lake was later drained in 1807. The chapel presents a delightful picture, especially in winter when decorated with snow.

HISTORY BUFFS

The drive from Seefeld to Scharnitz leads close to the former *Porta Claudia*, a Roman control point guarding the pass. Later, in the Napoleonic wars, an English colonel was appointed to command a garrison there and successfully repelled the French invaders under Marshal Ney. A small pathway leads from the village to the scene where it all happened.

south of Grän. The water of the lake reaches a temperature of 22°C, a little on the chilly side for some, but rowing boats are available to enjoy the surrounding countryside. From the village of **Tannheim**, (3km/ 2 miles) from Grän, it is a 5km (3-mile) drive south to the remote **Visalpsee**, another picturesque alpine lake. The area around here is a protected nature reserve and a walk around the lake takes about an hour. Even more remote is the **Traualpsee**, further south, which can only be reached on foot. Tannheim itself has an interesting **parish church**, designed by a local builder, Andreas Hofenegger in 1725, with ceiling frescos by Johann Keller, painted in 1800. On returning to Weissenbach the next turn-off point is at **Stanzach**, 10km (6 miles) south. From here a left turn leads into the **Namloser Tal** and the hamlet of **Namlos**, which means 'without name'.

Imst is situated on a slope and divided into an upper and lower part of town. Historically it is an old town, deriving its name from the Latin *oppidum humiste*, known in AD763. Although it received its market town charter in 1282, Imst had to wait another 600 years to get town status. Few other Tirolean towns have as many well-kept old burghers' houses as can be seen in the upper part of Imst. The local **museum** exhibits masks worn by the participants of the yearly *Schemenlauf*, a similar event to the *Schellenlauf* in Nassereith – both spectacles have the same object of symbolically driving out winter. The

museum also exhibits works of local art and handicrafts.

i Fremdenverkehrsverband

From Imst take the 171 east to Ötztal, the 186 to Oetz, then drive on the L13 through Nedertal and Sellraintal to Kematen in Tirol, and cross the Inn river to Zirl.

Zirl, Tirol

6 Zirl lies in the foothills of the Zirler Berg and its function as a control point for traffic northwards was recognised by the Romans. The later history of Zirl is intertwined with Emperor Maximilian I, who established his favourite residence in Innsbruck and used to hunt here.

The mighty **Martinswand** is the subject of a legend – according to which the Emperor once lost his way among the rocks during a hunting trip, but was rescued by a miracle. The spot, a grotto, is marked by a bust of the Emperor and can be visited from Zirl in an hour's walk. North of Zirl another narrow path leads to the **Ehnbachklamm**, a romantic gorge with a wild stream thundering down between the rocks. At **Martinsbühel**, 2km (1 mile) east of Zirl, stand the remains of Maximilian's hunting lodge.

i Fremdenverkehrsverband

From Zirl take the 177 north over the Zirler Berg with a steep gradient of 1 in 6 back to Seefeld.

Seefeld in Tirol – Leutasch 28 (17½)
Leutasch – Nassereith 40 (25)
Nassereith– Ehrwald 21 (13)
Ehrwald – Reutte 34 (21)
Reutte – Imst 52 (32)
Imst – Zirl 65 (40)
Zirl – Seefeld in Tirol 12 (7½)

Innsbruck's main street, Maria-Theresien Strasse

ⓘ Fremdenverkehrsverband Innsbruck-Igls, Burggraben 3

Leave Innsbruck and head south under the motorway to Igls.

Igls, Tirol

1 Igls lies only 6km (4 miles) from Innsbruck on an elevated plateau and is probably best known for its winter sports facilities. Its altitude (900m/2,950 feet above sea level) affords visitors an invigorating climate and welcome retreat from busy Innsbruck, where it can sometimes get very hot in summer.

ⓘ Fremdenverkehrsverband

From Igls continue on a small, narrow road via Patsch, St Peter and Pfons to Matrei.

Matrei am Brenner, Tirol

2 Matrei played a part in Celtic and Roman history, when crossing the Alps at the Brennerpass was considered to be the safest and most reliable way. The Romans called it *Matreium* and today it looks like a small medieval village, enhanced by the beautifully painted house façades. A 1916 fire and air bombardments in 1945 caused severe damage, but most of it has been restored. Look out for the partially rebuilt 13th-century **castle** and the 14th-century **parish church**.

ⓘ Fremdenverkehrsverband, Reuterplatz 3

From Matrei continue south to Steinach.

Steinach am Brenner, Tirol

3 Steinach's interesting parish church is dedicated to St Erasmus. The sumptuously decorated high altar is considered to be among the finest baroque-style choir

View over Innsbruck from the 15th-century Stadtturm

NORTH, SOUTH & EAST TIROL

Innsbruck • Igls • Matrei am Brenner • Steinach am Brenner • Gries am Brenner • Brennerpass Gossensass • Sterzing • Sarnthein • Bozen Völs • Seis • Brixen • Wolkenstein • Bruneck Kals am Grossglockner • Matrei Felbertauerntunnel • Mittersill • Krimml Innsbruck

Innsbruck has a magnificent setting enclosed by the Alps and is one of the most important junctions in Austria from north to south and east to west. The capital of Tirol since 1363, its name means 'bridge over the Inn'. The Herzog Friedrichstrasse leads through the very centre of town, whose focal point is the famous Goldenes Dachl (golden roof). Beautifully kept houses with colourful façades line the main street, with arcades on either side of the road sheltering the pavements from rain and snow. The centre is traffic-free, in summer lined by outdoor cafés and restaurants, thus offering visitors the joys of leisurely strolls when sightseeing or shopping.

BACK TO NATURE

9 East of Bozen a side road leads up to the Rittenplateau and the village of Klobenstein. From here, near the hamlet of Mittelberg, you can see a marvel of nature, the **Erdpyramiden**. These pyramids, reminiscent of stalagmites in caves, are up to 30m (100 feet) high and their formation is due to erosion of the soil after the Ice Age.

14 Before turning left into the Antholz valley after leaving Bruneck, continue on the SS49 further east to Welsberg, then take a right fork which leads, via Prags, to the **Pragser Wildsee**. This spot is a photographer's dream, with a lake varying in colour from dark green to blue at one end and a steep rock fall at the other forming the backdrop.

sections in Tirol. The altar paintings are the work of Martin Knoller, an artist from Steinach.

Turning west under the 700m (2,300-foot) long bridge into the **Gschnitz** valley) and the Gschnitz itself, a pleasant walk then leads via Obertal to the **Lapenis Alm**, an alpine pasture and starting point for many hikes. Another path leads from Gschnitz uphill to the **church of St Magdalena**, from where there are fine views over the valley.

⌷ Fremdenverkehrsverband

From Steinach continue south via Stafflach to Gries.

Gries am Brenner, Tirol

4 *En route* to Gries a stop at the small village of **Stafflach** is recommended as it provides access to two tranquil valleys – the 11km (6½-mile) long Schmirntal and the 8km (5-mile) long Valsertal, which ends in a nature reserve.

Gries is the last stop before the Brennerpass and a starting point for a 7km (4-mile) drive into the Obernbergtal and to the **Obernberg** village. A half-hour walk leads to the picturesque **Obernberger See**.

⌷ Fremdenverkehrsverband

Continue to the Brennerpass.

Brennerpass

5 Since 1919 the Brennerpass has formed the border between

Austria and Italy, when part of Tirol, called Südtirol, had to be ceded to Italy. By AD200 the Romans had laid a narrow path over this important Alpine crossing. Remnants of the old Roman road can still be seen at the small **Brennersee** (lake) near by. Nowadays the Brenner crossing carries a large volume of traffic, mainly between Germany and Italy, which unfortunately pollutes the Tirolean countryside.

From Brenner continue south on the SS12 to Gossensass.

Gossensass, Südtirol

6 A stop at Gossensass rewards the visitor with a first glimpse of Südtirol. The medieval burghers' houses in the centre are a reminder of the wealth created by the local mining industry. A chairlift from Gossensass takes visitors up to the **Hühnerspielalm** and a section near the top of the **Rollspitze**, 2,800m (9,186 feet) above sea level, which can be reached from the top in a half-hour walk.

⌷ Kurverwaltung

Continue on the SS12 for 5km (3 miles) to Sterzing (Vipiteno).

Sterzing, Südtirol

7 One of Sterzing's attractions are the colourful houses in the Neustadt, the main road in the centre of town. These buildings date

The Brenner motorway, linking Germany with Italy

back to the periods of late Gothic and Renaissance style in the Middle Ages. Many are adorned with decorative oriels. Look out for the **Deutschordenskommende**, a 15th- to 16th-century building erected for the Deutscher Orden, a brotherhood founded in 1198 by Christian knights and priests to look after the sick. It is now a museum.

Two impressive castles are in the vicinity. **Burg Sprechenstein** lies 1.8km (1 mile) north in a picturesque setting on a slope. Beautiful frescos decorate the castle's chapel, which contains a winged altar in late Gothic style. **Burg Reifenstein** stands on a rock 2km (1 mile) south of Sterzing. Still standing from the 12th century are the keep and the living quarters. The Deutsche Ritterorden (Order of the German Knights) erected additional buildings in front of the main castle in the 16th century.

⟦i⟧ Verkehrsamt, Stadtplatz

Continue south on the SS508 via the Penser Joch to Sarnthein.

Sarnthein, Südtirol

8 The village of Sarnthein lies tucked away from the main traffic routes. On a gentle slope stands 13th-century **Schloss Reinegg**, now one of the best preserved in South Tirol. The churches in Sarnthein and the nearby hamlets of **Nordheim**, **Astfeld** and **Gentersberg** were all built in the 12th to 14th centuries in Romanesque style, but Gothic features such as arcades were added later.

⟦i⟧ Verkehrsverein

Drive south on the SS508 for 19km (11 miles) to Bozen.

Bozen, Südtirol

9 Bozen (Bolzano in Italian) was for centuries an important trading centre. Wealthy merchants here employed Italian artists from Venice and Florence, and together with talented local craftsmen Bozen became a showpiece and meeting place for northern and southern cultures. Even in prehistoric times a settlement stood here and in 15BC the Romans erected a military post called *Pons Drusi* on this site.

The centre of Bozen is very similar to other Tirolean towns like Meran and Innsbruck, its pavements sheltered by arcades. South of the Waltherplatz (the main town square) stands the **parish church** on the site of an early Christian church, already in existence in the 5th century. The tower is 62m (203 feet) high; also notable is the 1729 high altar in marble. The old town of Bozen stretches out to the north of the Waltherplatz and is mainly a pedestrian precinct; the market plays an important role in the life of the local population and sells local produce.

For curiosity's sake you should also see the other side of Bozen, the Italian part called **Neu Bozen**. You enter it turning west across the Talfer river. Mazzini Square contains a fascist victory monument which has withstood several attempts to blow it up. Crossing back over the river you can stroll along the **Wassermauer Promenade** in a northerly direction to **Schloss Maretsch**. This is a lovely 13th-century castle, enlarged 300 years later and now a favoured venue for meetings and conferences.

Before leaving Bozen a trip further south should not be missed. **Salurn** (Salorna) is the last village of the German-speaking South Tirol.

FOR CHILDREN

When visiting Innsbruck take the children to the **Alpenzoo**, on the northern slopes of town. Here you can see animals from all parts of the Alps in a well-arranged natural setting.

9 From Bozen take the cable-car to Oberbozen. From here a rack railway runs through the meadows of the Rittenplateau to Klobenstein, a journey of 12km (7 miles). The railway used to run from the centre of Bozen, but the cablecar and the new road provide faster connections. The whole family will be enchanted by the beautiful countryside and magnificent views from up here, right to the Dolomites.

Gravestones here indicate it was a settlement during Roman times and the **Salurner Klause**, a narrow part of the Etsch valley, only 2km (1 mile) wide, represents a natural border. Steep mountains protect the valley, but throughout history this has been the scene of frequent skirmishes.

The **parish church of St Andreas** in Salurn was first documented in 1215 and its free-standing tower can be seen from far away. A visit to the ruins of **Burg Hadersburg** is also recommended. The return journey from Salurn to Bozen provides a real treat, a drive through the vineyards on the Südtiroler Weinstrasse. If you ask for red wine anywhere you will be offered **Kalterersee**, a light and fruity wine from this region.

ℹ Städtisches Verkehrsamt und Kurverwaltung, Waltherplatz 28

From Bozen take the Grosse Dolomitenstrasse (SS241) via Welschnofen and the Karersee to Hotel Latemar, then a sharp left turn towards the Nigerpass, just before the Karer Pass descends via Tiers. Take a right fork soon after Tiers, then turn north to Völs.

Völs, Südtirol

10 At the beginning of the ascent to the Seiser Alm, a well-known pasture, lies the village of Völs, with its late Gothic **parish church,** and Romanesque **St Peter am Bichl**, higher up the village. Some houses dating back to the 15th and 16th centuries are decorated with frescos or ornate portals. Nearby **Schloss Prösels**, 2km (1½ miles) south, shows interesting features from the 15th century: towers, portals, ramparts and medieval fortifications.

ℹ Verkehrsverein Völs am Schlern

From Völs continue north, then the road turns east to Seis.

Seis, Südtirol

11 Seis is the central point from which to explore the Seiser Alm, an alpine pasture with large green meadows surrounded by mountains.

Hiking near Innergschloss in the Hohe Tauern National Park

The popularity of the area threatens its natural beauty and plans are in hand to make it car-free, with public transport providing the necessary communications. A road east leads 9km (5½ miles) to **Schönblick**, from where the road is barred to private cars. From Schönblick several chairlifts transport visitors to enjoy the beauty of this alpine paradise.

ℹ Verkehrsamt Seis

Continue north for 3km (2 miles) to Kastelruth, take the first turning west, then north for 8km (5 miles) to Waidbruck, and on the SS12 north to Brixen.

Brixen, Südtirol

12 Brixen is the oldest town in Tirol. Founded in AD901 it soon gained importance and became a bishopric. The inhabitants, however, have not enjoyed their status happily over the centuries: the plague arrived in 1348 and 1636, and in 1444 a fire claimed most of the buildings. At the end of the 18th century Brixen had to endure the occupation of 12,000 French troops. When they were driven out, the Bavarians arrived for eight years, until 1814 when Brixen was reunited with Austria. Later in 1919, after World War I, South Tirol was ceded to Italy and the Italian occupation continues today.

The **cathedral** represents one of the most important church buildings in Tirol and its bishops rule over a wide area of the Catholic hierarchy in Tirol. It is well worth a visit – the cloister is particularly outstanding, and there are superb frescos. Located southwest of the cathedral is the former **castle of the prince-bishops**, which occupies the site of an earlier fortress from 1200. Now called the **Hofburg**, it was started in 1595 in Renaissance style, and completed only in 1710.

ℹ Kurverwaltung, Bahnhofstrasse 9

From Brixen take the SS12 south towards Klausen, cross

*the river and take the SS242d
to St Ulrich and Wolkenstein.*

Wolkenstein, Südtirol

13 The village of Wolkenstein is the last in the Grödner valley, before the Grödner Joch takes you into the next valley, the Gadertal. The ruin of **Burg Wolkenstein** is a reminder of the former aristrocratic rulers of the area. Their best-known son was the poet Oswald von Wolkenstein, who lived from about 1377 to 1445. The churchyard of Brixen's **cathedral** contains a plaque carved in stone, dedicated to the poet.

i Verkehrsamt Wolkenstein in Gröden

Take the SS242 east from Wolkenstein, then turn left on to the SS243, through the Grödner Joch and north on the SS244 down to the Gadertal to Bruneck.

Bruneck, Südtirol

14 One of the most famous medieval painters and wood-carvers, Michael Pacher, was born in Bruneck. His reputation took him far afield from this alpine region and it is considered a great honour to exhibit one of his many masterpieces in churches or museums. Bruneck's delightful centre around the Stadtgasse is now a pedestrian zone.

Directly above the town stands **Schloss Bruneck**, built between 1251 and 1336. The strong outer walls remain – the inside is interesting too. A **regional museum** in the suburb of **Dietenheim** was erected in the grounds of a former large farm, which was called Mair am Hof, and portrays the life and work of the farmers in the valleys of South Tirol.

From Bruneck, try an excursion 14km (8½ miles) north through the Tauferer Tal to **Sand in Taufers** and its **castle**. The fortified castle (Burg) was constructed in the 13th century and stands on a commanding hill above the village. Two drawbridges have to be crossed to enter the castle courtyard, which is flanked by the keep and another wide tower, containing the living quarters. The inner courtyard features a small smithy and the chapel is decorated with frescos from the workshop of Michael Pacher.

i Verkehrsamt, Bruneck

From Bruneck take the SS49 east and branch off after 10km (6 miles) north via Niederrasen into the Antholzer Tal (Antholz valley), over the Staller Sattel back into Austria and continue on the L25 through the Defereggental (Defereggen valley) to Huben. Then across the Iseltal on the L26 into the Kalser Tal (Kalser valley) and Kals.

Kals am Grossglockner, Osttirol

15 Kals is a good starting point for many mountain hikes in the area and several huts provide the necessary stopping points. The **Grossglockner**, at 3,797m (12,461 feet) is the highest mountain in Austria and, weather permitting, can be clearly seen from Kals. For a really magnificent panorama there is a chairlift called **Bergbahn Glocknerblick** leading up to 2,000m (6,562 feet). From there a world of 30 alpine peaks unfolds.

i Fremdenverkehrsverband, Kals

From Kals return to Huben on the L26, then turn sharp north on the 108 to Matrei.

Matrei, Osttirol

16 Matrei lies well positioned in a wider section of the Tauerntal (Tauern valley), already settled in prehistoric times. Matrei's landmark, **Schloss Weissenstein**, stands on a steep rock. It was built in the 13th century, but rebuilt in the 19th. A chairlift provides a pleasant ride up the mountain and from the top easy walks can be taken to enjoy the magnificent alpine panorama.

At **Bichl**, just outside Matrei, old Roman gravestones are exhibited, dating from 200BC. A trip to the end of the Virgental leads to the **Umbalfälle** (Umball waterfalls), which can be seen from a specially arranged path to get the best views.

i Fremdenverkehrsverband, Rauterplatz 3

From Matrei turn north towards the Felbertauerntunnel on the 168.

Felbertauerntunnel, Osttirol/Salzburg

17 It was only in 1967 that a road connection was established here through a tunnel, 5km (3 miles) long. From old pictures it can be seen that this crossing over the Alps was used much earlier, when loads were packed on horses and driven in convoys over the narrow trails. These convoys were called *Samerzug* and they are still organised from Mittersill to let the tradition live on.

From Felbertauerntunnel continue north to Mittersill.

Mittersill, Salzburg

18 Mittersill has become a busy junction where traffic meets from north and south, east and west, but is also a focal point for the National Park region of Hohe Tauern, where measures are taken to protect the environment. Mittersill has a very interesting local museum, the **Heimatmuseum**, housed in the **Felberturm**, a square-shaped tower where farmers once came to pay their rents. The ground floor displays agricultural tools and the upper floors exhibit a well-presented collection of alpine minerals and crystals. One of the emeralds found in the Rauris valley in the Hohe Tauern range is set in the British crown, part of the Crown Jewels in the Tower of London.

The **castle**, on the slopes overlooking the Pinzgau valley, was burnt down during the peasant revolt in 1525 and then rebuilt. It is now a privately owned hotel.

i Fremdenverkehrsverband, am Marktplatz 4

From Mittersill continue west on the 165 to Krimml.

SPECIAL TO...

The **Goldenes Dachl** (golden roof) in Innsbruck, with its balcony below, is one of the main attractions. The roof contains 1,657 gilded copper tiles and was commissioned by Emperor Maximilian I so that he could watch the goings on down below. Things have not changed much over the centuries, only now the people are looking up at the roof instead of the Emperor looking down.

2 The **Europabrücke** (Europa Bridge) near Schönberg is not only a superb technical achievement but also an attraction for visitors. Best seen from the old Brenner road below, it stands 190m (623 feet) above the valley and is counted among the most daring building projects of this century.

FOR HISTORY BUFFS

On **Bergisel**, south of Innsbruck, stands a monument to Andreas Hofer, looking down from the scene of the battles he fought so successfully for his country in 1809 against a vastly superior enemy. A pleasant park has been laid around the statue and near by stands the **Bergiselschanze**, built for the Olympic ski jump in 1964.

Krimml, Salzburg

19 Krimml is well known for its mighty waterfalls, claimed to be the largest in Europe. The water crashes down with tremendous force in three steps over a total distance of 380m (1,250 feet). Photographers should note that the best time for taking pictures is from 10am to 1pm from the upper fall – as the falls are flanked by steep mountains they are in shade for most of the time.

i Verkehrsverein Krimml, Salzburg

From Krimml continue on the 165 over the Gerlos Pass to Zell am Ziller, turn right on the 169 to Jenbach, then take the A12 west to Innsbruck.

The mighty Krimml waterfalls

Innsbruck – Igls 6 (4)
Igls – Matrei am Brenner 15 (9)
Matrei am Brenner – Steinach am Brenner 5 (3)
Steinach am Brenner – Gries am Brenner 5 (3)
Gries am Brenner – Brennerpass 6 (4)
Brennerpass – Gossensass 10 (6)
Gossensass – Sterzing 5 (3)
Sterzing – Sarntheim 44 (27)
Sarntheim – Bozen 21 (13)
Bozen – Völs 53 (33)
Völs – Seis 7 (4½)
Seis – Brixen 30 (18½)
Brixen – Wolkenstein 39 (24)
Wolkenstein – Bruneck 58 (36)
Bruneck – Kals am Grossglockner 81 (50)
Kals am Grossglockner – Matrei 22 (13½)
Matrei – Felbertauerntunnel 14 (8½)
Felbertauerntunnel – Mittersill 24 (15)
Mittersill – Krimml 33 (20½)
Krimml – Innsbruck 98 (61)

2/3 days – 312km (194½ miles)

THE LOWER LANDS OF THE TIROL

Rattenberg: during one of its music festivals which are common throughout the Tirol

ⓘ Verkehrsbüro, Münchner Strasse 2

From Kufstein take the A12 to Schwaz.

Schwaz, Tirol

1 Schwaz flourished during the 15th and 16th centuries when it played a leading role in the silver and copper mining industries of central Europe. The size of the **parish church** gives an idea of the wealth that mining brought to the town: the roof is covered with 15,000 copper plates. A former **silver mine** is open to visitors who are taken into the mountains on a special train and get a good idea of the construction and working conditions in medieval times. **Burg Freundsberg** has an imposing keep which houses a local museum exhibiting documents relating to silver mining in the 16th century.

ⓘ Fremdenverkehrsverband

Cross the Inn river and take the L215 east to Jenbach.

Jenbach, Tirol

2 Before entering Jenbach, branch off to your left at Ried to **Schloss Tratzberg**, which stands on a wide rock above the Inn valley. Built during the 16th century, many of its rooms contain original furnishings. The main attraction is a long wall painting depicting the family tree of the Habsburgs.

ⓘ Fremdenverkehrsverband

Drive northwest to the Achensee.

Achensee, Tirol

3 Pertisau, on the Achensee (Achen Lake), enjoys a favourable position on a small plain bordering the lake shores. It is also the end of the road, as the slopes of the Karwendel mountain range descend right to the lake. The area around Pertisau is a nature reserve and offers rewarding walks. As the mountains are fairly steep, a trip by cableway up to the **Zwölferkogel** is the most convenient way to conquer this hurdle and from there you can walk through the high alpine pastures to

Kufstein • Schwaz • Jenbach • Achensee
Alpbach • Brixlegg/Kramsach • Rattenberg
Wörgl • Kitzbühel • Prama • St Johann in Tirol
Fieberbrunn • Saalfelden am Steinernen Meer
Maria Kirchental • St Ulrich am Pillersee
Kufstein

The fortress at Kufstein was built by the Bavarians, but was conquered in 1504 by Emperor Maximilian I and has stayed in Austrian hands ever since, with the exception of two brief periods during the Napoleonic wars. One of the towers contains the Heldenorgel (Hero's Organ), played at noon every day (also at 6pm in summer) to commemorate the fallen in the two world wars. A good view of the town can be had from the Heldenhügel (Hero's Hill) which is crowned with a statue of the Tirolean hero Andreas Hofer. Between the Inn river below and the fortress lies the Römerhofgasse, an enchanting street in the old town, supposed to host the oldest wine bar in Tirol. A lift from here takes you up to the fortress and its museum.

enjoy the invigorating scenery. On the return you can stop at the village of **Maurach** and take the cableway up to the **Erfurter hut** to explore the Rofan mountain range which is known for its alpine flowers.

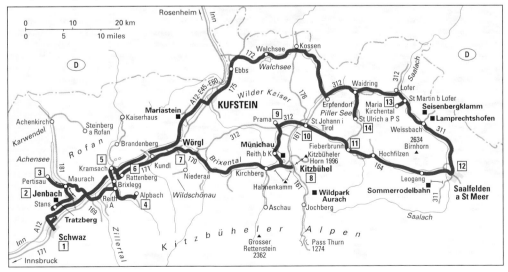

SCENIC ROUTES

8 From Kitzbühel it is a 20-minute drive via Jochberg to Pass Thurn. At first you travel through the villages of Aurach and Jochberg, then the road climbs up through woods and round bends to the pass itself, which is also the border between the provinces of Tirol and Salzburg.

12 From Saalfelden the route along the Saalach river takes you through forests on either side and if time allows, a stop in one of the valleys is very rewarding.

SPECIAL TO...

3 Since 1889 the steam-powered **Achenseebahn** has plied between Jenbach and Pertisau. It is a rack railway and takes 25 minutes to cover 3.5km (2 miles). The carriages date from 1889 and the trip is altogether nostalgic and enjoyable.

Achensee's attractions: lakeside beaches (above) and the steam cog railway (left)

ℹ️ Fremdenverkehrsverband Achenkirch-Tirol, Pertisau

From Pertisau join the 181 at Maurach. Continue south to Wiesing, cross the Inn river and drive northeast towards Brixlegg. Turn right at St Gertraud and continue via Reith to Alpbach.

Alpbach, Tirol

4 Alpbach created its own style of Tirolean houses, wide low wooden constructions with rich flower decorations on the balconies. In August it is the meeting place of the European Forum where leading international politicians, scientists, economists and artists hold lectures. The **parish church of St Oswald** stands right in the middle of the village and the colourful houses set on the slopes make it one of the most attractive centres in Tirol.

ℹ️ Fremdenverkehrsverband

Return via Reith to Brixlegg, then cross the Inn river for Kramsach.

Brixlegg/Kramsach, Tirol

5 On the return from Alpbach a stop at the village of **Reith** is suggested if it's warm weather – there are bathing facilities on a small lake, right in the centre. The water reaches a temperature of 24°C in summer, and boaters and anglers can also practise their skills on the lake.

Brixlegg was a mining town in the Middle Ages, and is surrounded by several old forts, most of them dating back to the 12th century. Over the river lies Kramsach, close to three lakes just east of town.

Going further east you come to the open-air **Höfe Museum**, which exhibits old Tirolean farming houses and their original furnishings. A chairlift from Mariatal, north of Kramsach, leads up to 1,800m (5,906 feet) and the idyllic **Ziereiner See**, a small alpine lake.

ℹ️ Fremdenverkehrsamt, Kramsach

From Kramsach cross the Inn river to Rattenberg.

Rattenberg, Tirol

6 Rattenberg is supposed to be the smallest town in Tirol, with only 600 inhabitants. Mining brought wealth to the town in the 15th century, but its decline has enabled the town to retain its medieval appearance. **Schloss Rattenberg** is now a ruin and the only part of the original Romanesque castle can be found in the base of the keep. In 1651 Wilhelm Biener, the Chancellor of Tirol, was executed here on false charges and in summer open-air plays are staged to mark this unhappy event. The Servite convent and church were first mentioned in AD988 and improved between 1400 and 1430.

ⓘ Fremdenverkehrsamt

Continue northeast on the 171 to Wörgl.

Wörgl, Tirol

7 Wörgl is an ideal centre for excursions into the nearby valleys and villages. Eight kilometres (5 miles) north, across the River Inn, stands **Burg Mariastein** on a free-standing rock. From the courtyard a spiral staircase leads up to the former chapel and further to the Hall of the Knights, which is now a museum.

The only ice and limestone cave in Tirol open to the public can be reached from Mariastein on foot via the Buchackeralm in about two hours, but you should enquire first at Wörgl for opening times.

Another trip from Wörgl leads south to Niederau and the Wildschönau valley. Luscious alpine meadows are strewn between the little villages with **Oberau** at the centre. The highest village is **Thierbach**, which can be reached by a small winding road. Thierbach represents a typically enchanting Tirolean village in an idyllic setting. The local liquor, *Rübenschnaps*, is unique.

Tauern range in the south, including Austria's highest mountains. From the top of the Kitzbühler Horn a path leads down through the **Alpenblumengarten**, an enclave on either side of the trail showing all the splendour of alpine flowers. The cableway tickets enable you to rejoin it on the lower Alpenhaus terminus.

Kitzbühel itself is a very attractive town with a long history – early finds date back to 1300BC. The old part stands on a raised level, with the colourful painted façades of the houses visible from below. It received its town charter in 1271 and rich mines in the area enabled it to flourish from the 15th century. The **museum**, at Hinterstadt 32, has three floors dedicated to the history and achievements of the town and its citizens. A **ski museum** draws attention to more recent activities.

Before leaving Kitzbühel explore its surroundings and the various facilities on offer. Driving west to Kirchberg, south to Aschau and then forking right uphill leads to an enchanting spot, the **Labalm**. Here you can sit in an alpine pasture, surrounded by little streams coming down the slopes. On the other side of the valley the panorama is completed by the view of the **Grosser Rettenstein**, 2,366m (7,740 feet).

Just east of Kirchberg, *en route* to Kitzbühel, is the terminus of the

FOR HISTORY BUFFS

8 Schloss Lebenberg was originally the seat of small country aristrocracy, and was called the Pfaffenberg. In 1548 a map describes the building for the first time as Lebenburg, sited on a hill. In 1696 the prince-bishop of Passau, Count Johann Phillip of Lamberg, acquired the castle and two other castles in the area, Münichau and Kapsburg.

The Lamberg family played an important part in the history of Kitzbühel. They administered the law courts from 1679 to 1840. In 1885 the castle of Lebenberg became the first tourist pension in town.

Typical mountain house on the Hahnenkamm, above Kitzbühel

ⓘ Fremdenverkehrsamt, Wörgl

From Wörgl take the 170 east to Kitzbühel.

Kitzbühel, Tirol

8 The town of Kitzbühel is situated between two mountains; cableways lead to the tops of both and the Kitzbühler Horn has the additional facility of access by a narrow road, which conveniently ends at a restaurant. The views are superb on a clear day and reach from the Wilder Kaiser mountain range in the north down to the high peaks of the Hohe

Fleckalmbahn to the Ehrenbachhöhe. From here a gentle stroll leads down to the Hahnenkamm, the top terminus of a cableway from Kitzbühel, from where there is a superb view of the town below and the surrounding mountains. Another route, the **Panoramaweg**, leads along the slopes of the mountain ridge back to the top terminus. On the walk you pass the starting point of the famous Hahnenkamm ski race. A glimpse of the first part of the course, even in summer, demonstrates why this race is so daring and exciting. On the return to Kitzbühel, the **Schwarzsee** and nearby **Gieringer Weiher** provide facilities for swimming, reaching

Maria Kirchental's church – a popular destination for pilgrims from all over the area

temperatures of 27°C in summer.

Kitzbühel offers a very eventful programme in summer. Nearly every weekend something happens. A vintage car rally usually takes place in June, open-air concerts are held twice a week, a tennis tournament is in late July and early August. The main summer event is the festival on the first Saturday in August. The centre of the town is then closed and filled with stands selling food and drink, usually until the early hours of the morning. Later in the season, on a Sunday morning, a bicycle race and a marathon start from the town centre.

i Tourismusverband Kitzbühel, Hinterstadt 18

From Kitzbühel take the 170 west and turn right at a signpost for Reith, then continue north to the 213 at Prama (Stangl).

Prama, near Going, Tirol

9 Shortly after the turn-off to Reith bei Kitzbühel the 500-year-old **Schloss Münichau** appears on the roadside to your left. Although now a hotel with all modern facilities, it has retained its old charm, with thick walls, Gothic arches and wooden beams in the bedrooms. The old Rittersaal (Hall of the Knights) acts as the dining room and conveys a truly medieval atmosphere. Interesting also is the typically Tirolean **farmhouse** opposite, where the interior has been converted into an extension of the hotel.

From Münichau continue for a short, pleasant drive to the main road and cross over the Stanglwirt at Prama. Here a wide variety of sports and facilities are available, including indoor and outdoor tennis, riding, squash, bowling, rafting, canoeing, paragliding and swimming. The main attraction for horse lovers is a visit to the stables and a ride on one of the Lipizzaners, the famous white horses of the Spanish Riding School in Vienna.

i Stanglwirt

From Prama, continue for 6km (4 miles) east to St Johann.

BACK TO NATURE

8 From Kitzbühel, south on the road to Jochberg, a well marked turning left leads to the **Wildpark Aurach** (game park). There you can wander around and see the animals, mainly red deer, roaming about in an enclosed area. Some rarer species, like lynx and ibex, are kept in open cages. The best time to visit is at 2pm, when they are fed.

FOR CHILDREN

12 Three kilometres (2 miles) south of Saalfelden a chairlift from Kehlbach leads up to the Huggenbergalm. From here a 1,600m (1 mile) long track of the **Sommerrodelbahn** (toboggan run) leads downwards, a ride for the whole family to enjoy.

St Johann in Tirol, Tirol

10 St Johann is a popular summer and winter resort and lies on a traffic junction, where a short cut from Tirol to the city of Salzburg via Bavaria branches off. The village features picturesque old Tirolean farmhouses. The **parish church** (1724–8) was built in baroque style on the site of a former Gothic building and is one of the first large baroque churches in the Tirolean lowlands. St Johann offers varied facilities at a **leisure complex** which contains both indoor and outdoor swimming pools. On the **Rüppenhang**, a mountain slope, two summer toboggan runs of 700m (2,297 feet) provide excitement, while a chairlift opens up an ideal walking and hiking area above the village.

i Fremdenverkehrsverband

From St Johann drive southeast on the 164 to Fieberbrunn.

Fieberbrunn, Tirol

11 Fieberbrunn is a long village and you have to watch out for the turn-off from the main road to the centre. The Countess Margarete Maultasch, Tirol's only female ruler, stayed here in 1354 and was supposedly cured of an outbreak of fever through the properties of the local spring, which contains high levels of iron. This gave the village its name (Fieberbrunn means 'Feverspring'). A cableway leads up to the top of the **Lärchfilzkogel**, 1,654m (5,426 feet) above sea level.

i Fremdenverkehrsverband

Continue east on the 164 to Saalfelden.

Saalfelden am Steinernen Meer, Salzburg

12 After Hochfilzen, the last village in Tirol, you cross into the province of Salzburg. The local **museum** in **Castle Ritzen** exhibits a unique collection of Christmas cribs and works by local artists.

ⓘ Fremdenverkehrsverband, Bahnhofstrasse 10

From Saalfelden turn north on the 311 to St Martin bei Lofer and continue on a short road to Maria Kirchental.

Maria Kirchental, Salzburg

13 On the way to St Martin a short stop at **Weissbach** leads to a fascinating gorge, the **Seisenbergklamm**. On the other side of the main road is the entrance to the caves of **Lamprechtshofen**, where guided tours are available daily, lasting 40 minutes.

Maria Kirchental is a little hamlet standing amid beautiful luscious alpine meadows. The **church** was designed by one of Austria's leading architects, Johann Fischer von Erlach, who was later responsible for many famous buildings in Salzburg and Vienna. Built between 1693 and 1701, it was one of his early works and shows how brilliantly he solved the problem of setting a church in a landscape surrounded by mountains.

ⓘ Fremdenverkehrsverband, Lofer

Drive back to St Martin, turn left on the 311 and left again at Lofer on the 312 to Waidring. Here another left turn leads to St Ulrich am Pillersee.

St Ulrich am Pillersee, Tirol

14 St Ulrich is a delightful village on the long and narrow **Pillersee** (lake). It is a good choice for anybody wanting to get away from the main tourist routes. Swimming, boat hire, windsurfing and angling are on offer. The small **pilgrim church of St Adolari** on the northern end of the lake is enchanting. It is a little gem among the many Tirolean churches and dates back to 1013; a glimpse inside is highly recommended.

ⓘ Gemeindeamt

Drive back to Waidring, turn left on the 312 to Erpfendorf, right towards Kössen, then left on the 172 and after 15km (9 miles) south to Kufstein on the 175.

Kufstein – Schwaz 46 (29)
Schwaz – Jenbach 7 (4½)
Jenbach – Achensee 11 (7)
Achensee – Alpbach 33 (20½)
Alpbach – Brixlegg/Kramsach 13 (8)
Brixlegg/Kramsach – Rattenberg 2 (1)
Rattenberg – Wörgl 14 (8½)
Wörgl – Kitzbühel 30 (18½)
Kitzbühel – Prama 12 (7½)
Prama – St Johann in Tirol 6 (4)
St Johann in Tirol – Fieberbrunn 12 (7½)
Fieberbrunn – Saalfelden am Steineren Meer 27 (17)
Saalfelden am Steineren Meer – Maria Kirchental 24 (15)
Maria Kirchental – St Ulrich am Pillersee 20 (12½)
St Ulrich am Pillersee – Kufstein 55 (34)

Kufstein's mighty fortress overlooks the town from its commanding rocky bluff

RECOMMENDED WALKS

8 Drive from Kitzbühel south to Mauring and take the chairlift up to the Bichlalm. From here a leisurely walk up on the slopes leads toward the Auracher Graben and down to the Aurach. A pleasant stroll leads back to the terminus of the chairlift and car park.

10 From St Johann take the 312 north to Erpfendorf. Turn right to the Lärchenhof, then take the trail leading down to the bottom of the valley and continue uphill through the Griesbachklamm (gorge) on a well-secured footpath. After the waterfall continue right to the end of the path, then turn left on a small dirt road and walk a short stretch uphill. Another trail starts on your left and leads back to the Lärchenhof, always gently descending on the right-hand side of the valley.

TIROLEAN VALLEYS

The mighty Münzturm (Mint Tower), symbol of Hall in Tirol. The first coin was struck in 1477

Kaunertal, Tirol

1 The Kaunertal lies between the Upper Inn and the Pitz valley and is bordered by the Glockturmkamm and Kaunergrat mountain ranges. From Imst a short way south leads to **Wenns** and – taking a right fork – to **Piller** and the **Pillerhöhe**, 1,559m (5,115 feet). A steep descent follows down to **Kauns**, a charming little village on the slope. Near by the River Fagge joins the Inn and here the Kaunertal really begins. A pleasant walk from Kauns leads to the ruins of **Schloss Berneck**, which was partly renovated in 1977 and can be visited on certain days (consult the information office in Kauns for opening times). The castle was the seat of the Lords of Berneck during the 13th and 14th centuries and changed owners frequently. The western keep, the eastern section of the living quarters and part of the outer wall belong to the original castle, the rest is 15th- and 16th-century.

The hamlets spread along the Kauner valley have been amalgamated for administrative purposes into *Gemeinden* (communities). The first one after Kauns, Kaunerberg, incorporates Obwals, Schnadigen, Mairhof and Prantach. There is an information office on the main road in Mairhof.

From Kaunerberg the road proceeds to **Feichten**, part of the Gemeinde Kaunertal, along with 10 other hamlets. The emphasis here is on sports and leisure. There are good camping facilities at **Camping Kaunertal**, 200m (650 feet) off the

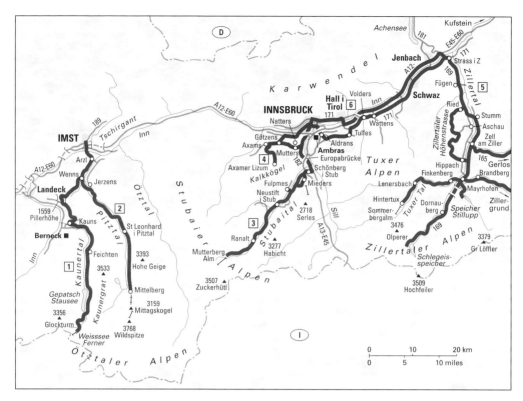

main road, open from May to October. Past Kaunertal the Gletscher Strasse (glacier road) begins a steep climb to the **Gepatsch Stausee** (reservoir). A stop at the beginning of the lake is the starting point for a pleasurable walk on the west side, which is closed to cars. Having passed the lake, the road winds along age-old pine forests and lush alpine pastures, finishing at the **Gletscher-**restaurant), 2,750m (9,022 feet) above sea level, at the Weisssee Ferner (Weisssee glacier). A chairlift takes visitors up to 3,000m (9,843 feet).

ⓘ Fremdenverkehrsverband Kauns, Kaunerberg and Kaunertal

Return to Imst on the same route or turn left at Kauns for Prutz and Landeck.

Pitztal, Tirol

2 South of Imst, across the Inn river, lies **Arzl**, a charming little village at the beginning of the Pitztal valley. From here an interesting trail leads through the **Pitzenklamm**, a gorge which is also called the Luis Trenker Steig, after a Tirolean film actor and director who starred in many black-and-white films of mountain dramas.

The next village, **Wenns**, lies perched on a terrace above the valley and warrants a stop to see the **Platzhaus**. Unlike other fresco-decorated façades, the artist here completed a fully painted front with pictures and ornaments.

After a short drive past the village of **Jerzens**, on the other side of the valley, the valley narrows and you enter the Inner-Pitztal, with **St Leonhard im Pitztal** as its main centre. The region, similar to the Kaunertal, comprises an area of over 20km (12 miles) along the valley, as far as **Mittelberg**. From here the **Pitzexpress**, a subterranean railway, takes visitors and summer skiers up to the **Mittagskogel**, 2,860m (9,383 feet) above sea level. The **Pitz-Panorama cableway** takes you further to the **Hinterer Brunnenkogel** (3,400m/11,155 feet). From here the views are superb and all-year skiing takes place on the glacier.

ⓘ Fremdenverkehrsverband Arzl, Wenns, St Leonhard im Pitztal

Mountain river in the Stubaital

Return to Imst on the same route.

Stubaital, Tirol

3 Proximity to Innsbruck makes the Stubai valley a very popular area for visitors. The old Brenner road from Innsbruck connects with the turn-off to **Schönberg**, but a stop is suggested just before, to see the **Europabrücke**, a magnificent bridge which spans the whole valley.

Mieders is only 2km (1¼ miles) from Schönberg im Stubaital. The slender spire of the **parish church** with traditional Tirolean houses surrounding it presents a very pleasing sight. The Serles chairlift provides easy access to one of the mountains and opportunities for numerous walks and hikes. The formidable view of **Serles Mountain** should not deter visitors from attempting a climb to the summit as access is easy from the rear. Magnificent views can be had from the top, right down to Innsbruck and the Nordkette mountains behind.

The next village is **Fulpmes**, set amidst gently sloping meadows.

Neustift im Stubaital

The rocky cliffs of the Kalkkögel mountains west of Fulpmes are sometimes called the Northern Dolomites. Since the 15th century blacksmiths have worked in Fulpmes, producing beautiful wrought-iron work. Lately, the market has extended to the manufacture of mountaineering gear. The **Schmiedemuseum** in the main square provides further insight into the art of forging wrought iron.

Further along, the road leads to **Neustift im Stubaital**, a popular tourist centre which caters for both summer and winter visitors. The former **Gasthöfe** (local inns) have been converted into four-star hotels and the choice is enormous. Leisure facilities include indoor and outdoor swimming pools and tennis courts, as well as discothèques. Schools teach parasailing and hang-gliding, and others advise on hiking and mountain climbing. Professional mountain guides are also available.

Past Neustift, the valley narrows and the road leads through delightful countryside, lined with fir trees. **Ranalt** used to be the end of the valley with sheer rocks forming a natural gate. The road has been extended, however, and leads up to the **Mutterberg Alm** with a cableway connection providing access to the popular summer skiing area above.

ⓘ Fremdenverkehrsverband Mieders, Fulpmes and Neustift im Stubai

Return to Innsbruck on the same route.

Axamer Lizum, Tirol

4 Axams, near Innsbruck, was a relatively unknown village before it became famous in 1964 and 1976, when nearby Axamer Lizum was developed to hold the Winter Olympic games. Cableways, a funicular and chairlifts service this very popular area.

The village of **Götzens** is known for its **parish church**, dedicated to the Apostles Peter and Paul. Built in the 18th century on the site of a former church, the comparatively simple exterior hides a surprisingly elaborate interior – it is said to be one of the finest rococo-style buildings. The ornaments on the main and side altars are exquisite and so is the pulpit. The church took only four years to build and a local man, Franz Singer, was responsible for its construction.

From Götzens it is not far to **Mutters**, which has received an award for being the most beautiful village in Tirol. Its inhabitants proudly point out a copper plate in the village square which records this event. The meticulous cleanliness, well-cared-for gardens and flower-decorated balconies will convince the visitor that this award was well deserved. The adjacent village of **Natters** is similarly attractive and offers bathing facilities on a small lake near by.

ⓘ Fremdenverkehrsverband Burggraben 3, Innsbruck, Axams and Mutters

Zillertal, Tirol

5 From Innsbruck the first suggested stop is at the **castle of Ambras**, which was recently restored and opened to the public. It was built between 1564 and 1589 in Renaissance style and is surrounded by a park, part of which was designed along the lines of a 19th-century English garden. It was the residence of Archduke Ferdinand II and his wife, who came from the wealthy Welser family from Augsburg. The Archduke was a collector of medieval harnesses, and weaponry, artefacts, coins and medallions are also on show, together with paintings in the portrait gallery. The castle was burnt down during skirmishes in 1133 and was given to Ferdinand II and his family, who lived here from 1563 to 1595. It is divided into the lower and upper castle. Between them stands the impressive Spanish Hall, which was built by Giovanni Luchese between 1570 and 1571. A carpenter from Innsbruck, K Gottlieb, was responsible for the wood-panelled ceiling.

The route continues to **Aldrans** and from here on an elevated road east through meadows and small villages until it descends to **Volders** and **Wattens**, an industrial town known for its production of Tirolean crystal. Opposite Jenbach, at **Strass im Zillertal**, the extensive Zillertal region begins. Many villages and valleys make up the Ziller valley, perhaps the most typical of all Tirolean valleys. **Zell am Ziller** is a centre which offers many cableways to the surrounding peaks and also lies at the entry to the Gerlostal.

The village of **Gerlos** lies 17km (10½ miles) east of Zell and is reached by a well-kept mountain road which provides a link with the province of Salzburg on the other side of the Gerlos Pass. Gerlos will appeal to those who enjoy plenty of activity. The nearby **Durlassboden reservoir** offers facilities for swimming, rowing, sailing and windsurfing. The village itself has tennis courts, indoor and outdoor swimming pools and you can hire mountain bikes or enjoy trout fishing, rafting or paragliding. Return to Zell am Ziller and proceed south to Mayrhofen.

Mayrhofen is the main town in the Zillertal. A strongly traditional way of life flourished here long before tourism arrived in the last century. The church and local inns were the focal points for the inhabitants. The town lies in the middle of a wide basin, where four alpine valleys merge. Two cableways connect with surrounding peaks. Mayrhofen itself gets very crowded in the summer, but there are many oppor-

Typical farmhouse in the Zillertal

SPECIAL TO...

5 If you are in Lanersbach in the Tuxer Tal (Tuxer valley) visit the old **water mill**, called the **Tuxer Mühle**, near **Juns**.

5 A folkloric feast called the 'Gauderfest' is celebrated at Zell am Ziller in May. Apart from various local competitions with prizes and other entertainments, a high-grade *bockbeer*, the **Gauderbier**, is brewed specially for the occasion, greatly adding to the overall enjoyment.

FOR HISTORY BUFFS

5 The **Zillertal railway** has a 760mm gauge. This was ordered by the Imperial Minister for War in 1878, so that in the case of war the rolling stock could also be used in Bosnia, which then belonged to the Austro-Hungarian empire.

5 The origin of the village of Zell am Ziller dates back to the 8th century, when a Christian monk erected a cell and founded the village. From 1188 the name Celle figures in deeds and the coat of arms of Zell shows a monk holding the cross in one hand and a church in the other.

year-round activities on the **Tuxer Ferner** (glacier).

On the return from Mayrhofen a left fork at Hippach leads to the **Zillertaler Höhenstrasse**, a winding road running high up on the western slopes of the Zillertal (Ziller valley). Ample time should be allowed for the drive as the road is narrow with bends, but the magnificent views and ever-changing scenery make it a trip well worth the effort. It is possible to rejoin the main road at **Aschau**, but a left turn at Zellberg ensures the continuation of this rewarding panoramic drive. The road finally ends at **Ried**, and 6km (4 miles) further lies **Fügen**, which has developed during recent years from a small village into a well-known resort. The **parish church** is dedicated to the Assumption of Our Lady and shows interesting early Gothic frescos which were painted during the 14th and 15th centuries. Woodcarvings by the local artist Franz Nissl were added later in 1770. The romantic **Haselbacher waterfall** can be seen on the opposite side of the valley, east of Hart.

Left: a welcome sign in Mayrhofen, the main town in the Zillertal. Set in its wide valley (below) Mayrhofen is the starting point for summer hiking

tunities to branch off into one of the adjacent valleys.

East of Mayrhofen the road through the suburb of **Strass** leads into the Zillergrund, named after the Ziller river which flows through the valley. Soon after Strass you can take a left fork up to **Brandberg**, a mountain retreat in a very picturesque setting. If you continue back through the Zillergrund the road leads past hamlets and inns to the **Speicher Zillergründl**, a reservoir and starting point for walks along the lake or into one of the valleys converging there.

Southeast of Mayrhofen the road leads steeply up the **Stilluppklamm** (gorge) to the **Stillup reservoir**, and from there it is a short walk along the lake to a waterfall and inn near by. Perhaps the most exiciting trip from Mayrhofen is 20km (12 miles) south to the **Schlegeisspeicher reservoir**, a large artificial lake created like many for hydroelectric schemes. The wall which regulates the flow of the water is 131m (430 feet) high and 725m (2,379 feet) long. A walk around the lake is very rewarding and the view over the reservoir towards the glaciers is superb.

The **Tuxer Tal**, west of Mayrhofen, should not be missed and the resort of **Lanersbach** offers a great variety of walks. Further along, **Hintertux** lies at the far end of the valley and a trip by cableway leads up to the **Sommerbergalm**, an alpine pasture. From here several hikes can be undertaken and the second section of the cableway takes you up into the snow region at 2,600m (8,700 feet). Summer skiers will wish to go even further up on one of the chairlifts to join in the

⒤ Fremdenverkehrsverband Zell
am Ziller, Dorfplatz 3a, Gerlos

*From Fügen continue on the 169
north to the A12 and drive west
to exit at Hall.*

Hall in Tirol, Tirol

6 Hall's salt mine finished production in 1967, but a **museum** at the Oberer Stadtplatz relives the 700 years of mining tradition in the town. A replica of an alpine salt mine, built according to original plans, shows the shafts and galleries, together with a mining drill and a slide used by the miners where walking was impossible. The mighty **Münzturm** (Mint Tower), which was part of the town's fortifications, is attached to the **Burg Hasegg**, the local castle. This tower has become the town's emblem. Archduke Sigmund transferred his mint here from Meran in 1477. In 1486 the first **Silbertaler** (silver coin) was struck here, a forerunner of the silver dollar in the US, as the word dollar derives from the medieval coin, the *taler*. The last coins were struck here in 1809, to commemorate Andreas Hofer, the famous Tirolean hero. In 1975 minting was briefly resumed for the Olympic coins. Also on view in the castle are the Fürstenzimmer, the duke's rooms with Gothic-style beamed ceilings, and the wedding

Hall in Tirol, the former salt town of the Inn valley

chapel of Emperor Maximilian I. The **Rathaus** (town hall) has an impressive Gothic roof and battlements decorated with coats of arms. It is claimed to be the most attractive town hall in Tirol.

Return to Innsbruck.

CARINTHIA & STYRIA

The southern part of the Austrian Alps, with an abundance of warm lakes encircled by forests and meadows, is explored in this region. Life is more leisurely than in the north and one of the highest mountain passes crosses the area. Gorges, spas and dramatic-looking limestone ranges are intermingled with green pastures and forests, providing the northern boundaries of the region.

In the southeast, Christendom had to be defended over centuries against marauding Magyars and Turks. Abbeys, castles and fortresses have been preserved and bear witness to an uneasy past. Industry has also left its mark, a whole mountain having gradually been reduced in size, step by step, to provide the iron ore for the ever-hungry furnaces of the iron- and steel-works. The Romans started this development in the area a long time ago, but there is still a lot of life left on the mountain before future centuries can return it to wilderness or leave it as a monument to human endeavour. Interest in past and present technology has brought tourism, and an old mountain railway built for transporting the ore has become a major attraction.

Woodlands and meadows cover the area in the southeast with the lower-lying parts being used for agriculture and vineyards. The capital of Styria, Graz, lost some of its importance when Austria's port of Trieste was lost to Italy, but culture is still very much alive here, a tradition which goes back to its imperial Habsburg past.

Heiligenblut's Gothic Pfarrkirche

Tour 7
The route commences north of the Lienzer Dolomiten range, a continuation of the main Dolomites lying further west. A turn eastwards leads through the Lesach valley, known for its scenery but also for its winding roads. Later the valley widens and a turn north leads to one of the many Carinthian lakes, the Millstätter See. A very rewarding trip follows through the picturesque Maltatal (Malta valley). The return follows the route back towards the Millstätter See and then continues west along the valley of the Drau river and Roman excavations, just before finishing at Lienz.

Tour 8
Many lakes are on the itinerary of this tour, including gorges and passes through the southern parts of Carinthia, right up to the border with Slovenia. The tour later visits Klagenfurt, the capital of Carinthia, and its large and most popular lake, the Wörthersee. A round trip of the lake and the smaller ones in its vicinity is included before the tour finishes at Villach.

The Grossglockner Hochalpenstrasse is the best way to see the mountains at their best

Tour 9

This tour starts from southern Carinthia and leads right up on one of Austria's famous mountain roads. The delightful village of Heiligenblut is a stopping place before the real ascent begins. The well-constructed road should not present any problems, apart from heavy traffic when you branch off to one of the popular view points. The descent into the province of Salzburg leads to the traditional spa of Badgastein. The absence of a road south over the mountains is solved by loading cars on shuttle trains through a tunnel.

Tour 10

Having passed two small lakes, the itinerary continues through an area called the Nockgebiet, where the mountain peaks are rounded off and the road has to wind its way between them. Having crossed another alpine pass, the route passes into the southeast of Salzburg province, only to turn very soon into Styria and the southern flank of the impressive Dachstein mountains. Turning south again, after a while you drive through a nature park in the lower Tauern range, where the peaks reach about 2,500m (8,000 feet) above sea level. There are famous abbeys and castles *en route* and the final ascent to the top of the Gerlitzen mountain concludes the tour.

Tour 11

From Graz, the capital of Styria, which is also the second largest town in Austria, the first visit along this tour is to the stud farm of the Lipizzaner horses at Piber. Passing through a stretch of the industrial part of the province the route continues to the remote area around Hinterstoder, which lies off the main tourist track. Then the drive leads through a famous gorge, the Gesäuse, to a mountain appropriately called the Erzberg, the 'ore mountain', which has provided and still provides that important raw material, iron ore. The visit to a spectacular grotto is another highlight of this tour.

Tour 12

The eastern part of Carinthia is explored on this tour, starting with the Lavant valley and then turning right to the confluence of the Lavant into the larger Drau river. The tour now turns back into Styria with visits to impressive castles and a pleasant, leisurely drive along the southern border, past vineyards and fields. The tour then turns north past a spa and mineral spring and along the Styrian castle road and the Feistritz river to a small lake providing the opportunity to relax. Interesting caves near by can be visited before returning through hilly countryside to Graz.

4/5 days – 340km (211 miles)

ALONG RIVERS & VALLEYS

Lienz • Sillian • Maria Luggau • Hermagor Feistritz an der Drau • Millstatt • Gmünd Maltatal • Steinfeld • Greifenburg • Lavant Aguntum • Lienz

Lienz, capital of East Tirol, lies in a wide basin between the Hohe Tauern mountain range in the north and the Lienzer Dolomiten in the south. The parish church of St Andreas has a long history. An early Christian place of worship existed here in the 5th century, followed by a Romanesque church, which was built in the 10th century and consecrated in 1204. Two tombstones of the last Counts of Wolkenstein were sculpted by Christoph Geiger. Schloss Bruck was built in 1280 by the Counts of Görz and became the property of Emperor Maximilian I, who sold it to the Freiherrn (barons) of Wolkenstein-Rodenegg. It is now a museum, with frescos on the ceilings and walls of great artistic and historic value.

[i] Fremdenverkehrsverband Lienzer-Dolomiten, Albin-Egger-Strasse 17, Lienz

From Lienz take the 100 southwest to Sillian.

Sillian, Tirol

1 Just east of town stands **Burg Heinfels**, near the entrance to the Villgratental. The medieval fortress belonged to the Counts of Görz in the 13th century. The fortifications, including 38 crenellations, were

Lienz's distinctive onion-domed clock tower on St Michael's church

added around 1600. The castle is now in decay, but a walk around the walls, keep and mighty *palas* (living quarters) provide a good insight into its construction and former appearance.

A rewarding detour into the Villgraten valley starts from here and you can drive for about 14km (9 miles) to the **Unterstalleralm**. From here a 20-minute walk across alpine meadows leads to the **Schwarzsee**, at 2,455m (8,054 feet) above sea level. The mountain flora around the lake is quite outstanding in its variety and beauty. Another excursion from Sillian, which leads into South Tirol and the Dolomites, is strongly recommended. Drive west on the main road to Toblach, then turn left, due south on the **51** to Schluderbach and continue on the **48b** to Misurina. From here you can already see the **Drei Zinnen**, the most spectacular of all mountains in the Dolomites. The shape of these three limestone rocks is quite unique and the sheer drop from their peaks attracts rock climbers from many countries. The return trip can be undertaken in half a day, as it is only 50km (31 miles) in each direction. In the peak season the road from Misurina to the Drei Zinnen can get very busy.

[i] Fremdenverkehrsverband Sillian

Take the 100 east for 2km (1 mile), turn right and continue east on the 111 to Maria Luggau.

Maria Luggau, Kärnten

2 The route through the **Tiroler Lesachtal** is very pleasant and is part of a series of roads which make up the **Karnische Dolomitenstrasse**. Having passed through the resorts of Kartitsch, Ober and Untertilliach, you enter the province of Carinthia at Maria Luggau. The **pilgrim church** was built in the first half of the 16th century and took 24 years to complete. Its decorative baroque tower is a landmark. Turning left just before St Lorenzen leads to old wooden **watermills**, some still in working order. A club in Maria Luggau takes care of the maintenance and the mills can be visited (inquire at Haus 15).

Nearby **St Lorenzen** features interesting farmhouses with the upper floor and balconies made of wood. Part of the balcony is reserved for drying maize, a typical feature of farmhouses in the Lesachtal (Lesach valley).

[i] Verkehrsamt

From Maria Luggau continue on the 111 east via Kötschach to Hermagor.

Hermagor, Kärnten

3 Hermagor is a small town with its share of medieval history. The **parish church** of the two saints Hermagoras and Fortunatus shows wall paintings in the choir section which date back to the 14th century depicting figures of the Apostles. The beautiful 15th-century winged altar in the **Wolkensteinkapelle** is decorated with carvings and paintings. **Schloss Möderndorf**, south of Hermagor,

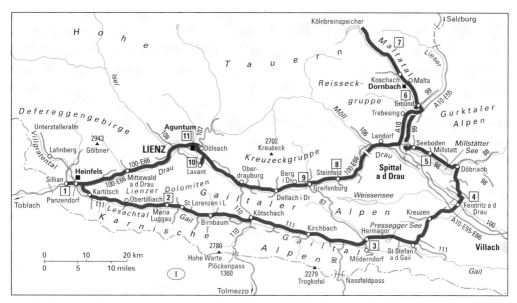

houses the local **museum**, which exhibits a Martin Luther bible of 1541.

The **Pressegger See**, a lake 6km (4 miles) east of Hermagor, is counted amongst the warmest lakes in Carinthia and, favoured by its sheltered position, reaches temperatures of 28°C.

South of Hermagor, the Gerlitzenbach joins the larger Gail river, but before the confluence it has to pass through a dramatic gorge, the **Gerlitzenklamm**. The entrance to the Klamm is just past the village of Mödendorf and the path through the gorge is open from June to September. An excellent system of bridges and trails leads over ravines and many waterfalls, but a good head for heights and surefootedness are needed on certain sections of the path. It takes about two hours to walk from one end to the other and a series of plaques inform the visitor about its geological history.

Alternative routes are available for the return to the car park, taking about two to three hours.

i Verkehrsamt

*Continue on the **111** east to St Stefan an der Gail, turn left after the village and take the **L33** north to Feistritz an der Drau.*

Feistritz an der Drau, Kärnten

4 In the centre of a late Roman fort in Feistritz, remains of an early Christian church were revealed. The **parish church of St George** is interesting because it is a mixture of styles. The core is Romanesque, later rebuilt in Gothic style and the interior features 17th-century baroque.

i Verkehrsamt

*Cross the Drau river and continue north to the **98** and then northwest to Millstatt.*

Millstatt, Kärnten

5 Millstatt lies on the northern shores of the Millstätter See and is a very popular resort. The **abbey**

The quayside at Millstätter See

was founded by Benedictine monks
in 1088 but in 1469 was handed
over to the order of St George,
created to fight the invading Turks.
From 1598 to 1773 the Jesuits were
in charge until the abbey was secularised. Outstanding among its
art treasures is the fresco by
Görtschacher, titled the *Last
Judgement* (1513–19) which had to
be transferred to the church interior
to avoid weather damage.

The town stages many cultural
events during the summer season,
and there are spring, summer and
autumn music festivals with internationally famous musicians and
orchestras. Master classes are
arranged for certain instruments and
an international forum for the arts
organises courses for performing
and graphic arts. The **abbey museum** portrays the history of Millstatt
during the Romanesque, Gothic,
Renaissance and baroque periods. A
dungeon from the first half of the
16th century still displays the original scrawled messages from prison-
ers who were held there. Another
section deals with the geology and
mineralogy of Upper Carinthia, displaying some of the oldest finds in
Austria and Europe. A visit to the
Romanesque cloister and the abbey
church are strongly recommended –
the church is also used for concerts.

> *i* Kurverwaltung Millstatt,
> Rathausplatz

> *Continue on the **98** northwest to
> Seeboden and after a right turn,
> on the **99** to Gmünd.*

Gmünd, Kärnten

6 Gmünd's importance during the
Middle Ages was its position on
the trade route between Venice and
Salzburg and it has maintained its
medieval appearance. The town wall
is nearly completely intact and the
four keeps are proof of its former
defences, which defied Turkish
attacks in 1478. The main square is
flanked by the upper and lower tower gates and is considered the architectural centre of the town. The old
castle is classified a ruin since it
was destroyed by a fire in 1886. The
western part, however, which was
converted into a Renaissance construction, survived and now houses
a theatre, gallery and restaurant. The
Neues Schloss, southeast of town,
was built between 1651 and 1654
and contains the local museum.

> *i* Verkehrsamt, Hauptplatz 20

> *Take the **L12** into the Maltatal.*

Maltatal, Kärnten

7 Malta is the main centre in the
Maltatal (Malta valley), which is
also called the valley of the cascad-
ing waters – many waterfalls are to
be found here. **Schloss Dornbach**,
on the other side of the river, surrounded by water and a high wall,
was built in the 15th century. The
crenellations from this period can
still be seen. Over many bridges,
past numerous waterfalls and
through tunnels, you reach the
Kölnbrein Speicher, the dam of the
reservoir. It lies 25km (16 miles)
from Malta, and is 200m (654 feet)
high, with a span of 626m (2,054

feet). A walk across the dam offers
impressive scenery of the high
mountains in the background, mir-
rored in the waters of the reservoir.

> *i* Tourismusverband Lieser-
> Maltatal, Rathaus, Gmünd

> *From Gmünd take the **A10** south
> to Lieserhofen, then west to
> Lendorf and continue on the **100**
> southwest to Steinfeld.*

Steinfeld, Kärnten

8 Steinfeld, in the upper Drau valley,
is an old village with traditional
burghers' houses. It is now a resort
which caters especially for families.
At nearby **Gerlamoos** the former
Romanesque **church** was modified
into late Gothic style in 1516.
Thomas von Villach, the major master
in late Gothic painting in Carinthia,
created the frescos around 1480 in
the small **church**, which is well
worth a visit. The frescos were
restored in 1979. The Renaissance
castle of Steinfeld lies in the foothills
of the Kreuzeckgruppe (Kreuzeck
mountain range).

> *i* Verkehrsamt

> *Continue west on the **100** to
> Greifenburg.*

Greifenburg, Kärnten

9 The castle of **Greifenburg** consists of two baroque wings with a
Gothic centre. The **parish church of
St Katharina** was completed in
1521 by Lorenz Rieder in late Gothic
style – the interior is mostly decorated in late baroque style.

Nearby **Berg im Drautal** suffered greatly during the Middle Ages from invading Turks and Hungarians. As a result the late Romanesque **parish church** dedicated to the birth of Our Lady had to be converted into a fortified late Gothic building in the 15th century. In 1987 a fire covered all the frescos with a layer of dust, but all damage has since been remedied. The tower has also been saved from collapse and the façade renewed.

☞ Verkehrsamt, Greifenburg

From Greifenburg continue on the 100 and take a left turn to Lavant.

Lavant, Tirol

10 The village of Lavant attracted attention through the discovery of the site of an early Christian church. It is presumed that the building on the site dates back to the 4th century and was later modified on several occasions until it was destroyed by a rockfall in the 6th century. An 'emergency church' was established on the western parts of the ruin, but in 1000 a new **church of St Ulrich** was first mentioned. Remodelled into late Gothic style in 1500, it was again redesigned in 1770 by Thomas Mayr in baroque style. Another **church**, dedicated to St Peter and St Paul, was built on an early Christian place of worship in the 15th century. Fragments of Roman stones, decorated with reliefs, were discovered in 1956 and it is presumed that some of the

stones used in the church building also date back to Roman times.

☞ Fremdenverkehrsverband

From Lavant take the local road northwest, crossing the Drau river, and take a left turn to Aguntum.

Aguntum, Tirol

11 Four kilometres (2 miles) east of Lienz, near the village of Dölsach, lies the site of excavations of the Roman military fort of Aguntum, which was declared a city by Emperor Claudius around AD50. Later wars destroyed the settlement, which was eventually covered by a landslide. The excavations are still going on and the site can be visited.

☞ Fremdenverkehrsverband Lienzer-Dolomiten, Albin-Egger Strasse 17, Lienz

Return to Lienz.

Lienz – Sillian 31 (19)
Sillian – Maria Luggau 29 (18)
Maria Luggau – Hermagor 60 (37)
Hermagor – Feistritz an der Drau 34 (21)
Feistritz an der Drau – Millstatt 23 (14)
Millstatt – Gmünd 19 (12)
Gmünd – Maltatal 6 (4)
Maltatal – Steinfeld 90 (56)
Steinfeld – Greifenburg 6 (4)
Greifenburg – Lavant 33 (20½)
Lavant – Aguntum 5 (3)
Aguntum – Lienz 4 (2½)

The church at Lavant

BACK TO NATURE

2 *En route* between Maria Luggau and Hermagor, turn right at Kötschach and take the **B110** to the **Plöckenpass.** Botanists and nature lovers will enjoy the many flowers to be found on the **Mauthner Alm** and the **Hinterjoch mountain.** A **nature trail** takes visitors through this unique sea of flora. In **Kötschach** trekking, boat trips, rafting and kayak courses are on offer.

RECOMMENDED WALKS

7 At the Kölnbrein reservoir, a walk from the Berghotel Malta on the northern shore of the lake should not be missed for the exhilarating scenery.

5 days – 261km (161 miles)

THE SOUTHERN LAKES

Villach • Faaker See • St Jakob im Rosental
Ferlach • Eisenkappel • Eberndorf • St Kanzian
am Klopeiner See • Völkermarkt • Klagenfurt
Maria Wörth • Keutschacher See • Viktring
Pörtschach am Wörther See • Velden am
Wörther See • Villach

Villach is the second largest town in Carinthia, and has a long history. The most ancient finds are the burial sites found on the Napoleonwiese, near town, dating back to the Stone Age. The Römerweg, built by the Romans, is a path paved with stones. The Carolingians, who occupied the town after the Romans, called it Fillac, and in 1007 Villach became the domain of the bishops of Bamberg in Bavaria. In 1240 it received its town charter. Heavily bombed during World War II, later modernisation spoilt the former medieval character of the town.

☐ Fremdenverkehrsamt der Stadt
Villach, Europaplatz 2

From Villach take the 84 to Maria Gail and Drobollach on the Faaker See (Faaker lake).

Faaker See, Kärnten

1 About halfway from Villach to the Faaker See lies the **parish church of Maria Gail**. There was an early Romanesque church on the site but

Water-skiing, a favourite pastime

the present building has only a few parts of the original church in the nave and the massive tower above the choir section. The late Gothic winged altar is a masterpiece of carving and painting. Its main theme is the crowning of Our Lady by God and His Son.

The Turks set up camp near the Faaker See at the end of the 15th century on one of their forays into Austria and the church became one of their targets. It had to be reconsecrated in 1486 after they were driven out. A century later another disaster, an earthquake, damaged the church again, but the benevolent family of Grotto zu Grottenegg, from nearby Finkenstein, restored it.

The Faaker See is one of the southernmost lakes in Austria and Carinthia and reaches temperatures of 27°C. Its flat shoreline makes it an ideal recreation area for swimmers, windsurfers, sailors and anglers. Motorboats are not allowed, but rowing and electro-boats are there for hire. Horse-riding along the lakeshore is available for enthusiasts.

☐ Fremdenverkehrsverband, Drobollach

Continue southeast on the 84 to the junction with the 85 and then east to St Jakob im Rosental.

St Jakob im Rosental, Kärnten

2 The artificially created lake at St Jakob provides good opportunities for water enthusiasts. Anglers, in particular, are well catered for on the **Feistritzer Stausee**. About 5km (3 miles) northwest, near **Rosegg**, an old forest has become a wild animal reserve – over 150 animals from different parts of the world are kept in natural surroundings. Bison from the US, yaks from Manchuria and mouf-flon from Sardinia are to be seen along with local deer. The bird world is well represented with cranes, ducks and wild geese. A special station occupied in July and August holds diurnal birds of prey. The park is open from April to the end of October.

☐ Verkehrsamt

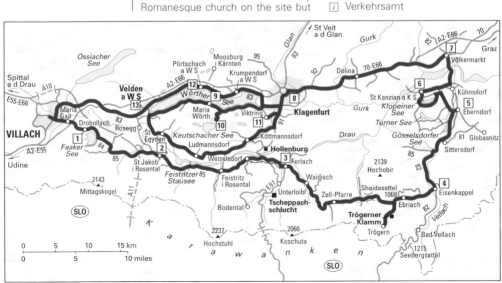

Gunmaker's sign, Ferlach

From St Jakob continue on the 85 east via Feistritz im Rosental to Ferlach.

Ferlach, Kärnten

3 A stop at Ferlach gives you a chance to visit the **Büchsenmacher Museum** (Gunsmith Museum) in the **Rathaus** (town hall), where the history of making weapons for hunting is on display. Do not miss a trip south to **Unterloibl**. From here a 1.5km (1-mile) walk to the inn, **Zum Goldenen Brünnl**, leads to the entrance of the **Tscheppaschlucht** (gorge). It takes about an hour to go through the gorge and as the path is secured with a handrail it is suitable for all ages. From the exit another exciting trail leads up to the **Bodental**. At one point the path runs through an arch in the rocks called the **Devil's Archway** and then to the **Tschanko waterfall**.

⧉ Fremdenverkehrsverband

Take the L103 southeast via Zell-Pfarre up to the Schaida Sattel (pass), now the L108, then turn right (south) to Trögern, back to the turn-off and east on the L131 for the last 8km (5 miles) to Eisenkappel.

Eisenkappel, Kärnten

4 Having turned south you reach the **Ebriachklamm** and past it the **Trögener Klamm**, the main attraction of this part of the tour. The road leads through both gorges and the latter is flanked by bizarre limestone rocks – its natural beauty is so impressive it has been placed under a preservation order. The Austrian talent for *Gemütlichkeit* (comfort) and catering has placed an inn at either end of the Trögerner Klamm. The hamlet of **Trögern** lies at the end of the road and can be used as a starting point for hikes into the surrounding mountains.

Eisenkappel was originally called Kappeln, after a *kapelle* (chapel) from AD1050. The prefix Eisen was only added after 1890 to denote its function as a marketplace for iron from the Lavant valley. A trip to the **Tropfsteinhöhlen** and the **Obir caves** is recommended. The visit takes you into the silent world of stalagmites and stalactites, enhanced by a magnificent *son et lumière* display.

South of the town, at the entrance to the Leppen valley, springs called the **Carinthia-Lithion-Quellen** produce water with healing properties for circulatory problems.

The **Seebergsattel** (pass), 14km (9 miles) south now forms the border with newly created Slovenia, which has seceded from former Yugoslavia. Before World War I it was part of the Austro-Hungarian empire. The drive from Bad Vellach leads over 5km (3 miles) up to 1,215m (3,645 feet) and the reward lies in magnificent views over the Karawanken mountain range.

⧉ Fremdenverkehrsamt

From Eisenkappel take the 82 north to Eberndorf.

Eberndorf, Kärnten

5 The large keep at the entrance to the **abbey** is a reminder of the defences erected in the Middle Ages against the marauding Turks. The abbey was built in the first half of the 12th century but in the latter half of the 15th century a wall and ditch had to be added to increase security. A fire in 1723 damaged the whole complex and in 1751 it was rebuilt to its present state. The tomb of the Knight Christoph Ungnad, who showed great courage when fighting the Turks, is considered to be a masterpiece of artists from Salzburg and Carinthia. It was erected in the 15th century out of Salzburg marble.

The **Gösselsdorfer See**, a lake 3km (2 miles) south of Eberndorf, provides a good spot for relaxation through its quiet position and bathing facilities. A detour of 6km (4 miles) southeast to the village of **Globasnitz** reveals interesting Roman remains. The settlement here was called *Luenna* and these excavations show foundations of Roman houses with their magnificent underfloor central heating. A visit to the local **museum** provides additional information and also exhibits finds from the nearby **Hemmaberg**, 2km (1 mile) west of Globasnitz. The Celtic settlements on the summit of the Hemmaberg were destroyed around AD600 and replaced by early Christian churches, the foundations of which can be seen in the **open-air museum** on the site. A wall surrounded the settlement and parts can still be seen.

⧉ Fremdenverkehrsverband

Take the local road northwest to the Klopeiner See, drive west along its south shore and turn north to St Kanzian.

SCENIC ROUTES

8 The drive from Klagenfurt along the southern shore of the Wörther See is very attractive and offers many opportunities for stops at any one of several small places for a swim.

10 Turning southeast after Velden into the Rosental valley leads along the River Drau. Looking south the imposing limestone mountains of the Karawanken range come into view. From Köttmannsdorf a short detour southeast leads to Unterschlossberg and the banks of the Drau river. A visit to **Schloss Hollenburg** is recommended. The plain-looking exterior of the castle stands in total contrast to its interior. Rows of flowerbeds adorn the Renaissance-style arcades and exude a delightfully friendly atmosphere. Near by the **Maria Rains'** pilgrim church is a little jewel standing on a hill among the lush meadows.

SPECIAL TO...

3 Every Saturday afternoon, from the beginning of June to early September, a steam train runs from Ferlach to Weizelsdorf and back. The journey takes about one hour in each direction through the lovely Rosental valley. For photographers a special stop is arranged to take a shot of the train 'drawing up', and the whole trip is a nostalgic delight.

FOR CHILDREN

8 The **Minimundus** open-air exhibition displays more than 150 models of well-known international and Austrian buildings at a scale of 1:25. A harbour basin contains model ships and a model railway runs through the whole area. The exhibition is open daily from the end of April to October. Late openings are Wednesdays and Saturdays, when you can see the models illuminated. The profits are donated to the Austrian Save the Children fund.

St Kanzian am Klopeiner See, Kärnten

6 St Kanzian boasts the first electrically operated observatory in Carinthia, equipped with a 17cm Newton telescope. The lake is noted for its temperature of 28°C and rates amongst the warmest in Carinthia. Windsurfing, horse-riding, golf and tennis are available as well as bathing. The nearby **Turner See** will appeal to those who prefer a smaller, more tranquil setting.

i Fremdenverkehrsamt

Take the local road east towards Kühnsdorf and then a left turn north on the 82 to Völkermarkt.

Völkermarkt, Kärnten

7 Before reaching Völkermarkt you cross the reservoir on a long, low-level bridge. The town was at its peak in the 16th century, when the Fugger merchants from Augsburg

From Völkermarkt take the 70 west to Klagenfurt.

Klagenfurt, Kärnten

8 Klagenfurt, capital of the province of Carinthia, was founded in the 12th century by Duke Hermann von Spanheim on a shallow site by the River Glan, which gave it the name the Furt an der Glan (ford on the Glan). A century later Duke Bernhard transferred the settlement to the foothills of the Kreuzberg mountain. During the Middle Ages peasant uprisings and the danger of Turkish attacks threatened Klagenfurt. In 1514 a fire nearly devastated the whole town; fortifications were then erected which made it one of the best defended towns in the Alps. In 1809 French troops blew up the town walls and inadvertently encouraged the extension and modernisation of Klagenfurt.

The town centre is still the **Alter**

Klagenfurt's famous Lindwurm

met their Venetian counterparts here. The foundations of Völkermarkt were established in the 11th century by Count Engelbert von Spanheim. Two hundred years later the Dukes of Spanheim built a bridge across the Drau river and so created the conditions for the development of the area as a trading centre. Turkish attacks made it necessary to fortify the town and this has helped the preservation of houses in the old part. The **heritage museum** explains local customs and history and is open from May to the end of October.

The imposing keep of the **Herzogsburg** (Duke's Castle) on the north end of the main square is witness to the former defence capabilities of the town. The **Altes Rathaus** (Old Town Hall) with its attractive arcades was constructed in the 15th century. Around 1715 the **Pestsäule** (Plague Column) was erected in the square as a memorial and now crowds enjoy themselves here every Wednesday, the traditional market day.

i Fremdenverkehrsamt, Hauptplatz 1

Platz (Old Square). The houses along this oblong square were once the residences of the noble burghers and wealthy merchants. The façades and courtyard arcades have all been restored to their original baroque style. In line with old traditions, they still bear names like Goldene Gans (the Golden Goose), Zur blauen Kugel (the Blue Ball) and Zum goldenen Anker (the Golden Anchor). The street numbers were added much later. The **Goldene Gans** dates back to the 15th century when it was the town hall. A little tower in the **Arkadenhof** (courtyard) is presumed to be a remnant of the old town wall which stood here.

The most important religious building is the **cathedral**, which was built by the Protestants around 1578–91. It is basically early baroque in style with late Gothic features incorporated in the interior. Interesting is the use of 11 different kinds of marble in the chapels on the eastern side. The **Landhaus** near by is closely linked with the history of the town. It was finished in 1590, when it was called the

Schloss (castle). It kept its original character although the façade and elegant arcades of 1740 altered its appearance. Inside the Grosser Wappensaal (Great Heraldic Hall) 665 painted coats of arms of the religious and secular aristocracy decorate the walls. Josef Ferdinand Fromiller was the artist responsible for most of the coats of arms, also for the historical paintings on the north and south sides of the hall and the ceiling. The Kleine Wappensaal (Lesser Heraldic Hall) contains the coats of arms of local rulers.

The emblem of Klagenfurt is the **Lindwurm**, a horrific dragonlike beast connected with the legend of the town's origins. The saga refers to the original foundations of the town on a murky swamp, inhabited by a dragon which was later slain. The monument stands in the **Neuer Platz**, the new town square. Ulrich Vogelsang sculpted the monster out of one single block of stone in 1590. It was erected in 1605 and later partnered with a statue of Hercules. The Lindwurm is now used as a fountain.

[i] Fremdenverkehrsamt, Rathaus

*Leave Klagenfurt south on the **91**, turn right for the **L96** and continue west to Maria Wörth.*

Maria Wörth, Kärnten

9 Maria Wörth enjoys an enviable position on the shores of the Wörther See. In the 9th century it was still an island. It is the oldest Christian settlement in Carinthia; the surrounding water provided security and shelter for the inhabitants in earlier years and in the 12th century when the Bishops of Freising, Bavaria, selected Maria Wörth as a base for spreading the Christian faith in Carinthia. The Gothic **parish church** is a landmark, but the interior is baroque and the crypt is in Romanesque style. The imposing high altar signifies the power of the Counter-Reformation and the Jesuits, who took over the church in 1598.

A small Romanesque church, the **Rosenkranz** (rosary) or **Winterchurch**, stands west of the parish church and is decorated with Romanesque frescos from the 11th century. Maria Wörth was connected to the mainland in 1770 and is now a charming small holiday resort on the warm Wörther See.

[i] Verkehrsamt

*Take the **L96** for a short drive east, then turn right to Keutschacher See.*

Keutschacher See, Kärnten

10 The Keutschacher lake is only 2km (1 mile) long and 1km (½ mile) wide, sheltered from wind and away from heavy tourist traffic. No motorboats are allowed here and it is an ideal retreat from the bustling Wörther See, which is only 3km (2 miles) away. A road leads right up to the top of the nearby **Pyramidenkogel** (850m/2,789 feet). From here a lift takes visitors up the viewing tower, from where you can get a good orientation of the surrounding area and splendid views of the Wörther See. Campers will enjoy the lakeside which offers three designated camping sites.

[i] Verkehrsamt

*Drive back to Maria Wörth and continue west on the **L96**, bypass Velden am Wörther See and turn south along the north side of the Drau river and on the **L99** east to join the **91**. Drive north on the **91**, and after a short distance turn left to Viktring.*

Composer Gustav Mahler found the small town of Maria Wörth an inspiring summer home

FOR HISTORY BUFFS

12 The **Carolingian Museum** at **Moosburg im Kärnten** is 5km (3 miles) north of Pörtschach. It is dedicated to King and Emperor Arnulf of Carinthia who ruled in the 9th century, and Moosburg's ancient history. Showcases present the unearthed finds from excavations around Moosburg and its castle. Roman pottery, ancient weapons, documents and jewellery share space with Carolingian stone carvings, maps and facsimiles of illuminated manuscripts. A model of the former imperial palace is also on show. The towering ruins of Arnulf's stronghold, surrounded now by tall trees, complete the visit. The museum is open from early June to the beginning of September; other times by prior application.

BACK TO NATURE

5 Nature lovers will be delighted at the naturist holiday centre near Eberndorf, called the **Rutar Lido**. A large area has been developed offering indoor and outdoor pools, a landscaped lake, saunas and a cosy restaurant. An apartment hotel, holiday homes and caravans are available, as well as 365 camping plots.

RECOMMENDED WALK

6 The **Klopeiner See** has two smaller lakes close by, all within walking distance. A suggested circular walk starts from St Kanzian west to the Klein See, then south to the Turner See and back north to St Kanzian. The walk leads through pleasant wooded countryside between the lakes.

Viktring, Kärnten

11 Viktring has been incorporated into the municipality of Klagenfurt but has its own history, which is closely associated with its famous **abbey**. One of the most important monasteries in Carinthia, it was founded in 1142 by Count Bernhard of Spanheim and subsequently used by Cistercian monks. The monks came from Lotharingia, now in France, and brought with them their late Romanesque building style from Burgundy. The purposely functional and plain interior of the building conforms with the puritanical outlook of the Cistercians. Notable are the three stained-glass windows in the choir section of the church which were erected around 1400. The windows are of great artistic value and depict the Apostles and other religious scenes.

☐ Rathaus, Klagenfurt

*Return to the **91**, drive north, then take the Klagenfurt ring road west and the **83** to Pörtschach.*

Pörtschach am Wörther See, Kärnten

12 Pörtschach is a well-known resort on the Wörther See with a long history. In 1166, the Leonsteiner dynasty erected a **castle** here, now a ruin. In the 16th century a new **Schloss Leonstein** was built near the old one. Pörtschach is divided into a western and eastern half by a peninsula which juts out into the lake and enables visitors to enjoy gentle strolls on the promenade along the lake. The town has extensive sport and leisure facilities. Watching the waterski jumping is a favourite pastime. The lake offers excellent opportunities for sailing, and motorboats are also on hire. Tennis players have a choice of 42 courts and two halls with indoor courts. International championships take place here during the season. Golfers have the nearby Golf Club Austria at **Moosburg**. Other clubs can be found further afield.

☐ Information, Gemeindeamt

The mainly industrial town of Villach is best explored on foot

*From Pörtschach continue on the **83** west to Velden.*

Velden am Wörther See, Kärnten

13 Velden lies on the west side of the lake and is the most exclusive of the lakeside resorts, favoured by the wealthy. It represents the social and cultural centre of the Wörther See. There is proof of human settlement here 7,000 years BC. Burial places found at Frög date from 750 to 400BC. **Schloss Velden**, which stands near the shore, was built between the 16th and 17th centuries in Renaissance style by Bartholomäus Khevenhüller, with an early baroque entrance. By the end of the 16th century it was a meeting place of the local aristocracy, but in 1891 it was rebuilt for use as a hotel. The opening of the railway line from Klagenfurt to Villach in 1864 provided the necessary infrastructure for the first public bathing complex on the lake, which opened in 1865. The facilities for sport and leisure offered are extensive and the Kurverwaltung provides the necessary contacts.

☐ Kurverwaltung, Seecorso 2

*From Velden go west on the **83** to Villach.*

Villach – Faaker See 7 (4½)
Faaker See – St Jakob im Rosental 15 (9)
St Jakob im Rosental – Ferlach 22 (13½)
Ferlach – Eisenkappel 38 (24)
Eisenkappel – Eberndorf 15 (9)
Eberndorf – St Kanzian am Klopeiner See 10 (6)
St Kanzian am Klopeiner See – Völkermarkt 13 (8)
Völkermarkt – Klagenfurt 26 (16)
Klagenfurt – Maria Wörth 17 (10½)
Maria Wörth – Keutschacher See 5 (3)
Keutschacher See – Viktring 47 (29)
Viktring – Pörtschach am Wörther See 19 (12)
Pörtschach am Wörther See – Velden am Wörther See 9 (5½)
Velden am Wörther See – Villach 18 (11)

The Grossglockner is Austria's highest mountain

ⓘ Fremdenverkehrsamt der Stadt Villach, Europaplatz 2

From Villach take the 100 to Spittal an der Drau.

Spittal an der Drau, Kärnten

1 The town of Spittal is often referred to as Spittal am Millstätter See, due to its proximity to the lake. It lies at the confluence of the Lieser and Drau rivers and its name comes from *Spittel*, an old German word meaning hospital. In 1191, a small church and hospital for pilgrims stood here. Previously a market place, the town only received its charter in 1930. One building outshines the rest, the Renaissance **Schloss Porcia**. It is also called the Schloss Salamanca after the Spanish Count Salamanca, who, as chancellor to Archduke Ferdinand of Austria, had the palace built between 1533 and 1597. It is one of the few Austrian buildings in true Renaissance style, and it incorporates some exquisite Italian designs. The focal point is the courtyard with three-storeyed arcades built on a square base. The upper floors house the local **Bezirksheimatmuseum** (District Museum) which gives information on the different ruling houses of the area and local folklore. A **miniature castle** in the park exhibits a collection of minerals and a **mining museum**.

The remnants of a Celtic settlement, called *Teurnia* (which under the Romans became *Tiburnia*) can

OVER THE ALPS TO FAMOUS SPAS

Villach • Spittal an der Drau • Obervellach Flattach • Döllach im Mölltal • Heiligenblut Grossglockner Hochalpenstrasse • Dorfgastein Bad Hofgastein • Badgastein • Mallnitz Villach

Although the town of Villach spreads out on both sides of the Drau river, the old centre lies on the right bank. The Hauptplatz (main square) is surrounded by burghers' houses, the most famous being no 18, where the physician and scientist Theophrastus Bombastus von Hohenheim (called Paracelsus) spent his youth (see page 55). The house is notable for its inner courtyard and decorative Renaissance arcades. Other interesting houses are the Hirscheggerhaus at no 20, with a three-storeyed courtyard and the Gasthof Post, no 26, which dates from 1525. The parish church of St Jakob also stands on the main square and has a 95m (312-foot) Romanesque tower. Inside the church are impressive gravestones of members of important 16th-century families, including the Khevenhüllers.

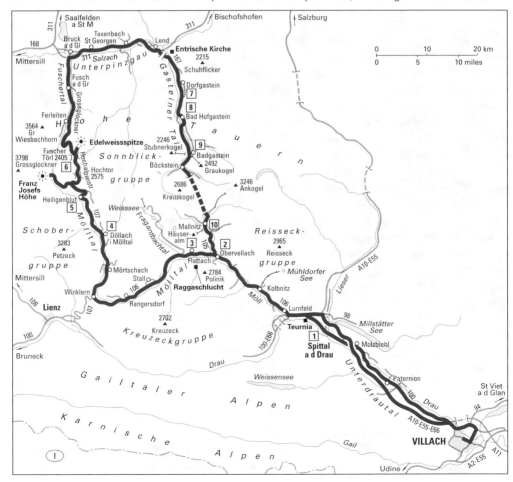

SCENIC ROUTES

4 The really attractive part of the Grossglockner Hochalpenstrasse (High Alpine Road) begins after leaving Döllach. Meadows and trees gradually give way to alpine pastures and are followed by a region of rocks and ice. The panoramic views from the **Edelweissspitze** are claimed to include 37 alpine peaks in excess of an altitude of 3,000m (9,843 feet).

be seen at **St Peter in Holz**, about 5km (3 miles) northwest of Spittal. The scattered remains lie between the main road and the confluence of the Fischerbach into the Drau river. The **Teurnia Museum** and an **open-air exhibition** provide additional insight into the early cultures and civilisations of the region.

i Fremdenverkehrsamt, Burgplatz 1 (Schloss Porcia)

From Spittal continue northwest on the 100 to the junction at Lurnfeld and take the 106 northwest to Obervellach.

Obervellach, Kärnten

2 Obervellach became known in the 16th century for its gold and copper mining industries. It was during this time, when the town flourished, that the local **parish church of St Martin** was built and attracted the famous Dutch painter Jan van Scorel in 1520, a pupil of Albrecht Dürer. Although one of his early works, the altar triptych in the northern chapel is judged to be a masterpiece of the Renaissance period.

i Fremdenverkehrsamt

Continue on the 106 west to Flattach.

Flattach, Kärnten

3 Flattach is the starting point for two excursions. South lies the entrance to the **Raggaschlucht** (gorge), to which a visit is recommended. The walk extends over 800m (2,625 feet) and climbs 200m (650 feet). There are secured walkways along the rocks and over bridges, which make this an enjoyable and fascinating exercise. The gorge is open daily from May to October.

The former gold and silver mining centre of Döllach im Mölltal

The trip north leads by road through the Fragantbachtal to the **Weissseehaus**. A cableway then takes you to the **Wurtenkees glacier**. The views from up here are very rewarding and extend as far as the highest peaks of the Eastern Alps.

i Gemeindeamt

From Flattach continue on the 106 to Winklern and then north on the 107 to Döllach.

Döllach im Mölltal, Kärnten

4 Up in the valley of the Möll river lies Döllach, the main centre of the newly created community resort of **Grosskirchheim**, which takes in a number of small villages in the vicinity. The **Schloss** was built in the 15th century and once housed the administration of the gold and silver mining in the area. Its imposing buildings are interconnected by walls and now incorporate an interesting **museum**, which explains the development of gold mining in the Hohe Tauern mountains – already practised in Roman times. A collection of minerals, old furniture, tools, arms and artefacts from Upper Carinthia supplement the exhibition.

i Verkehrsamt

The little town of Heiligenblut comes as a welcome relief after the almost relentless parade of nature's wonders

From Döllach continue on the 107 north to Heiligenblut.

Heiligenblut, Kärnten

5 Heiligenblut is perhaps one of the most photographed places in Austria because of its position, its attractive church and superb background. The name means Holy Blood and legend recalls the story of St Briccius, who wanted to take a sample of the blood of Jesus from Constantinople (now Istanbul) back to Denmark. He was killed by an avalanche, but later found and buried. A chapel was erected above his grave and the precious relic was later stored in the **parish church** of Heiligenblut. The church was erected by the miners' guild with the help of local farmers between 1483 and 1491 in true Gothic style. The wood-carved altar comes from the workshop of the famous Michael Pacher, the man responsible for many of the masterpieces in Alpine churches. The relic is kept in the **Sakramenthäuschen**, a shrine in the choir section. You should not miss the crypt. Steps lead down to a hall which is impressive in its noble simplicity and style. The church is surrounded by a beautiful church-yard and graves with wrought-iron crosses above them.

ℹ️ Verkehrsamt

From Heiligenblut continue on the 107 north to the Hochtor and Fuscher Törl.

Grossglockner Hochalpenstrasse, Kärnten/Salzburg

6 Soon after leaving Heiligenblut the real ascent starts and as the maximum gradient is only 1 in 8 this should not cause any problems, especially as the road is superbly engineered. Problems which could arise are caused by the road's popularity in the summer months, when parking areas near the viewpoints can be full and it is advisable to walk for the last stretch. After 8km (5 miles) the road to the Franz-Josefs Höhe branches off to the left. A hotel stands here and you are overwhelmed by one of the most majestic views in the Eastern Alps from a height of 2,362m (7,086 feet). The **Grossglockner**, Austria's highest mountain, stands right in front of you and a lift from the car park leads

SPECIAL TO...

5 The tourist office in Heiligenblut hires out equipment for those interested in gold washing in the surrounding streams. The former mines were used until the 15th century when they iced up, but the rocks in the riverbeds still contain particles of gold. You won't get rich, but it is an entertaining pastime, and who knows, someone may be lucky and bring home some grains of the precious metal.

RECOMMENDED WALKS

1 Between Spittal and Obervellach a stop is suggested at **Kolbnitz** in the Mölltal. The **Reisseck mountain railway** takes visitors up to the Reisseck Lake Plateau in 45 minutes. The large and small **Mühldorfer Seen** are both natural alpine lakes and are now being used as reservoirs. Well-marked trails lead visitors through the area for enjoyable walks and hikes. The **powerhouse** at Kolbnitz can be visited and will be of special interest to the technically minded.

5 From Heiligenblut start northwest of the village via Winkl to the romantic Gössnitzal and the 100m (327-foot) waterfall.

Above: view of the Grossglockner mountain (nearly 3,800m/12,500 feet high) and the Pasterze Glacier (below)

down to the glacier. It is 9km (6 miles) back to the turn-off point and then 7km (4 miles) of zigzags and bends up to the highest point, the **Hochtor**, at 2,575m (8,420 feet), which is also the border between the provinces of Carinthia and Salzburg.

From the Hochtor, the road leads down to the Fuscher Törl and a side road from there up to the **Edelweissspitze**. This is also a superb viewpoint which should not be missed. From then on it is downhill all the way!

ⅰ Franz-Josefs Höhe

Drive from the Edelweissspitze down to Fuscher Törl, turn right and continue on the 107 to Bruck an der Glocknerstrasse. Take a right turn and continue on the 311 to Lend and turn right for the 167 to Dorfgastein.

Dorfgastein, Salzburg

7 When entering the Gastein Tal (Gastein valley) a surprise awaits the visitor. Near the ruin of **Klammstein** is the entrance to a cave, called the **Entrische Kirche** (literally translated as the 'frightening church'). It is a large cave, divided into many subterranean halls. An upper floor, recently discovered, is a great attraction. The cave can be visited from June to September.

A short drive leads to the resort of Dorfgastein, a small restful village surrounded by meadows and pastures. A chairlift leads up to the 1,500m (4,920-foot) **Brandlalm**.

ⅰ Verkehrsamt

From Dorfgastein continue on the 167 to Bad Hofgastein.

Bad Hofgastein, Salzburg

8 This spa resort gets its warm water from a nearby spring. The water is known for its healing properties for rheumatic disorders. One of the main attractions is the swimming pool in the **Kurzentrum**, where the water temperature in the three separate indoor pools is 32°C and swimmers can reach the outdoor pool without leaving the water. If you find this too warm, the sport swimming pool is kept at 24°C. No spa is complete without a **Kurpark**, where you can stroll, and the park in Bad Hofgastein is laid out with alpine flora, affording views of the glaciers of the Hohe Tauern mountain range.

The **parish church of Our Lady** was first built in 894 and was reconstructed several times during the 15th and 16th centuries. It also benefited from donations and gifts during the period 1400 to 1560, when gold mining created many benefactors of great wealth. The church is now one of the finest Gothic-style buildings in the province of Salzburg. The high altar inside is enriched with a statue of the Madonna sitting on a throne. The **Weitmoserschlösschen**, southwest of the town, stands in a commanding position on a hill, representing a **Gewerkensitz** (guildhall), and also the residence of mine owners from the boom years during the 16th century, in typical Salzburg style.

[i] Kurverwaltung

Continue for 8km (5 miles) on the 167 south to Badgastein.

Badgastein, Salzburg

9 The waterfall of the Gasteiner Ache, the river which gushes through the town, is Badgastein's landmark. If you are stopping overnight it is suggested you stay a certain distance from the falls as the noise of the thundering waters is loud. As in many other spas, the Romans were the first to discover the healing qualities of the thermal springs. The first person, however, to analyse the benefits of the springs, was the physician and researcher Theophrastus Bombastus von Hohenheim (see page 51). All kinds of cures are available under doctors' orders, especially for sufferers from asthma, rheumatism and circulatory problems. The **Felsenbad Gastein** offers similar facilities as the one at Bad Hofgastein.

For golfers a nine-hole golf course is available from May to October. As

FOR HISTORY BUFFS

6 East of the village of Bruck, after the descent on the Grossglockner Hochalpenstrasse, lies **St Georgen**. In 1732 a linden tree was planted here to commemorate the expulsion of the Protestants. The tree is still standing and is now a natural monument. Also interesting is the **parish church**, a neo-Gothic building. It contains a picture of Maria auf dem Eis (Our Lady of the Ice) of around 1500.

FOR CHILDREN

Draupromenade 12 in the centre of Villach is the location for the **Villacher Fahrzeug Museum** (automobile museum) which will be of interest to children and adults alike. The museum pays homage to the post-World War II vehicles of the '50s, when owning a car was only a dream to many. The exhibition covers cars, scooters, motorbikes and mopeds and is open daily.

The Gasteiner Ache cascades through the centre of Badgastein

Badgastein is also a winter sports resort a number of lifts are available to take you up to higher altitudes. The Stubnerkogel cableway from the station leads up 2,246m (7,369 feet); the Graukogel chairlift from the Hotel Schillerhof goes up to 1,985m (6,512 feet), while from the Bellevuehotel, another chairlift provides an easy connection to the Almbar, with an open-air pool. Needless to say, good Austrian catering can be found at all three destinations.

A short way south of Badgastein, near **Böckstein**, an old **gold and silver mine** is being used for hot-air treatments. The therapeutic mine shaft has temperatures between 37 and 42°C and humidity of between 80 to 97 per cent. Entry to the **Heilstollen** (treatment shaft) is strictly supervised and a prior visit to a physician is obligatory.

i Kurverwaltung

Drive 4km south to Böckstein. Cars are put on shuttle trains and taken through the tunnel to Mallnitz.

Mallnitz, Kärnten

10 It takes about 10 minutes from Böckstein to Mallnitz by train. Mallnitz is a resort just south of the high Alpine peaks of the Hohe Tauern range and a good centre for walking tours and mountain hikes. The town is 1,200m (3,937 feet) above sea level and the mountain air is crisp and clean.

The Ankogel cableway, about 4km (2 miles) north of Mallnitz takes visitors up to 2,722m (8,930 feet) and apart from the breathtaking views over the snow-covered mountains the terrain offers gentle walks and hikes. You can take the double chairlift to the 1,900m (6,234-foot) **Häusleralm** which starts only 1km (½ mile) south of Mallnitz. Very pleasant walks can be taken from the top terminus on the surrounding plateau.

i Fremdenverkehrsverband

*From Mallnitz take the **105** south to Obervellach, then the **106** southeast to Lurnfeld, the **100** east to Lendorf and join the **A10** southeast to Villach.*

Villach – Spittal an der Drau 41 (25)
Spittal an der Drau – Obervellach
    31 (19)
Obervellach – Flattach 5 (3)
Flattach – Döllach 37 (23)
Döllach – Heiligenblut 10 (6)
Heiligenblut – Grossglockner
    Hochalpenstrasse 31 (19)
Grossglockner Hochalpenstrasse –
    Dorfgastein 66 (41)
Dorfgastein – Bad Hofgastein 8 (5)
Bad Hofgastein – Badgastein 8 (5)
Badgastein – Mallnitz 6 (4)
Mallnitz – Villach 77 (48)

Gilded cherub inside Strassburg's Gothic parish church

ⓘ Fremdenverkehrsverband der Stadt Villach, Europaplatz 2

From Villach drive north on the 98 to Radenthein, turn right and continue east on the 88 via Bad Kleinkirchheim to Patergassen. Turn left on the 95 and take a left fork soon after Ebene Reichenau for the Nockalmstrasse to Kremsbrücke. Turn north and continue on the 99 to Rennweg. From here the route continues either through the tunnel or over the Katschbergpass to St Michael.

St Michael im Lungau, Salzburg

1 The Gothic parish church of St Michael was first documented in 1147. Inside, the oldest part is the choir section, where Romanesque features are apparent, and there are some interesting frescos. At the northern entrance to the church is a Roman gravestone.

About 6km (4 miles) east lies 13th-century **Schloss Moosham**. During the 17th and 18th centuries witch-hunt trials took place here and the actual spot where the inquisitions were carried out can still be seen.

ⓘ Fremdenverkehrsamt

Continue on the 99 east for 3km (2 miles), then take a right fork for the 96 to Tamsweg.

Tamsweg, Salzburg

2 Tamsweg is the main town of the Lungau area and was granted its charter as a market town in 1246. The pilgrims' church of St Leonhard, south of the town, stands on an elevated position above the Mur river with fortifications added in 1480. Notable inside are the stained-glass windows, especially the Goldfenster (golden window), painted in 1450.

During August the *Preberschiessen* takes place on the Prebersee, a lake 9km (5½ miles) northeast of Tamsweg. Participants have to aim at the mirror image of a target on the lake. In theory, their bullets will then be reflected on course!

ⓘ Fremdenverkehrsverein Lungau, Rathaus

From Tamsweg take the 95 west for 11km (7 miles) to Mauterndorf.

Mauterndorf, Salzburg

3 Impressive **Burg Mauterndorf** was built in the 12th century on Roman foundations. It was used by monks from Salzburg to collect the *Maut* (tolls) from passing trade. It became a ruin at the beginning of the last century but was expertly restored between 1894 to 1901. The building consists of two floors and the courtyard and inn on the first floor are open to visitors during the summer.

ⓘ Fremdenverkehrsamt

Take the 99 north for 39km (24 miles) to Radstadt.

FAMOUS ABBEYS & ANCIENT CASTLES

Villach • St Michael im Lungau • Tamsweg Mauterndorf • Radstadt • Schladming Gröbming • St Lambrecht • Friesach • Gurk Strassburg • St Veit an der Glan • St Georgen am Längsee • Burg Hochosterwitz Magdalensberg • Maria Saal • Gerlitzen Villach

A popular trip from Villach leads to the remains of Castle Landskron, only 6km (4 miles) northeast. Although mostly in ruins, the layout of the castle with its surrounding walls and fortifications can still be clearly seen. It stands perched on a mountainside and affords panoramic views over Villach and the Ossiacher See. The Great Hall is used for medieval banquets on Tuesday evenings.

Turning northwest from Villach via Fellach the road takes you to Bad Bleiberg, an old mining village, now a health resort. The thermal spa was only opened in 1988 and many cures are available under medical supervision. On the southeast corner of Villach lies the Warmbad Villach, a waterpark that uses the thermal spring water. A waterfall, rapids and the 'longest chute in Europe' provide fun and relaxation.

Radstadt, Salzburg

4 Historically, Radstadt developed as a medieval town built to guard the strategic route over the Radstädter Tauern. A large section of the town's fortifications are still intact. Three mighty **round towers** linked by remnants of the town wall enhance its medieval character and the remains of the former moat are now called the **Stadtteich**, the town pond. A steep road north of the town leads up to the **Rossbrand mountain**, 1,770m (5,807 feet) high and provides breathtaking views over many peaks in the area.

ⓘ Verkehrsverband, am Stadtplatz

SCENIC ROUTES

The route from Villach to St
Michael leads through the
Nockgebiet, a designated
nature park. Drivers will
negotiate many bends round
these unusually shaped
mountains, called the Nocks.
Of volcanic origin, they are
special to this area of
Carinthia. With their rounded
shapes they create a most
attractive landscape, quite
different from other alpine
areas.

4 The route from Radstadt to
Schladming via the Ramsau
leads through one of the
most attractive parts of
Austria, called the Ramsau
after its main village. The side
road leading up to the
Türlwand hut enables visitors
to admire the sheer rock fall
on the southern side of the
Dachstein mountain, the
Dachstein Südwand. One of
the most challenging climbs
in the Alps, it has claimed
many lives. A cableway
leads up to the nearby
Koppenkarstein, which offers
magnificent views over the
Alps.

*Continue on the 99 west to Eben
im Pongau, take a right turn and
drive northeast to Filzmoos. Take
a sharp left turn north at
Filzmoos to Unterhofalm for a
detour and return. Continue from
Filzmoos east and take a left turn
about 4km (2½ miles) before
Ramsau am Dachstein, then
north for 5km (3 miles) to the
Türlwand-hütte. Return to the
road leading east to Ramsau,
then, having passed Ramsau,
take a right turn to Schladming.*

Schladming, Steiermark

5 Schladming lies in a very attractive
position with the mighty
Dachstein mountain range in
the north, the Schladminger
Tauern in the south, and the
Enns river running between
them in the valley.
Schladming had its boom time in the
Middle Ages, when silver was
mined here. In 1525 it was the centre of the peasants' and miners'
revolt. When this rebellion failed,
the town was burnt down as a
punishment, though subsequently
rebuilt. The **Salzburger Tor** is a remnant of the old fortifications. In more
recent years Schladming has manu-
factured the water-repellent *Loden*
cloth.

ⓘ Verkehrsverein, Hauptplatz

*From Schladming continue east
on the 146 to Gröbming.*

Gröbming, Steiermark

6 Gröbming lies on an elevated
plateau above the Enns river. The
parish church contains one of the
most beautiful and elaborate altars
in late Gothic style and depicts
Jesus on a throne surrounded by
the 12 Apostles, with the story of
the Passion portrayed on the wings
of the altar.
The **Stoderzinken Alpine Road**
starts near the church and leads
towards the 2,047m (6,715-foot)
Stoderzinken mountain and the
Friedenskirchlein (Chapel of
Peace). The view from there is
superb.

ⓘ Verkehrsverein

*From Gröbming take the local
road south to Stein an der Enns
and continue south on the L704
(Erzherzog Johann Strasse), over
the Sölkpass to Schöder.
Continue south on the L501 until
the junction with the 96. Turn left
and pass Murau, then turn right
following the road south via
Lassnitz to St Lambrecht.*

St Lambrecht, Steiermark

7 The road from Gröbming leads
through the **Naturpark Sölktal**.

RECOMMENDED WALKS

Take the Villacher Alpenstrasse into the Dobratsch mountain range and then a chairlift up to the top terminus at 1,958m (6,423 feet). From here a two-hour walk leads up to the top of the Dobratsch mountain, 2,166m (7,106 feet) above sea level. The panoramic views from here take in three countries, Italy, Slovenia and Austria (Carinthia).

5 Schladming in Styria is an excellent centre for walks and hikes south of the town. A mountain road leads up to the Hochwurzen, with a trail to the top of the Guschen peak. Alternatively, take the cableway up to the Planei peak, southeast of the town. From here very rewarding walks to nearby huts and alpine pastures are suggested. The views towards the Dachstein range are superb.

Friesach: the town square (above) and (below) a sculpture of the Madonna

Here you cross the Nieder Tauern until the Mur river is reached at Murau. St Lambrecht is closely associated with the Benedictine **abbey**. The Romanesque minster of 1103 collapsed in 1327 and it took nearly 100 years to build the present Gothic church; of note is the abbey building, which was erected in the 17th century by Domenico Sciassia in Renaissance style. The Kaisersaal (Emperor's Hall), Konklavesaal (clergy meeting room) and the Refektorium (dining hall) are worth visiting – they are decorated in 18th-century baroque style. The abbey museum exhibits some of the original furniture, Roman sculptures and inscriptions.

[i] Verkehrsverein

Continue northeast and follow the bend southeast on the L502 to Neumarkt in Steiermark. Then join the 83 south to Friesach.

Friesach, Kärnten

8 Friesach claims to be the oldest town in Carinthia. It reached its peak period under Archbishop Eberhard II of Salzburg who ruled between 1200 and 1246 and the town became the second largest ruled by Salzburg. Many historical figures have stayed here: Archbishop Konrad in 1122, Emperor Friedrich Barbarossa in 1170, King Richard the Lionheart in 1192 and Duke Leopold VI of Austria, who invited all rulers between the Danube and the Adriatic Sea to Friesach for a meeting and great tournament in 1224. Friesach was occupied in the 13th

SPECIAL TO...

7 A stop at **Murau**, *en route* to St Lambrecht, gives the chance to experience a ride on a **narrow-gauge railway**, the **Murtalbahn**. In spite of many technical problems arising from the mountainous terrain the line was completed in just 316 working days on 8 October 1894. The **Murtalbahn Betriebsleitung** in Murau gives further details about timetables and opportunities for a nostalgic ride on the footplate of one of the steam engines.

century by Bohemians and in the 15th century by Hungarian troops. At the end of the 15th century it was attacked by Turks and in 1797 was occupied by French soldiers.

Its association with the powerful Archbishops of Salzburg and its religious orders means there are numerous churches in Friesach. The **parish church** is noteworthy for its stained-glass window in the choir section. This dates from 1280 and depicts the five wise virgins, waiting for their bridegrooms from heaven, while the five foolish ones seek worldly pleasures. The **Dominikanerkirche**, at 74m (243 feet) long, is the longest church in

BACK TO NATURE

En route from Villach to Radenthein, west of the Feld or Brennsee, an alpine **Wildpark** (game park) invites visitors to wander about and see animals in natural surroundings. Deer, moufflon, ibex, mountain goats, wild boar, foxes and bears can be spotted and there is a special section for petting animals. Around 80 animals live here. An adjoining **museum** exhibits a selection of all kinds of fish from the area.

Carinthia. Its most important treasure is the sculpture of Our Lady, the Friesacher Madonna, which dates back to the early 14th century. The **church of the Holy Blood** contains Romanesque columns from a former building on the site. The **Deutschordenskirche of St Blasius** is basically a Romanesque-style building with interesting carvings. The **Stadtbrunnen**, the town fountain, is the work of an Italian master of 1563. In summer visitors to Friesach are entertained by amateur performers at the *Sommerspiele*. Plays are produced at the **Burghof**, and many other festivals take place in the town.

[i] Fremdenverkehrsbüro, Hauptplatz 1

Take the L62 northwest to Metnitz and follow the bend leading south to the L63 to Kleinglödnitz. Turn east on the 93 to Gurk.

Gurk, Kärnten

9 Gurk's cathedral is counted among the most beautiful and famous Romanesque churches in Austria. The foundations were laid in 1140 and the main buildings were finished 80 years later. The founder of the convent was Countess Hemma, and her remains were transferred into the crypt under the choir in 1170. The high altar is a masterpiece by Michael Hönels. It is over 14m (46 feet) high, modelled in Spanish Imperial baroque style. Seventy-two carved figures have been incorporated in the altarpiece, which took six years to complete. The figure of Thomas Becket stands next to Pope Leo, the saints Florian and George, with the patroness Hemma and Empress Kunigunde

Strassburg Castle

crowning the main alcove – Romanesque and Gothic frescos adorn the porch and bishop's chapel. A conducted tour includes a visit to the crypt with its 100 columns supporting the upper parts of the cathedral.

[i] Marktgemeindeamt, Dr Schnerich Strasse 12

From Gurk continue northeast on the 93 for 4km (2½ miles) to Strassburg.

Strassburg, Kärnten

10 Strassburg is a medieval town crowned by a **castle** which was formerly the seat of the prince-bishops of Gurk. The two keeps and the Romanesque Mauritius chapel are the only remains of the fortress, founded in 1147 under Bishop Roman I. Earthquakes and subsequent alterations changed the shape from its original design. Five hundred years of architectural history can be observed in the structure of the buildings – from Romanesque and Gothic via the Renaissance to baroque – signifying the change from a medieval fortress to a castle.

[i] Fremdenverkehrsamt

From Strassburg return to Gurk and take the L67 south to St Veit.

St Veit an der Glan, Kärnten

11 Originally surrounded by a 10m (33-foot) high wall, St Veit was the capital of Carinthia from 1170 until 1518. Parts of the **town wall** are well preserved and still stand. The **Hauptplatz** (main square) is the focal point of the town. It is 200m (656 feet) long and contains the

Pestsäule (a column commemorating the plague), a **fountain** (commemorating a famous medieval entertainer) and the **Schlüsselbrunnen**, with the statue of a miner. The **Rathaus** (town hall) with its baroque-style façade and inner arcades spanning over three floors, is a beautifully designed building. Above the portal is a plaque made of forged iron depicting a citation, a crown and a coat of arms. Higher up, on the centre part of the roof, is a relief of the imperial crown. The former **Herzogsburg** (ducal castle) in the Burggasse was built between 1523 and 1529 to house the local armoury and is now the **municipal museum**.

[i] Fremdenverkehrsamt, Hauptplatz 1

From St Veit take the 82 east, then turn north after 5km (3 miles) to St Georgen.

St Georgen am Längsee, Kärnten

12 The convent of St Georgen was founded between 1002 and 1008 for the nuns of the order of St Benedict and is one of the oldest in Carinthia. Times have been hard on the convent; it was attacked by the Hungarians in 1259, looted by the Turks in 1473 and damaged by fire in 1527. Roman columns were uncovered during recent renovations. Stones from about AD300 were used in the arches of the cloisters and the north wall of the church. A modern **watersports centre** has been created on the lake and from here you can hire rowing and sailing boats, as well as swim.

[i] Verkehrsamt

From St Georgen am Längsee drive back south to the 82, continue east and after 2km (1 mile) turn into a side road to Hochosterwitz.

Burg Hochosterwitz, Kärnten

13 The origins of this fortified castle probably date back to a Roman fort. A rock cone 170m (558 feet) high provided the ideal base for a fortress in the Middle Ages. Fourteen gates had to be crossed to reach the top and inner centre. Having first captured the settlement, Georg Freiherr von Khevenhüller, a civil servant at the Imperial Court, bought the castle and remodelled it into its present appearance. The intricate fortifications withstood all attacks, particularly from the Turks between 1570 and 1586. Impressive collections of suits of armour and medieval weapons together with coins, medals and works of art from the Renaissance are displayed in showrooms in the castle. The Khevenhüller family still own the

Through the gateway of the town hall in St Veit an der Glan there is an inner court with tiered arcades

FOR CHILDREN

When taking an excursion to **Bad Bleiberg** from Villach, do not miss a visit to the **Terra Mystica**, which is both educational and entertaining. A lift takes you 250m (820 feet) down a mine shaft. The journey begins on a former mine railway, passing through an exhibition on the creation of planet Earth and the solar system after the 'big bang'. The workings of the original mine are also explained.

In **Bad Kleinkirchheim**, a small village just past Radenthein, a model railway exhibition next to the Römerbad will be of interest. One hundred and thirty engines, 450 carriages and all the necessary accessories will provide a pleasant break during your journey.

to be erected to fortify the building against threats of attack by the Hungarians – who did attack in 1480 but were repulsed. Stones from the Roman period were incorporated in the outer wall and of note here is a stone relief of a Roman carriage, which is believed to come from the nearby Zollfeld. Apart from important works of art, including the baroque-style high altar, there is a colourful fresco depicting the Three Kings on horseback, which was uncovered in 1884 but dates back to 1435. It is presumed to be the work of an artist from upper Italy. Also within the wall stands a Gothic spire, the **Totenleuchte** (Lantern of the Dead). This was erected to house an ever-burning light to repel demons from the church cemetery. Behind it stands a unique octagonal Romanesque **charnel house**, which was also used for defence purposes when needed.

About 5km (3 miles) north lies the site of the Roman town of *Virunum*. Excavations started in the late 18th century and this former provincial Roman capital has been reconstructed on this location.

[i] Fremdenverkehrsamt, Am Platzl 7

> *From Maria Saal take the L83 south to Annabichl, a suburb of Klagenfurt, turn right and join the 95 near Fesching. Drive north via Moosburg to Feldkirchen, turn left for the 94 to Bodensdorf and the mountain road to Gerlitzen.*

Gerlitzen, Kärnten

16 The panoramic, winding drive from Bodensdorf takes you past many inns and trails leading off the road, inviting a stroll to enjoy the superb views. The highest spot is at the **Berger Alpine Hotel**, 1,800m (5,905 feet) above sea level. **Ossiacher See** (Lake Ossiach), the town of Villach and the Karawanken mountain range in the south offer a scene which will be difficult to forget.

[i] Verkehrsamt, Bodensdorf

> *From Gerlitzen return to Bodensdorf and continue on the 94 to Villach.*

FOR HISTORY BUFFS

15 Five kilometres (3 miles) north of Maria Saal lies the Zollfeld and at its centre stands one of the most significant finds in the area, the **Kärntner Herzogsstuhl**. Many stories exist about this throne, made of Roman stones from the former town of *Virunum*, which stood here. The massive double throne was used by Carinthian rulers in the 8th and 9th centuries as a symbol of their power. Judgement was dispensed from here and until 1651 the dukes used it to receive people who came to pay their tributes.

property and guided tours are available from Easter to October.

[i] Schlossverwaltung

> *From Hochosterwitz follow the L83 southwest to St Michael am Zollfeld, turn left for 2km (1 mile) to Meiselberg and take a left fork to Magdalensberg.*

Magdalensberg, Kärnten

14 In 1948 excavations were started on the Magdalensberg which revealed remnants of a Romano-Celtic town. Most of the buildings have been combined to form an **open-air museum** on the site, which is open to visitors from May to mid-October.

The top of the mountain was sacred to both Celts and Romans. Now the **church of SS Helena and Magdalena** stands here with its late Gothic main altar. The focal point is a woodcarving of Helena, the mother of the Emperor Constantine, who, according to legend, rediscovered the Holy Cross on Mount Golgotha.

[i] Freilichtmuseum

> *From Magdalensberg, return to Meiselberg, turn sharp left to Ottmanach, then sharp right via Rosendorf to Maria Saal.*

Maria Saal, Kärnten

15 The church of Maria Saal was consecrated in AD751–2 and was the see of the bishop until 1052, when it became a centre for pilgrimage. In the first half of the 15th century, modifications were undertaken to the church and in the latter half of the century a surrounding wall had

---

Villach – St Michael im Lungau 101 (63)
St Michael im Lungau – Tamsweg 15 (9)
Tamsweg – Mauterndorf 11 (7)
Mauterndorf – Radstadt 39 (24)
Radstadt – Schladming 60 (37)
Schladming – Gröbming 16 (10)
Gröbming – St Lambrecht 74 (46)
St Lambrecht – Friesach 30 (18½)
Friesach – Gurk 59 (37)
Gurk – Strassburg 4 (2½)
Strassburg – St Veit an der Glan 24 (15)
St Veit an der Glan – St Georgen am Längsee 7 (4½)
St Georgen am Längsee – Burg Hochosterwitz 4 (2½)
Hochosterwitz – Magdalensburg 17 (10½)
Magdalensburg – Maria Saal 10 (6)
Maria Saal – Gerlitzen 50 (31)
Gerlitzen – Villach 27 (17)

5 days – 434km (269 miles)

The wooded spur of the Schlossberg overlooks historic Graz (below). The clock tower in the middle (seen close-up right) is the city's emblem

ℹ Fremdenverkehrsamt, Herrengasse 16

From Graz take the 70 to Voitsberg.

Voitsberg, Steiermark

1 Leopold VI founded the town of Voitsberg below the **castle of Ober-Voitsperch**, now a ruin. The centre of the building within surrounding walls and the Zwinger compound are still standing. **Schloss Greisenegg** is believed to have been Leopold's downtown **castle of Untervoitsberg**, which he founded at the same time as the town. It became the Landhaus in the 19th century, the seat of local government.

Four kilometres (2½ miles) north of Voitsberg, via Bärnbach, stands **Schloss Kainach**, a Renaissance castle from 1526, now an intriguing museum of castles. It can be visited all year round.

ℹ Fremdenverkehrsamt

Continue west on the 70 to Köflach.

Köflach, Steiermark

2 Köflach grew in the 18th century when deposits of coal were discovered here. Now it is better known for its proximity to the village of **Piber**, where the famous Lipizzaner horses are bred. The stud farm was originally founded in the village of Lipica, near Trieste, by Archduke Karl. Spanish and Neapolitan horses, often of oriental descent, were interbred, resulting in the distinctive white horses. After

THE GREEN LANDS OF STYRIA

Graz • Voitsberg • Köflach • Knittelfeld Judenburg • Rottenmann • Spital am Pyhrn Admont • Eisenerz • Leoben • Bruck an der Mur Frohnleiten • Graz

Graz is the second largest city in Austria and capital of the province of Steiermark (Styria). Its name derives from the Slavonic *gradec*, a small castle. Excavations in the Schlossberg area have shown there were settlements here from around AD800. The Habsburgs took great interest in the development of Graz – the castle was enlarged, town gates erected and the cathedral rebuilt. In 1478 the Turks arrived and were repulsed, but they devastated the land around Graz. The result of these attacks was the building of a chain of fortifications from Vienna via Graz to the Adriatic sea. The Counter-Reformation in the 16th century brought the Jesuits into prominence and this increased the political and cultural importance of Graz.

SPECIAL TO...

1 A visit to the **glass centre** in **Bärnbach**, near Voitsberg, is recommended. Guided tours show the production of glass and the museum exhibits, among many other items, include glass from about AD200. It is open daily, Sundays and holidays, mornings only. Information is also provided in English.

FOR HISTORY BUFFS

5 Burg Strechau stands on a crag 3km (2 miles) west of Rottenmann. It was built in the 13th century and became the centre of the Protestant movement in Styria in the 16th century. Visitors can see the outer parts and bastions of the castle.

World War I Austria lost Lipica and the stud farm was moved to Piber to continue the long-standing Austrian tradition. Horse lovers can visit the farm from Easter until the end of October and guided tours are available in the morning and afternoon.

⌐i⌐ Fremdenverkehrsbüro, Bahnhofstrasse 24

From Köflach take the 77 northwest for 29km (18 miles) and then take the right turn for Kleinlobming. Proceed via Grosslobming on the L504 to Knittelfeld.

Knittelfeld, Steiermark

3 Knittelfeld's round tower and remains of the medieval town wall still stand. Bombed in 1945, the town has been completely rebuilt since then and is now an industrial centre. The Österreich-Ring west of the town used to be part of the Grand Prix Formula 1 circuit. Now courses in advanced driving are held here and it is known

in the 14th and 15th centuries to become the largest and most important trade centre of Styria. Literally translated Judenburg means the 'Jews' castle' and refers to a Jewish settlement here on the northwest outskirts of the town. This lasted until 1496, when the Jews were expelled. The head of a Jew, carved in stone and about 500 years old, can still be seen on an oriel of the Post Hotel.

⌐i⌐ Bezirksfremdenverkehrsverband, Kapellenweg

From Judenburg take the 96 west to Mitterdorf and branch off on a right fork for the 114 to Trieben and the 113 to Rottenmann.

Rottenmann, Steiermark

5 Rottenmann was awarded its town charter in 1279 and remnants of its old town wall still stand. During the Middle Ages it was an important trading post for iron ore and salt. In the **parish church** a

BACK TO NATURE

On the return from Frohnleiten to Graz a visit to the **Lurgrotte** near Peggau is recommended. It is one of the most extensive caves in Austria and apart from impressive stalagmites and stalactites, it also shows a rebuilt skeleton of a cave bear. The grotto is open all year round.

Knittelfeld's motor racing circuit – a change from history

to be one of the most picturesque car-racing tracks. **Schloss Spielberg** stands between the town and the circuit and can be seen from some distance. It was erected by an Italian architect/builder around 1570 and is a famous local landmark – it contains beautiful antiques.

⌐i⌐ Fremdenverkehrsamt

Take the S36 southwest to Judenburg.

Judenburg, Steiermark

4 Judenburg's history goes back to the 7th century BC. The **Strettweger Kultwagen**, found at nearby Strettweg, not only testifies to an early settlement but also shows that great artists must have lived here long before the arrival of the Romans. The Kultwagen is a delicately formed miniature carriage on four wheels carrying riders on horseback. It is now on display at **Schloss Eggenberg**, near Graz (see page 67).

Five important trade routes met here, and the town started to grow

painting by the famous Kremser Schmidt and the prayer stool of Emperor Friedrich III can be seen.

⌐i⌐ Fremdenverkehrsamt

Continue on the 113 via Selzthal to Liezen and then north on the 138 to Spital.

Spital am Pyhrn, Oberösterreich

6 The route from Liezen over the Pyhrnpass to Spital was once used by the Celts and Illyrians. The Romans later built the first road connection from here to the Donau (Danube) valley further north. The **church of Maria Himmelfahrt** (Assumption of Our Lady) takes pride in its richly decorated interior, which was executed by great artists. It was built between 1714 and 1730 and the superb frescos were the work of Bartolomeo Altomonte. The high altar is a masterpiece by Veit Königer, who built it in 1763. The side altars are the work of two artists, Martin Altomonte and Martin 'Kremser' Schmidt, a reference to his home town of Krems an der Donau.

⌐i⌐ Tourismusverband

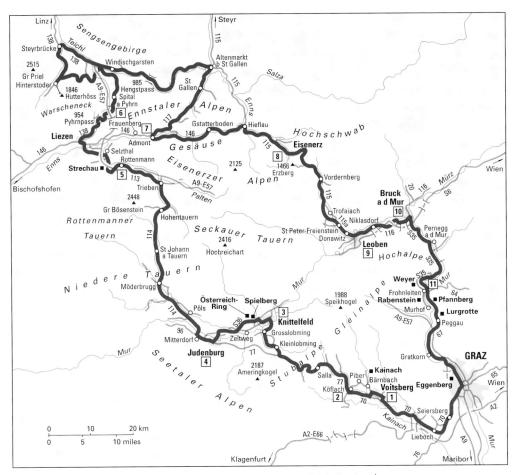

From Spital continue on the 138 north to Windischgarsten, take a left turn on the L551 to Hinterstoder, then a right turn for the L552 to Steyrbrücke and drive southeast on the 138 back to Windischgarsten. Continue on the L550 east to Altenmarkt bei St Gallen and turn sharp right on the 117 southwest to Admont.

Admont, Steiermark

7 Admont is well known for its Benedictine **abbey**. It was founded in the 11th century by Archbishop Gebhard of Salzburg and Countess Emma from Carinthia helped by donating large properties in the Enns valley. One of the most important abbeys in Austria, it was destroyed by fire in 1865. Using what was left from the original abbey, Wilhelm Bucher rebuilt the basilica and parts of the abbey in neo-Gothic style. The main hall of the famous library represents true baroque style with ceiling frescos by Bartolomeo Altomonte, which provide a splendid setting for the books. The main dome is decorated with frescos by Martin Altomonte portraying the protection of art and science by religion and the church. Josef Thaddäus Stammel created 18 sculptures to decorate the hall, four with the motto 'The last four things', showing death, the final judgement, heaven and hell. The library contains about 145,000 volumes and thousands of manuscripts. It is counted amongst the largest abbey libraries in the world. The **Natural History Museum**, housed in a side wing of the abbey, contains a surprising collection of 250,000 insects.

Nearby **Schloss Röthelstein**, southwest of the town, sustained heavy damage in World War II, but some features are still intact, including the Rauchküche (curing kitchen) and a painting on wallpaper depicting a legend of the prodigal son. A very attractive building, only a short drive west from Admont, is the **pilgrim's church of Frauenberg**. Standing in a commanding elevated position, it was rebuilt between 1683 and 1687 with a beautifully painted baroque style façade.

ⓘ Fremdenverkehrsbüro

From Admont take the 146 east to Hieflau, turn right and continue on the 115 to Eisenerz.

Eisenerz, Steiermark

8 Eisenerz cannot belie its connection with the Erzberg, the mountain once 1,534m (5,033-feet) high, but now only 1,466m (4,809 feet), which contains 32 per cent pure iron. The ore is believed to have been mined by the Romans, since when open-cast and subterranean mining has continued to this day. The open-cast mining can be viewed from the **Schiftturm** (shift tower), which is equipped with a bell announcing the shift changes. The underground mining is best viewed by joining a conducted tour. Over 10 million tons of iron per year are mined in the open-cast operations and then transported to the steelworks at Donawitz and Linz.

The **parish church of St Oswald** is said to be the only fortified and fully intact church building in Austria. It was consecrated in 1512 during the time of the Turkish assaults.

FOR CHILDREN

8 Children and adults will enjoy a ride on the **Erzbergbahn**, a railway which was completed in 1891 for the transport of iron ore from the Erzberg to the blast furnaces in Vordernberg and Donawitz. The track is now managed by railway enthusiasts and runs over steep gradients, six viaducts, five tunnels and both round and through the Erzberg mountain. Timetables at Erzberg station.

RECOMMENDED WALKS

6 The area around Spital and Hinterstoder appeals to walkers and hikers. From Spital a walk or drive to the Gasthaus Grünau leads to the Vogelsang Klamm (gorge). A secure and well-designed path takes you through the gorge. At the other end of the gorge you can either walk to some of the huts further up or return to the car park at Gasthaus Grünau.

SCENIC ROUTES

6 The detour from Windischgarsten to Hinterstoder and then along the valley of the Steyr river to Steyrbrücke leads through beautiful alpine woods and meadows, surrounded by mountains. A trip by cableway from Hinterstoder up to the Hutterhöss peak offers rewarding views over the **Totes Gebirge** (the Dead Mountains), so called for their bare and remote appearance. If enough time is available, the trip can be extended from Hinterstoder towards Weissenbach and the end of the valley.

7 One of the best known routes in Austria runs from Admont through the Gesäuse to Hieflau, offering very dramatic scenery. A narrow valley leaves just enough space for the river Enns, a railway line and the road. The gushing waters and rapids are frequently used by kayak enthusiasts and provide a strong challenge for their skill.

Beautiful arcades on Bruck an der Mur's Kornmesserhaus

ⓘ Informationbüro, Hieflaustrasse 19

From Eisenerz continue on the 115 (on the last section the 115a) south to Leoben.

Leoben, Steiermark

9 Leoben was first mentioned in AD982 as an important junction on the trade routes to Italy. King Ottokar of Bohemia transferred the siting of the town in 1262 to a strategically better position on a bend of the River Mur. The new town was properly planned to fulfil the needs of a market place. A wall supplemented by watchtowers surrounded the town and its castle, the **Stadlburg**. This later became a Jesuit monastery. Part of the wall and the **Mautturm** (Toll Tower) are still standing. Notable also is the red painted façade of the **Hacklhaus**, built around 1680 and elaborately decorated with statues and ornaments.

ⓘ Verkehrsbüro, Hauptplatz 12

Take the 116 east to Bruck.

Bruck an der Mur, Steiermark

10 Bruck was granted the privilege to store salt in 1230, and awarded its municipal charter in 1277. The focal point of the main square is the **Kornmesserhaus**, which was built by the wealthy trader Pankraz Kornmesser. It took six years from 1499. His design was inspired by a trip to Venice. Beautifully shaped arcades on the ground floor combine with additional smaller ones on the first floor, forming a loggia. A skilfully ornamented Renaissance fountain adorns the central square. A good view of the town can be obtained from the clock tower of the ruin of **Schloss Landskron**. This tower was the only part of the castle to survive the fire of 1792.

ⓘ Reisebüro der Stadt Bruck an der Mur, Kollomann-Wallisch Platz 25

From Bruck take S35/335/S35 to Frohnleiten

Frohnleiten, Steiermark

11 Frohnleiten was once a market town which controlled the traffic on the Mur river. Delightful old narrow streets enhance its medieval appearance. The town uses its favourable position away from through traffic to develop its efforts into the leisure and tourist industry, together with vantage points in the vicinity.

Murhof, 4km (2½ miles) south boasts an 18-hole golf course in a magnificent setting. The ruin of **Schloss Pfannberg** houses the grave of the *Minnesänger* (medieval entertainer) and poet Hugo von Montfort, who lived here and was governor of Styria until his death in 1423.

Burg Rabenstein, 2km (1 mile) south, was privileged to have the old transit road run right through its courtyard, so that the owners could collect considerable tolls from passing traffic by road as well as from boats on the river below. In summer, medieval banquets are held here from time to time. **Schloss Weyer** is a moated building dating from the 13th century and has an attractive courtyard flanked by arcades.

ⓘ Fremdenverkehrsamt

From Frohnleiten take the 67 south to Graz.

Sculptures decorate the church walls in Wolfsberg

ℹ️ Fremdenverkehrsamt der Stadt Graz, Herrengasse 16

*From Graz take the **70** southwest to Lieboch to the **A2** and continue west as far as the Packsattel (pass) exit. Continue on the **70** southwest to Wolfsberg.*

Wolfsberg, Kärnten

1 Wolfsberg is perched on a hill above the shoreline of the river and is a delightfully romantic-looking medieval town. **Schloss Wolfsberg** was originally Gothic but was converted in 1846 to the English Tudor style. Sadly, it is not open to the public. The Romanesque **basilica of St Markus** has also Gothic and baroque-style features and contains an interesting altarpiece called 'Markus with the Lion', which was painted in 1777 by the famous Kremser Schmidt.

ℹ️ Fremdenverkehrsverband, Bambergerstrasse 100

*From Wolfsberg continue on the **70a/70** south to Griffen.*

Griffen, Kärnten

2 Opposite the **parish church of Griffen** lies the entrance to a fascinating **cave**. Estimates put the age of the limestone at 200 million years. The showcases at the entrance display bones of animals which lived here during the Ice Age, while other discoveries suggest a Stone Age human presence. The special features of the show cave are the colourful stalagmites and stalactites, in addition to the great variety of stone formations which were created over millions of years. Guided tours are conducted daily from May to September and last approximately 20 minutes.

ℹ️ Fremdenverkehrsamt

4 days – 425km (264½ miles)

MEDIEVAL TOWNS & FORTRESSES

Graz • Wolfsberg • Griffen • St Paul im Lavanttal
Deutschlandsberg • Leibnitz
Bad Gleichenberg • Feldbach • St Johann
Weiz • Graz

The cathedral of Graz, the Domkirche St Ägydius, has an inscription on the western entrance: AEIOU. Its original Latin *Austria erit in orbe ultima* means 'Austria will always exist'. The provincial government of Styria sits in the Landtag. The Arkadenhof (courtyard), in the centre of the building, has three storeys of arcades, all in Renaissance style. The Landeszeughaus (arsenal) exhibits armour and weapons from the 15th to 18th centuries, in all about 30,000 items. Schloss Eggenberg, 3km (2 miles) west of Graz, is a masterpiece of baroque style, completed in 1635. The most precious item in the castle museum is the 3,000 year old Strettweger Kultwagen, a delicately executed miniature of immeasurable cultural and artistic value (see page 64).

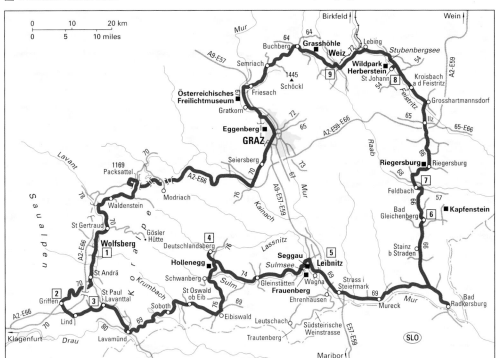

The lower town of Wolfsberg,
set beside the River Lavant

*Take the L127 south to Lind,
take a sharp left turn and continue on the L126 to St Paul.*

St Paul im Lavanttal, Kärnten

3St Paul is a small market town,
surrounded by three churches,
with a troubled past which included
assaults by Hungarian and Turkish
armies. The foundation of the
Benedictine abbey dates back to
1091, which explains the dominant
Romanesque features, well
expressed on its portal. The roof
inside has Gothic vaulting, while the
furnishings and the pulpit are in
baroque style. It was the famous
Michael and Friedrich Pacher from
South Tirol who, in 1470, created
the 'sky' of the church in a manner
very true to life. The fresco by
Thomas von Villach, shows the
founders of the abbey being
recommended for a place in heaven
by St Benedict. You can also detect
a portrait of the artist himself, which
he added in 1493. The west wing of
the abbey contains a valuable collection of paintings, including some by
Peter Paul Rubens, a huge library
and other beautiful objects.

ⓘ Fremdenverkehrsamt

*Continue southeast to
Lavamünd, take the 69 northeast
via St Oswald ob Eibiswald to
Eibiswald, then turn left on the
76 north to Deutschlandsberg.*

Deutschlandsberg, Steiermark

4High above a gorge of the Lassnitz
river stands the keep of the
fortress Deutschlandsberg, built
around 1130 but now ruined. Here,
on 1 January 1292, the Styrian
aristocracy met and decided to rebel
against Albrecht I of Habsburg.
Deutschlandsberg enjoys a soft,
southerly climate and claims 280
days of sunshine a year, which has

helped to establish a thriving wine
industry in the area. Five kilometres
(3 miles) south stands Renaissance
Schloss Hollenegg, open to visitors
by prior appointment.

ⓘ Fremdenverkehrsamt

Take the 74 east to Leibnitz.

Leibnitz, Steiermark

5Leibnitz dates back to Roman
times. Excavations at nearby
Frauenberg have unearthed temple
remains which confirm the existence of a shrine to the goddess Isis
on this spot – the **museum** is worth
a visit.

Nearby **Schloss Seggau** stands
at the confluence of the Sulm and
Lassnitz rivers, and displays ancient
reliefs and mosaics in the courtyard.
The Fürstenzimmer (Halls of the
Princes) are richly decorated with
paintings. Below the foothills of the
Seggau mountain lies the **Sulmsee**,
a lake with possibilities for swimming, rowing and fishing.

ⓘ Fremdenverkehrsamt

*From Leibnitz take the 67 south
to Strass in der Steiermark and
turn east on the 69 to Bad
Radkersburg, then north on the
69/66 to Bad Gleichenberg.*

Bad Gleichenberg, Steiermark

6Bad Gleichenberg was a spa in
Roman times. Its thermal springs,
known for their healing properties,
gush with water at a temperature of
28°C. Drinking and bathing cures are
available for sufferers from circulatory problems. The water is also a
well-known brand of Austrian mineral water. Ten kilometres (6 miles)
east lies **Schloss Kapfenstein**, the
12th-century home of the dreaded
Raubritter (robber knights). These
medieval gangsters would descend
on hapless travellers and relieve
them of their valuables. Happily, the
castle now offers only attractive
views and culinary delights.

SCENIC ROUTES

5The Südsteirische
Weinstrasse (South Styrian
wine road) leads through
very pleasant and attractive
countryside. It starts at
Ehrenhausen, south of
Leibnitz and runs west
through vineyards and a hilly
landscape, along the Austrian
border to Schloss Trautenberg
and Leutschach.

SPECIAL TO...

At **Stübing**, north of Graz,
stands the **Österreichisches
Freilichtmuseum** (Austrian
open-air museum). Over 80
buildings from every Austrian
province are on show here
and document the life and
work of Austrian farmers. An
old grocery shop, a former
classroom and old kitchens –
called **Rauchküchen** (curing
kitchens) on account of their
open fires – are exhibited. A
special section called **Bauern
in Tirol** (Farmers in Tirol)
describes the hard life of
mountain farmers.

ⓘ Kurverwaltung

From Bad Gleichenberg continue on the 66 north to Feldbach.

Feldbach, Steiermark

7 The *Steinerne Metzen*, the old official measure for grain, stands on Feldbach's main square as a symbol of the town's importance as a trading centre in the Middle Ages. The triangular market square shows remnants of a *tabor*, a defence wall against invading Hungarians and Turks. Inside this wall the houses were built close together and their cellars were used to store supplies. A passageway ran along the wall through all the houses to enable quick and safe movement of the defenders. The local **museum** is situated in one of these houses.

Ten kilometres (6 miles) north stands the **fortress of Riegersburg**, one of the mightiest Christian bastions against the Turks. It was built by a formidable lady who earned the nickname Naughty Liesl because of her robust lifestyle.

ⓘ Fremdenverkehrsamt

From Feldbach take the 66 north to Ilz, continue north to Grosshartmannsdorf and take a left fork northwest via Kroisbach an der Feistritz to St Johann.

St Johann, Steiermark

8 St Johann is renowned for the **castle of Herberstein**, which dates from 1300 and has been occupied for 700 years by the same family. The public rooms

Schloss Eggenberg

and family museum can be visited by prior arrangement. Nearby **Stubenbergsee** lies amidst an attractive, hilly landscape: rowing and sailing boats are for hire and trout fishing is also on offer.

ⓘ Gemeindeamt

Continue along the Feistritz river and turn left at Lebing to Hart, then take another left turn and continue southwest on the 72 to Weiz.

Weiz, Steiermark

9 Weiz is called 'the friendly town' because of its position on a basin, sheltered by surrounding mountains. The **church** is dedicated to St Thomas à Becket, and was fortified with a *tabor* (defensive wall) in 1689, which was later turned into living accommodation.

ⓘ Fremdenverkehrsamt

From Weiz take the local road to Steinberg, then the next turning on your right north via the Gollersattel to Buchberg and Seilnergraben. Continue southwest via Neudorf to Semriach and Friesach and south on the 67 to Graz.

Graz – Wolfsberg 88 (55)
Wolfsberg – Griffen 23 (14)
Griffen – St Paul im Lavanttal 16 (10)
St Paul im Lavanttal –
  Deutschlandsberg 72 (45)
Deutschlandsberg – Leibnitz 37 (23)
Leibnitz – Bad Gleichenberg 60 (37)
Bad Gleichenberg – Feldbach 12 (7½)
Feldbach – St Johann 41 (26)
St Johann – Weiz 23 (14)
Weiz – Graz 53 (33)

FOR HISTORY BUFFS

The **mausoleum** of Emperor Ferdinand II, who died in 1637, stands south of Graz cathedral and is reached by climbing up an impressive array of steps. The building was started in 1614 according to plans by Giovanni Pietro de Pomis and the interior was designed by the eminent Austrian architect Fischer von Erlach between 1687 and 1699. Leading artists of the time were commissioned to undertake the work and, besides Emperor Ferdinand II, the mausoleum contains the marble sarcophagus of his mother, Maria of Bavaria.

BACK TO NATURE

8 Wildpark Herberstein lies adjacent to the castle. Apart from about 70 deer, there are foxes and wolves to be seen roaming around in large open enclosures. Other animals there include mountain goats and ibex.

FOR CHILDREN

9 Seven kilometres (4½ miles) north of Weiz lies the entrance to the **Grasslhöhle**, an interesting cave which is suitable for children. Guided tours last about 45 minutes and the main attraction is called the *Riese*, the Giant. It is a stalagmite, 10m (33 feet) high and 2m (6 feet) thick.

Children may also enjoy a ride on the **narrow-gauge steam train** from Weiz to Birkfeld, which is in operation during the summer.

RECOMMENDED WALKS

1 Five kilometres (3 miles) northeast of Wolfsberg lies St Gertraud. From here, 14km (9 miles) east on the **L148** you drive up to the **Gösler Hütte**. This is an ideal starting point for many walks through the pastures and up to the top of the Koralpe mountain range, which is well away from crowded tourist resorts.

SALZBURG & UPPER AUSTRIA

The town of Salzburg has also given its name to the province, which only became part of Austria in 1816. Before then it was under the strong and independent rule of its Archbishops. Its famous son, Wolfgang Amadeus Mozart, is therefore strictly speaking not Austrian by birth, but by his choice to live in Vienna.

Salzburg is a jewel amongst Austrian towns and it is no coincidence that it attracts so many visitors from all over the world. The Salzburg Festival is a major cultural event and the standard of the performances complements the superb setting and atmosphere of the town.

The province of Salzburg extends into valleys leading up to high mountains and the area bordering Tirol and Carinthia has been declared a nature reserve. Traffic into some of the narrow side valleys has been banned apart from shuttle taxis, which take visitors up in the morning, then bring them back again in the evening. The region east of Salzburg had grown into a well-known tourist area long before the arrival of the motor car and was favoured by the Emperor Franz Josef himself. The Salzkammergut lakes acquired fame as stage settings for operettas and musicals. The opportunities offered for leisure and tranquillity there have a proven record and with the cultural centre of Salzburg so near, are hard to beat.

The scene in the province of Upper Austria is quite different, although not so evident in the Salzkammergut, which is shared by both provinces, and Styria. The influence of Bavaria, the western neighbour of Upper Austria, is apparent in its similar landscape and its agricultural background. The province is also a great producer of wealth through its heavy industry, and the capital Linz is one of the fastest-growing towns in Austria. Most modern steelworks and large chemical plants are on the outskirts and are now linked with the west and east through the Rhine, Main and Danube canal.

North of the Danube (Donau) lies an area still off the main tourist routes. Traditional crafts are carried on here and where they are no more economical they are demonstrated in museums. The northern border is formed by the Böhmerwald, the largely unspoilt area of the Bohemian woods which will attract many visitors who appreciate nature left in its original state.

Tour 13

After a detour into one of the side valleys the route from Saalfelden leads east over two mountain passes and offers stunning views over the Salzburg limestone mountains. Back in the main valley a round trip from Bischofshofen allows you to explore the remote scenery of the Kleinarl valley. Two spectacular gorges are next on the itinerary and a detour into the Rauris valley provides insight into an area formerly known for its gold and precious stones. There are also visits to two of Austria's main hydroelectric schemes which not only provide information about one of the country's major assets, but also offers views over the stunning alpine panoramas.

Tour 14

This tour starts with visits to a salt mine, rock and ice caves, then some of the country's most romantic lakes, the Gosau and Hallstätter See. Salt is still on the agenda in the area of the 'Ausseer Land', Bad Aussee and Alt Aussee. Turning north the town of

Bad Ischl, with its former imperial association, is passed and the route leads past the Traunsee and Attersee to the traditional Salzkammergut resorts of St Wolfgang, St Gilgen, Mondsee and Fuschl, which still retain their delightful old-world charm, before returning to Salzburg.

Tour 15

This tour explores one of the lesser known regions of Austria up to now not greatly exposed to tourism. It will be of interest to those who want to explore new pastures and enjoy the tranquillity of unspoilt nature. A stretch along the Danube leads to a turn north into the Mühlviertel (a district of the Mühl river), where its northern frontier is provided naturally by the Böhmerwald, an extensive ridge of forest. One of the most attractive parts lies in the northwest corner near the point where Austria, Bavaria and Bohemia meet. The tour then turns south towards the Danube, which can be crossed by ferry, but no through road exists on the northern shore and the return to Linz has to be taken inland.

Tour 16

From Linz, the capital of the province, the tour leads through the town of Wels and then via the abbey at Kremsmünster to Steyr, well known for its heavy industry. Fortunately the industrial revolution has been kept away from its delightful, well-preserved medieval centre. The tour then follows a stretch into the neighbouring province only to return through Enns to the abbey of St Florian, a highlight of the tour.

Tour 17

This tour leads along the southern shores of the Danube river right up to the Bavarian border town of Passau. The direction changes from here and the tour continues along the Inn river and the border towns of Schärding and Braunau. The route then turns in an easterly direction right through one of the province's agricultural centres at Ried and turns back to Linz, stopping at an old Benedictine abbey *en route*.

Zell am See, the centre of one of Austria's principal sporting areas

3/4 days – 293km (181½ miles)

MOUNTAINS, LAKES & DAMS

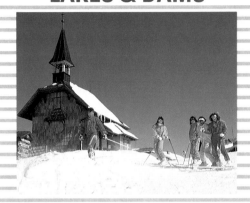

**Zell am See • Saalbach • Bischofshofen
St Johann im Pongau • Liechtensteinklamm
Goldegg im Pongau • Rauris • Kaprun
Enzingerboden • Zell am See**

Zell am See is one of the best known Austrian resorts. It benefits from its uniquely picturesque position, but tends to get very crowded during July and August. Nothing much remains from the old settlement apart from the Vogtturm (tower), which stands in the Stadtplatz and 16th-century Schloss Rosenberg, now the town hall and host to the town museum. The parish church of St Hippolyte was founded in the 10th century. Facilities for recreation are extensive. The lake is fed by water from melted glaciers and its temperature is therefore on the chilly side, reaching about 20°C. However, heated outdoor pools are available for the not-so-hearty. Watersports enthusiasts will find a sailing and windsurfing school, and sailing, rowing, pedal and electroboats are available for hire. Thumersbach, on the eastern shore, has a waterski school.

Perfect conditions at the all-round sports resort of Zell am See

ⓘ Kurverwaltung, Brucker Bundestrasse

Leave Zell am See on the 311 north and turn left at Maishofen for Saalbach.

Saalbach, Salzburg

1 Although better known as a winter sports resort, Saalbach will appeal to visitors who prefer a quieter atmosphere. Covered and open-air pools offer plenty of opportunities for swimming and the village is an excellent centre for walkers and hikers. The **Schattberg cableway** takes you up to the mountain, 2,018m (6,600 feet) above sea level. The cableway can transport 850 people an hour, which helps to avoid queues. The wide panoramic view from the top is of the limestone peaks of the Loferer Steinberge and south to the permanent ice fields of the Grossvenediger mountain. You shouldn't miss turning further along the valley of the Saalach river right to the end of the road. Lush alpine pastures border each side of the river and botanists should walk along the **Pflanzenlehrpfad**, an interesting trail which gives explanations of the various local plants.

ⓘ Fremdenverkehrsverband

From Saalbach return east on the L111 to Maishofen, turn left for the 311 to Saalfelden and turn right to continue east on the 164 to Bischofshofen.

St Johann im Pongau's twin-spired church is a distinctive landmark

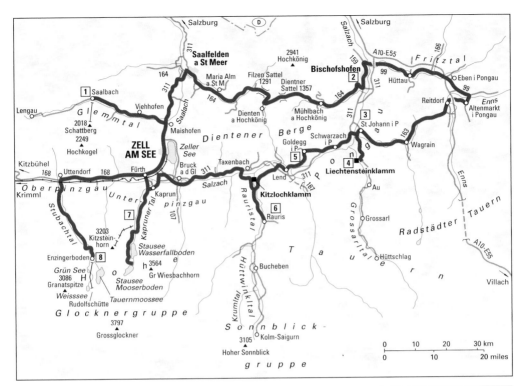

Bischofshofen, Salzburg

2 Bischofshofen is a winter sports resort – ski-jumping was pioneered here. The **parish church of St Maximilian** dates back to the 15th century. The **Rupertikreuz** is a copy of the original from AD800 and is kept in the parsonage. A short walk west of the town leads to the **Bachsfall ruins**. Dating back to the 12th century, they can be seen above the Gainfeld waterfall, which has been designated a national monument. Prehistoric artefacts have been found at **Götschenberg**, a little further on, also the ruins of a medieval citadel and former copper mine.

☐ Fremdenverkehrsverband

Drive 4km (2½ miles) north to the 99 and turn east via Altenmarkt im Pongau and Wagrein to St Johann.

St Johann im Pongau, Salzburg

3 Approaching St Johann the two towers of the **parish church** can be seen from some distance away. The church is also called the Pongauer Dom, the cathedral of the Pongau district. The old parish church burnt down completely in 1855 in a fire which affected practically the whole village. Reconstruction started almost immediately and within six years a new church stood there again, without losing its former imposing stature over village and valley. The architects, Schneider and Wessiken, chose neo-Gothic as the most suitable style. The **Annakapelle** contains an old carving of Heinrich II and his wife Kunigunde on a throne, which dates from 1530.

An alpine road and a chairlift east of the town lead up to the **Hahnbaum**, from where the Hochkönig mountain to the northwest and the peaks of the Hohe Tauer range to the south are the main points in view.

☐ Fremdenverkehrsamt

From St Johann take the L109 south to the Liechtenstein-klamm.

Liechtensteinklamm, Salzburg

4 Only 4km (2½ miles) south of St Johann, via Plankenau, lies the well signposted parking place for the Liechtensteinklamm. This gorge is one of the most picturesque in the Alps, nearly 2km (1¼ miles) long. There is a well thought out and safe path through the gorge, which had to be blasted in parts during its construction. The end of the walk is marked by the spectacle of the **Schleier waterfall**, where the water plunges down 60m (197 feet). If time allows, a trip further up the valley to Grossarl and Hüttschlag is suggested. Apart from beautiful scenery visitors can take a look at the **Kösslerhäusl**, an old miner's cottage from 1600, when copper was still mined there. It stands between Grossarl and Hüttschlag.

☐ Fremdenverkehrsamt, St Johann

From Liechtensteinklamm drive back to St Johann and take the 311 south to Schwarzach and a right fork to Goldegg.

Goldegg im Pongau, Salzburg

5 A small village on a small lake, this is an ideal place for a short stay. **Schloss Goldegg** stands in an elevated position. Totally surrounded by water in the 14th century, it was formerly a citadel and the original wooden claddings from this period can still be seen in the living rooms and bedrooms. During the 16th century the building was enlarged into a castle and the Rittersaal (Hall of the Knights) shows impressive frescos and wall paintings in Renaissance style. The castle also houses the **Pongau folk museum**, which exhibits tools and implements once used in trades and crafts which have long since vanished (open May to September).

ℹ Fremdenverkehrsamt

Take the local road southwest to Lend, turn right then take a left fork to Kitzlochklamm and south to Rauris.

Rauris, Salzburg

6 The Kitzlochklamm, at the beginning of the Rauris valley, is another of the exciting gorges which flank the river bend. The Klamm is open for visitors daily from May to October and its main attraction is a 100m (328-foot) high waterfall.

Rauris was discoverd by the Celts as a source for precious metals. The Romans later started a gold rush, but most of the finds were made in the late Middle Ages, which also brought wealth to the village. It was during this period that the **parish church** and **guild houses** were built. Even in the 19th century gold mining was still carried on, but later the high operating costs stopped production. A visit to the **Heimatmuseum** (Local Museum) in Rauris gives an insight into the flourishing times of the village. The local tourist office organises gold-wash excursions to the upper parts of the Rauris river. You won't become rich but it can be a lot of fun. A drive further into the valley to Kolm-Saigurn leads to the end of this attractive valley, where you can still see the slag heaps, collapsed mine shafts and former houses of the miners.

ℹ Verkehrsamt

From Rauris drive north on the L112 to Taxenbach and turn left to continue on the 311 via Bruck to Schüttdorf. Take the road for 5km (3 miles) south to Kaprun.

Kaprun, Salzburg

7 One of the largest hydroelectric combines in Austria lies high up in the Kapruner Tal. About 80 per cent of the country's electricity is provided by water power. Additional benefit for the country is that this method is environmentally sound and avoids pollution. Arrangements for visitors to see the dams and reservoirs are well organised and even in the high season delays are kept to a minimum.

Driving past Kaprun village you come to a barrier and are directed to one of the nearby parking areas, depending on whether you want to go up to the Kitzsteinhorn or just see the Kaprun installations. Coaches are then provided to take you up through the many tunnels and bends on the former construction road. Transport is arranged in stages and one steep hill, the Lärchenwand, is tackled by an open-air platform taking visitors up the mountainside. The last stage is another bus ride to the top reservoir at Moserboden.

The **Heidnische Kirche** (Pagan's Church) marks the spot where Protestants met in secret during the Counter-Reformation. A walk across the dam is very rewarding, as nature can be seen in all its glory, glacier peaks reflected in the blue waters of the reservoir and green pastures in the valley below. Return to the start and a short walk from here leads down to the **Stollenbahn**, a subterranean railway, which takes you up on the journey to Kitzsteinhorn. From the 2,450m (8,038-foot) high Alpincentre, a cableway connects with the Kitzsteinhorn terminus, which is located just 200m (656 feet) below the summit. A breathtaking panorama unfolds here and extra distraction is provided by watching the snow machines and summer skiers roaming around on the glaciers below. Both trips can be undertaken in one day, provided you start in the morning.

i Fremdenverkehrsverband, Salzburger Platz

From Kaprun drive north to the 168. At Fürth turn left to Uttendorf and left again through the Stubachtal to Enzingerboden.

Enzingerboden, Salzburg

8 From Enzingerboden a two-stage cableway leads up to the **Rudolfshütte**, 2,252m (7,382 feet) above sea level. The views from here are truly spectacular. The lake reflects the deep blue of the sky and the white of the surrounding snow-covered mountains. Climbing up a short path, Austria's highest mountain, the Grossglockner, comes into view and looking downwards you can admire the colour of the **Grün See** (Green Lake), a reservoir near the first stage of the cableway. A ski-lift for skiers only takes the sporty one stage further up for a run down, but summer skiing here is usually restricted to mornings only as the strong sun melts the snow from midday onwards.

i Enzingerboden

From Enzingerboden drive back north to Uttendorf, turn right and continue on the 168 east to Schüttdorf, then turn left for the 311 north to Zell am See.

Zell am See – Saalbach 18 (11)
Saalbach – Bischofshofen 68 (42)
Bischofshofen – St Johann im Pongau 44 (27)
St Johann im Pongau – Liechtensteinklamm 4 (2½)
Liechtensteinklamm – Goldegg im Pongau 16 (10)
Goldegg im Pongau – Rauris 22 (13½)
Rauris – Kaprun 28 (17½)
Kaprun – Enzingerboden 52 (32)
Enzingerboden – Zell am See 41 (26)

Zell am See's attractive lakeside setting contributes to its charm

FOR CHILDREN

Adults and children alike will enjoy a thrilling ride on the **narrow-gauge railway** from Zell am See to Krimml. Try for the steam-powered trains every Tuesday and Thursday in July and August, and every Saturday in September.

RECOMMENDED WALKS

6 The Tauerngold circular trail leads from Kolm-Saigurn along the historic gold mining sites and takes about 90 minutes.

6 days – 386km (240½ miles)

SALZBURG & THE SALZKAMMERGUT

Salzburg • Hallein • Golling an der Salzach
Werfen • Gosau • Hallstatt • Bad Aussee
Bad Ischl • Ebensee • Gmunden • Altmünster
Mondsee • St Gilgen • St Wolfgang im
Salzkammergut • Fuschl • Salzburg

The area around Salzburg has a long history. Finds on the Rainberg date from 5000BC to 2000BC, when there was continuous settlement in the region. The Illyrians occupied the area later, followed by the Celts and the Romans. Salzburg's greatest period, however, commenced with the beginning of the 17th century, which gave the city its present baroque appearance. Famous architects like Fischer von Erlach and Lucas von Hildebrandt were drawn here, commissioned by the ruling Archbishops. Salzburg only became part of Austria in 1816, having endured a brief Napoleonic and Bavarian rule. Music became an important stimulus for cultural life in the 19th century and this acquired worldwide recognition through the annual festival.

SCENIC ROUTES

8 The route along the Traunsee from Ebensee to Gmunden is very attractive – look out for the imposing Traunstein mountain, dominant on the other side of the lake.

10 Drive south from Schörfling along the west side of the Attersee to Unterach. The road often leads right along the shoreline of the lake and the scenery gets more and more dramatic the further you go. At Unterach the mountains of the Höllengebirge stand right on the opposite side of the lake and present a stunning picture.

ℹ️ Stadtverkehrsbüro, Auerspergstrasse 7

From Salzburg take the 150 then the 159 south to Hallein.

Hallein, Salzburg

1 Hallein is very much connected with the mining and processing of salt. The village of **Dürrnberg** became part of Hallein in 1938, and it is a spa for cures which depend on saline waters. Its main attraction, however, is the **salt mine**, which can be visited from May to September. The tour through the mine is extensive and well organised. One shaft even crosses a subterranean border with Bavaria. Overalls and miner's caps are provided and enjoyable slides and rides through chutes will be fun for everybody. Opposite the **parish church**

Statuary, fountains and sculpture augment Salzburg's architecture

on the Gruberplatz stands the house of the organ player Franz Gruber (1787–1863), the composer of *Silent Night* (*Stille Nacht*) who died in 1863. In the **Keltenmuseum** (Celtic Museum) you can see local finds and the original score of the famous Christmas carol.

ℹ️ Fremdenverkehrsverband, Unterer Markt 1

From Hallein continue south on the 159 to Golling.

Golling an der Salzach, Salzburg

2 In the **castle** look out for the prehistoric cave drawings on show. The village is a good centre for short trips into the outgoing area. The Golling waterfall lies 3km (2 miles) west and can be reached by pleasant footpaths. The water there cascades down from a height of 76m (249 feet) and this spectacle with its surroundings has inspired many a painter seeking a romantic scene.

Eastwards, a short drive leads to **Scheffen**, which has a remarkably large church for a small village. Gothic-style ornaments on the door fittings and paintings of horses on the windows refer to the former function of this church as a centre for pilgrimages on horseback, presumably for blessings. Driving further along the valley you reach the Lammer Klause. A secured footpath, chiselled into the rocks, leads through the **Lammer Öfen**, a narrow gorge of the Lammer stream. The rocks on either side are fascinating, the result of water erosion over thousands of years.

ℹ️ Fremdenverkehrsamt

From Golling continue south on the 159 to Werfen.

Werfen, Salzburg

3 The old market town of Werfen is now a favourite spot for visitors to one of nature's wonders, the **Eisriesenwelt** (giant ice cave). It claims to be the largest in the world, 42km (26 miles) long. The various monuments in ice are created by a natural airflow. In summer the warm air from outside enters the caves and melts the ice. In winter the molten ice freezes again and both phenomena interact and create spectacular formations, which depend on the direction of the wind. All are given names and are enhanced by clever illuminations. To reach the entrance, take the road north to the Fallstein car park. From here it is a 10-minute walk to the **Rasthaus** (rest house) and then four minutes by cableway to the **Dr F Oedi Haus**, the starting point for guided tours through the cave.

Also recommended is a visit to the fortress **Hohenwerfen**, which was erected in 1077 and extended by Archbishop Konrad in 1122. After the peasants' revolt between 1525 and 1526, further defensive measures were taken but the fortress acquired its present-day appearance in 1563 under Archbishop Lang. Emperor Franz I renovated the complex in 1824, as he wanted to retain this 'picturesque remnant of old times'. In 1931 a fire devastated the fortress, but it was restored yet again. The focal points inside are the *palas* – the living quarters – and the bell tower with its Renaissance bell of 1563.

ⓘ Fremdenverkehrsverband, Hauptstrasse

From Werfen continue south on the 159 towards Bischofshofen, take a left turn for the 99 east to Niedernfritz, turn left for the 166 and continue to Gosau.

Gosau, Oberösterreich

4 After a steep descent from Pass Gschütt, a right turn in Gosau leads to the **Vorderer Gosausee**, an alpine lake 937m (3,074 feet) above sea level, which is surrounded by sheer rocks and offers a most stunning view towards the Gosau glacier and the Dachstein mountain beyond. This particular view is very well known in Austria and has been chosen as a motif for many landscape painters in search of a romantic setting. A cableway from the western shore of the lake is available up to the 1,587m (5,207-foot) **Zwieselalm**. From here a far-reaching panorama lies before you, suggesting many other delightful places to explore.

ⓘ Fremdenverkehrsverband, Gosau

Continue on the 166 east to Gosaumühle and south to Hallstatt.

View across the Vorderer Gosausee to the Gosau glacier

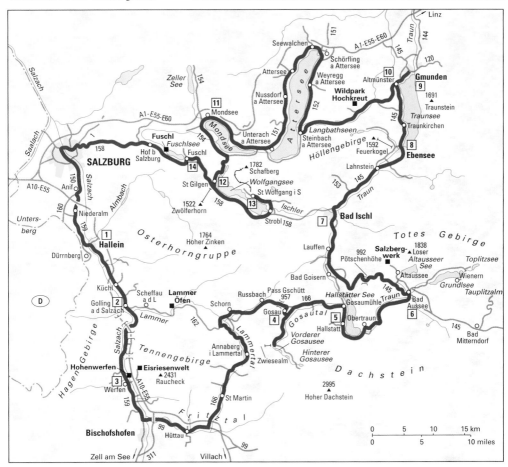

SPECIAL TO...

Anif, south of Salzburg, will be of interest to music lovers. The simple grave of one of the greatest conductors of our century, Herbert von Karajan, lies in the churchyard next to the parish church. Also of interest here is a very picturesque moated **castle**, which can only be seen from the outside as it is private property.

FOR HISTORY BUFFS

1 Although there are many Roman sites in this region, you rarely find those of the Celtic civilisation which preceded them. At Hallein Dürrnberg there is an **open-air exhibition** of a Celtic farmstead and a reconstruction of a royal grave. Open daily from the beginning of May to the beginning of October.

Hallstatt, Oberösterreich

5 The village of Hallstatt is a rewarding subject for any photographer – especially those prepared to take a boat out on to the lake to get a good shot. The village lies perched between the lake and the foothills of a mountain and its reflection on the surface of the lake provides an unforgettable image. Hallstatt's history goes back to 900BC. Many graves have been found since excavations started in the 19th century. For safety, the people of the early Iron Age lived in wooden houses on stilts on the shores of the lake. Salt mining became a lucrative business here early in village history. A five-minute trip by funicular takes you up to the entrance of the **salt mine**, which is open to the public from May to October. The visit starts with a slide down to the salt works and finishes with a circular walk round the illuminated salt lake. The **museum** at Marktplatz is also open from May to October, giving information on prehistoric times and the old methods of salt mining. Also on show are finds from the **graveyards** of the **Salzberg** (Salt Mountain). A regular motorboat service connects with other villages on the lake.

☐ Fremdenverkehrsverband, Seestrasse 56

Continue south to Obertraun and northeast to Bad Aussee.

Bad Aussee, Steiermark

6 Bad Aussee owed its growth in the Middle Ages to its large deposits of salt. The **Kammerhof** on the Oberer Marktplatz houses the **museum** which exhibits local artefacts and costumes, but also has a special section dealing with cave exploration and salt mining. In the 19th century Bad Aussee's salt water was first used for medical cures. Now it is also a popular tourist resort. Nearby **Altaussee** had the first salt works before they were transferred to Bad Aussee by Duke Albrecht in 1290. The old **salt mine** (*Salzbergwerk*) lies northwest of Alt Aussee and can be visited daily. The guided tours last about an hour and a half. During World War II the mine was used to store precious works of art. The **Salzkammergut Panoramastrasse** (Panorama Road) leads from north of the town to Augstsee (10km/6 miles), an ideal spot for hikers who can climb up to the top of the Loser mountain in about an hour. Superb views from here make it worth the effort. Another lake in the area is the **Grundlsee**, which is by the village of the same name. You can follow the road to the other end of the lake and further on to the **Toplitzsee**. Rumour has it that treasures were sunk here before the end of the last war, but so far nothing of value has been recovered.

A detour is suggested from Grundlsee south to the **145** and east to **Bad Mitterndorf**. From here a narrow road leads up to the **Tauplitzalm**, a large plateau with many small lakes. Return to Bad Aussee on the **145**.

Halstatt, squeezed in at the foot of the steep Dachstein range

i Kurverwaltung

From Bad Aussee take the 145 northwest to Bad Ischl.

Bad Ischl, Oberösterreich

7 Bad Ischl is a well known spa, the discovery of Emperor Franz Josef I.

Emperor Franz Josef with his beloved hounds at the Kaiservilla

It was his favourite spot and summer residence, and he had his own villa built here. The **Kaiservilla** is open to visitors and shows the Emperor's

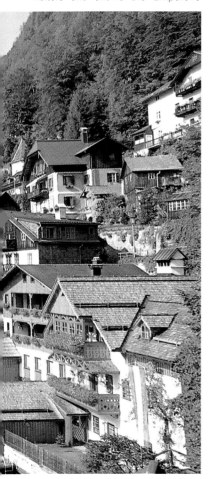

fondness for a simple and disciplined lifestyle. The composer of the operetta *The Merry Widow*, Franz Lehár, also had a house here, now the **Franz Lehár Museum**. Bad Ischl flourished in the 19th and beginning of the 20th century, when the European aristrocracy was at its most glittering. There is also another **salt mine** on view from mid-May to the end of September.

i Kurdirektion, Bahnhofstrasse 6

From Bad Ischl continue on the 145 northeast to Ebensee.

Ebensee, Oberösterreich

8 Ebensee lies on the southern end of the **Traunsee** and is bordered on its west side by the formidable **Höllengebirge** mountain range. A cableway leads from Ebensee up to the **Feuerkogel** peak, 1,594m (5,223 feet) above sea level, which offers fine views of the area. A rewarding side trip leads 8km (5 miles) west of Ebensee to the **Langbathseen** (lakes), which lie in a designated nature park to preserve their remote and unspoilt environment.

i Gemeindeamt

From Ebensee continue north on the 145 to Gmunden.

Gmunden, Oberösterreich

9 Gmunden lies at the top end of the Traunsee and is an old established holiday resort. A bridge over the Traun river connects the two parts of Gmunden and this is also the town centre. Its attractive lakeside position lured many visitors in bygone times and, as a result, a number of castles were built here for the wealthy. In the part of Gmunden called Traundorf stands **Schloss Cumberland**, which was built between 1882 and 1886 by the last King of Hanover. The most notable castle is **Schloss Orth**, erected in the 17th century on an artificial island and connected to the mainland by a 130m (426-foot) long wooden bridge. The products of Gmunden's ceramics factory are well known in Austria and the **Rathaus** (town hall) has a unique carillon using ceramic bells.

i Kurverwaltung, Am Graben

Drive southwest to Altmünster.

Altmünster, Oberösterreich

10 Altmünster was founded by the Romans and later became a market town. The name of the town, the 'old minster', refers to an early Benedictine monastery which only had a short lifespan. In the chapel of the **parish church of St Benedict** is a notable epitaph engraved in red marble, which refers to Count Herbersdorf, who was governor of the area and hated for his cruelty in putting down the peasants' uprising in 1526.

A peasant later took revenge and killed him. An old Roman gravestone has been taken into the church to avoid further erosion by the weather.

i Verkehrsamt

Take the L544 southwest to

FOR CHILDREN

10 The route from Altmünster to the Attersee Lake takes you past the **Wildpark Hochkreut**, a game park on an elevated meadow. It warrants a stop to see the enclosures with ibex, moufflon and bison which are kept there in relative freedom. Petting animals like ponies and goats will delight the children. Open from the beginning of April until the snows fall.

14 From Fuschl you can take the children to the summer tobogganing run, which lies 3km (2 miles) south.

Steinbach am Attersee, turn right on the 152 to Schörfling and continue on the other side of the Attersee on the 151 to Unterach am Attersee and northwest to Mondsee.

Mondsee, Oberösterreich

11 Mondsee is now a thriving holiday resort. It was already a settlement in 3000BC, when people lived in dwellings on stilts by the lakeshore. The finds established the name 'Mondsee Culture' which was given to similar settlements on other lakes in the Eastern Alps. After the Romans left, a Benedictine abbey was founded in AD748 by the Bavarian Duke Odilo II. The former **abbey church of St Michael** has five baroque-style altars by Meinrad Guggenbichler, one of which is called the Corpus Christi altar and depicts appealing statues of children carrying grapes. Incidentally, this church featured in the film *The Sound of Music*. Three museums can also be visited in Mondsee: the local **Heimatmuseum** with works by Guggenbichler; and the Austrian **Pfahlbaumuseum**, which shows stilt dwellings and brings to life the Mondsee Culture period are both located in the former abbey; the third museum is called the **Mondseer Rauchhaus**, an open-air museum which displays one of the oldest farmhouses of the area, fully furnished in the rural style of the time.

🛈 Fremdenverkehrsverband, Dr Franz Müller Strasse 3

From Mondsee take the 154 southeast on the west side of the lake to St Gilgen.

St Gilgen, Salzburg

12 A plaque on the magistrates' court in St Gilgen commemorates the birthplace of Mozart's mother, Anna Maria Pertl, who was

Michael Pacher's 15th-century masterpiece – the high altar of St Wolfgang's parish church

born here in 1720. Later, Mozart's sister, Nannerl (Marianne), lived here from 1784 to 1801. The **Mozartbrunnen** (fountain) in front of the town hall is a further reminder of the famous family and has become St Gilgen's landmark. This well-established lakeside resort offers many leisure and sports facilities and hikers can take a 10-minute ride by cableway up the Zwölferhorn mountain to wander around the top and enjoy the breathtaking view over seven lakes and the glaciers of the Dachstein to the south.

🛈 Verkehrsverein, Mozartplatz 1

From St Gilgen take the 158 southeast to Strobl and from there take a left turn to St Wolfgang.

St Wolfgang im Salzkammergut, Oberösterreich

13 As St Wolfgang gets very congested in the summer, it may be advisable – as well as pleasant – to leave the car in St Gilgen and complete your journey by lake steamer. St Wolfgang is perhaps the most famous village in the Salzkammergut area. Music lovers will recognise the setting of **The White Horse Inn**, the Weisses Rössl, which stands right on the lake. Inside, this old inn is full of tradition and sitting on the lakeside terrace enjoying a meal or a drink is one of the great pleasures of the visit. The **parish church** can be seen from many points around the lake and the interior contains a splendid work of art in the altar by Michael Pacher. The wood-carved altar was commissioned in 1471 and it took the artist 10 years to complete the work; it then had to be transported over the Brennerpass from Pacher's home in Bruneck, Tirol. This was quite a feat when you consider the height of the altar (12m/ 39 feet) and the transport facilities of the time. The Pacher Altar is in Gothic style, elaborately worked and painted. The wings are closed during the week, but opened on Sundays when it is revealed in all its glory. It is well worth spending a bit of time studying the intricate carving and getting to understand the details, so perfectly arranged and executed on this quite unique masterpiece.

☐ Kurdirektion

Turn back to St Gilgen and continue on the 158 northwest to Fuschl.

Fuschl, Salzburg

14 The village of Fuschl is surrounded by forests and mountains and a comparatively small lake, which makes the area more intimate. On a peninsula above the dark waters of the lake stands **Schloss Fuschl**, built in the 15th century as a hunting lodge for the Archbishops of Salzburg. Its exclusive position makes it a favourite spot for visitors and it now functions as a luxury hotel. Visitors can sit on the terrace overlooking the lake and surrounding mountains enjoying the view and the delightful atmosphere. In the castle grounds are a **hunting and pipe museum** and a **game park**.

☐ Gemeindeamt

From Fuschl take the 158 west to Salzburg.

Salzburg – Hallein 16 (10)
Hallein – Golling an der Salzach 12 (7½)
Golling an der Salzach – Werfen 16 (10)
Werfen – Gosau 54 (34)
Gosau – Hallstatt 31 (19)
Hallstatt – Bad Aussee 16 (10)
Bad Aussee – Bad Ischl 28 (17½)
Bad Ischl – Ebensee 18 (11)
Ebensee – Gmunden 31 (19)
Gmunden – Altmünster 3 (2)
Altmünster – Mondsee 75 (47)
Mondsee – St Gilgen 14 (8½)
St Gilgen – St Wolfgang im Salzkammergut 19 (12)
St Wolfgang im Salzkammergut – Fuschl 27 (17)
Fuschl – Salzburg 26 (16)

The view of Salzburg enjoyed by patrons of the Café Winkler. Its terrace can be reached by lift

BACK TO NATURE

The **Untersberg**, south of Salzburg, has been designated a nature park. It stretches from the foothills of the mountain right up to the top at 1,853m (6,079 feet) above sea level, and also forms the border with Bavaria. Sheer rock faces, alpine pastures with forests and meadows are a delight. Other attractions include a quiz trail through the woods, an adventure playground and game enclosures for deer and moufflon.

3 days – 271km (169 miles)

FORESTS & MEADOWS

Linz • Mauthausen • Gutau • Kefermarkt
Freistadt • Rohrbach • Aigen-Schlägl
Ulrichsberg • Schwarzenberg im Mühlkreis
Neufelden • Linz

Linz is the capital of Upper Austria: formerly a Roman army camp, the name Linz appears for the first time in AD799. The composers Mozart and Anton Bruckner worked here and in 1832 the first horse-drawn railway in continental Europe opened, linking Linz with Budweis in Bohemia. In 1898 the electric train service up to the Pöstlingberg near Linz was inaugurated. This technical feat managed the steepest gradient in Europe without a cogwheel.

[i] Tourismusverband, Pfarrgasse 9

From Linz take the 3 southeast to Mauthausen.

Most of Linz's finest buildings are in the Hauptplatz and Altstadt

Mauthausen, Oberösterreich

1 In 1208 the ruling Babenbergs erected houses here to collect traffic tolls on the Enns river, which joins the Donau (Danube). The shape of the castle facing upriver looks like the keel of a ship and it was built to function as a breakwater. It now houses a local **museum**. The **parish church of St Nicholas** is a late Gothic-style building; the precious picture on the high altar is by Kremser Schmidt, who painted it in 1796–7. In the quarries north of the town stands a memorial to the victims of the Mauthausen concentration camp.

[i] Fremdenverkehrsverband

Take the 123 north to Pregarten, continue on the local road north to Selker and take the right fork to Gutau.

Gutau, Oberösterreich

2 A short stop in Gutau is suggested to visit the **Färberei** (dye works) **Museum**, the only one of its kind in Austria. The museum is located in one of the 17th-century dye-works, which is under a preservation order. It is open Wednesday mornings and Friday afternoons between May and October, and at other times by arrangement.

[i] Fremdenverkehrsverband

From Gutau drive northwest for 8km (5 miles) on the local road to Kefermarkt.

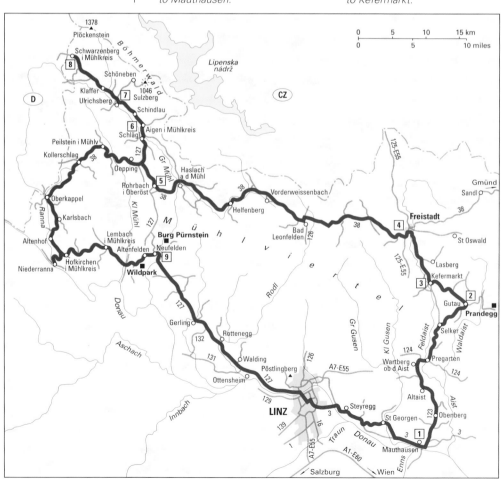

SCENIC ROUTES

2 The route from Gutau to Freistadt via Kefermarkt leads through unspoilt woodlands and gentle hills which ensure a memorable drive.

6 The area between Aigen-Schlägl, Ulrichsberg and Schwarzenberg lies in the foothills of the Böhmerwald range, which is known for its beautiful forests and rivers. The detour to Schöneben is very attractive and offers wide panoramic views into Bohemia.

SPECIAL TO...

4 The Hinterglas Museum at Sandl lies 11km (7 miles) northeast of Freistadt. The village became known in the 19th century for its special art form of painting on the reverse side of glass (*Hinterglasmalerei*). This technique makes it necessary to reverse the normal way of painting and the artist has to deal with the foreground first, having previously drawn the outlines of the contours. The finished painting is then framed and hung with the painted side on the back. Any dirt on the surface of the glass can then just be wiped away without disturbing the paint. The museum arranges courses in different painting techniques and is open for visitors daily from May to October.

Kefermarkt, Oberösterreich

3 Christoph von Zelking, who ruled in **Schloss Weinberg** from 1467 to 1491, donated the altar to the church of his favourite patron saint, St Wolfgang. The high altar is 13.5m (44 feet) high and 6.3m (20½ feet) wide and constitutes one of the main works of carving in the late Gothic period. The artist is unknown, and in the past the altar has been afflicted by woodworm – a threat now happily eradicated. The castle was first mentioned in 1305, before it had been converted into a Renaissance building. In the main part, the Halls of the Emperor, Ancestors and Knights are well worth seeing, especially the beautifully carved ceilings.

i Fremdenverkehrsverband

> *Take the local road north to Freistadt.*

Freistadt, Oberösterreich

4 Freistadt is the centre of the area north of the Danube which is called the **Mühlviertel**. The well-preserved medieval fortifications, the double walls around the town and its many gates and towers are quite unique. The town was founded to guard the old salt road to Bohemia. The main square is surrounded by houses designed by Italian architects. The **castle** was built in 1365 and is worth a visit: the collection of 14th-century *Sandler Hinterglasbilder* (pictures painted on the reverse side of glass) in the chapel is especially lovely (see **Special To...**). In the evenings the night watchman calls out the hours, as has been done for centuries.

The splendidly carved high altar of the church in Kefermarkt

i Fremdenverkehrsamt, Hauptplatz 12

> *Take the 38 west to Rohrbach.*

Rohrbach, Oberösterreich

5 Before reaching Rohrbach you might want to stop at **Haslach an der Mühl** and see the **weaving museum** (open mornings, daily all year round). Children will also like to visit the **Kaufmannsmuseum**, an old grocery store still selling sweets wrapped in paper cones.

The centre of Rohrbach consists of medieval burghers' houses with colourful façades set around the **Rathaus** (town hall), with traditional ground-floor arcades. An old tradition is still practised in Rohrbach: when one of its citizens dies, his or her name is called out from the church tower in all four directions.

i Tourismusinformation, Rathaus

> *From Rohrbach take the 127 north to Aigen-Schlägl.*

Aigen-Schlägl, Oberösterreich

6 The two adjoining villages of Aigen im Mühlkreis and Schlägl are often combined for practical reasons, although they are administered separately. The Hussite and peasant wars badly damaged the 13th-century **abbey** and the **church** and the outbuildings were rebuilt in the 17th century in their present baroque style. The abbey evaded secularisation by Emperor Josef II and began to flourish in the 19th century, when Abbot Fähtz acquired many paint-

FOR HISTORY BUFFS

4 The Ledermühle at St Oswald, 8km (5 miles) east of Freistadt, is one of the only remaining mills in the area. First documented in a bill of sale dated 20 August 1413, it has been owned continuously by the Kerschbaummayr family since 1656. It was only in 1967 that the miller, Ernst Kerschbaummayr, decided to terminate its commercial function. The mill now works only for visitors, managed by volunteers. You can see the different mechanical installations in operation. The mill is open from Easter to the end of October, Sundays and holiday afternoons.

BACK TO NATURE

9 The game park of Altenfelden lies just south of the village of Neufelden. It covers a large area and contains about 94 different species of animal. Although the park focuses on European stag deer, it also contains some exotic breeds. Look out for ibex, wild horses, antelope, otters, lynx, wild boar and red and polar foxes, among others. The park is just over 20 years old and very extensive, but there are plans to develop further. A marked path leads visitors past separate enclosures and dispensers are available for appropriate animal feeds; a useful map is handed out with information about the various paths and animals. The park is open daily all year round.

FOR CHILDREN

2 A wooded area 2km (1 mile) north of Gutau has been marked out with a trail which informs visitors about the world of birds: the **Vogellehrpfad**. Ten tree trunks have been hollowed out to house the birds, and children can press a button to listen to their sounds. To fit in with the general theme of a close relationship with nature, the energy for the appliances is provided by solar cells. Along the trail are 30 plaques explaining the life and migratory patterns of birds and other displays describe the six different environments suitable for the chosen varieties.

RECOMMENDED WALKS

7 Ulrichsberg lies in the hilly Böhmerwald, with natural forests stretching along the border with Bohemia. This makes the village an ideal starting point for a variety of walking tours. The local information office has suggestions for many walks and hikes beside rivers and through fascinating forests.

ings and built a neo-baroque library which contains 60,000 volumes, prints and manuscripts. The picture gallery holds around 200 paintings by old masters and many woodcarvings. The abbey cellar with its vaults provides a suitable backdrop for those who seek earthly pleasures and *Gemütlichkeit* (comfort), enjoying a glass of wine sitting inside large empty cut-away barrels.

i Tourismusverband, Marktplatz 6

From Aigen-Schlägl take the L580 for 7km (4 miles) northwest to Ulrichsberg.

Ulrichsberg, Oberösterreich

7 Ulrichsberg has a permanent exhibition, **Glass im Böhmerwald** (Glass in the Bohemian forest), a reminder of the traditional glass industry. The town now features a golf club with a nine- and 18-hole championship golf course and a **Jazzatelier** which attracts jazz fans and performers alike. Hikers and cyclists are also catered for with mapped trails and bike hire.

i Tourismusbüro, Markt 20

Continue on the L580 to Schwarzenberg.

Schwarzenberg im Mühlkreis, Oberösterreich

8 The village of Schwarzenberg flourished from the 17th century onwards, when glass production in the area reached its peak. Three glass works were erected here but the demand for their delicate products declined in the middle of the last century and their work can now only be seen in museums. The **Heimatstube** was installed in the old primary school and provides an insight into village life.

i Tourismusverband, Gemeindeamt

From Schwarzenberg take the L580 back to Aigen-Schlägl, then the 127 south until the junction with the 38. Continue west on the 38 to Kollerschlag and south to Oberkappel. The L584 leads south to Hofkirchen and the L587 to Niederranna on the Danube. Return to Hofkirchen and continue on the L587 east to Lembach and the junction with the L585, then turn sharp left and take a right fork to Altenfelden and east to Neufelden.

Neufelden, Oberösterreich

9 Neufelden's wealth was based on linen, and 17th- and 18th-century merchants built the distinctive and individual houses which line the market square. Today, beer has replaced linen as the local industry. **Burg Purnstein** dates from 1170 and although part is now in ruins, the main castle with its magnificent array of steps is impressive.

i Fremdenverkehrsverband

Take the 127 southeast to Linz.

Linz – Mauthausen 22 (13½)
Mauthausen – Gutau 25 (15½)
Gutau – Kefermarkt 8 (5)
Kefermarkt – Freistadt 12 (7½)
Freistadt – Rohrbach 56 (35)
Rohrbach – Aigen-Schlägl 11 (7)
Aigen-Schlägl – Ulrichsberg 7 (4½)
Ulrichsberg – Schwarzenberg im Mühlkreis 11 (7)
Schwarzenberg im Mühlkreis – Neufelden 85 (53)
Neufelden – Linz 34 (21)

A street scene in Linz

The house of Salome Alto in Wels. She was mistress of Wolf Dietrich, Bishop of Salzburg in 1587

[i] Tourismusverband, Pfarrgasse 9

From Linz take the 1 to Wels.

Wels, Oberösterreich

1 Wels was an important colonial town in Roman times, then called *Ovilava*. In AD776 the **castle** on the crossing of the Traun river was first mentioned as the seat of the powerful Count of Wels and Lambach. The town is now an important agricultural trade centre for the surrounding area. The historical **Stadtplatz** (town square) is considered to be the jewel of the town and one of the most attractive enclosed squares in Austria.

[i] Fremdenverkehrsamt, Stadtplatz 55

From Wels take the 138 south to Sattledt and take a left turn for the 122 to Kremsmünster.

Kremsmünster, Oberösterreich

2 The **abbey** is one of the oldest, largest and, according to art historians, one of the most important in Austria. It was founded in AD777 by the Bavarian prince Tassilo, and stands 50m (164 feet) above the Krems river in extensive grounds. The abbey church is a Romanesque and early Gothic-style basilica with strong baroque influences, the work of Carlo Antonio Carlone from 1680 onwards. Notable is the Gunthergrab, the tomb of Gunther, which was erected around 1300 and depicts the dramatic saga of the abbey's foundation. The art collection is housed in the main abbey building and exhibits one of the great treasures from the Middle Ages, the **Tassilokelch**, a gilded chalice on a copper base and a beautiful example of the work of medieval goldsmiths. The observatory is claimed to be the first high-rise block in Europe, erected between 1748 and 1758, and was also used as a museum devoted to the important branches of nature and science – geology, mineralogy, botany, zoology, physics, astronomy and anthropology.

In **Schloss Kremsegg**, about 5km (3 miles) east of Kremsmünster, a **motor museum** exhibits over 100 cars and motorcycles, including vintage models.

[i] Fremdenverkehrsbüro

Take the 122 northeast to Unterrohr and turn right to Bad Hall.

Bad Hall, Oberösterreich

3 There are over 10 springs in Bad Hall which offer hydropathic cures due to their iodine content – the **Paracelsus Institute** houses an iodine research station. A walk through the **Kurpark** is very relaxing. It contains exotic trees and provides a perfect setting for open-air concerts in summer.

[i] Kurverwaltung

From Bad Hall continue east on the 122 to Steyr.

FAMOUS ABBEYS

Linz • Wels • Kremsmünster •Bad Hall • Steyr Waidhofen an der Ybbs • Seitenstetten Markt Enns • Markt St Florian • Linz

Linz's main bridge, the Nibelungenbrücke, connects the two halves of the town. The Hauptplatz (main square) starts on the southern shoreline of the river and extends into the Landstrasse, both pedestrian precincts. The Linzer Schloss was erected around 1600 to take the place of old fortifications and recently underwent a total restoration. Part of it now houses the provincial museum and is worth a visit. The Altes Rathaus, the old town hall, still shows features of the original building constructed by Master Christoph after a fire in 1513–4, such as the octagonal turret with the lunar clock. The middle of the Hauptplatz is graced by the Dreifaltigkeitssäule, a pillar dedicated to the Holy Trinity, which was erected in 1723 out of white Salzburg marble.

The abbey of Kremsmünster

Steyr, Oberösterreich

4 Steyr lies at the confluence of two mighty alpine rivers, the Enns and the Steyr. Its **castle** was built in a strategic position on top of a rock between the two rivers. The river Enns was once used to transport iron ore from the Erzberg in Styria further north to the Donau (Danube). Formerly the iron ore was melted

SCENIC ROUTES

4 The road from Steyr to Weyer Markt runs along the bends of the Enns river through often changing scenery, which makes the drive very enjoyable.

SPECIAL TO...

4 In Steyr a unique **museum** has been established which illustrates the development of manufacturing from trades and guilds to modern industrial production. The human factor receives special attention and to compare the changes in working conditions a model of an old shoemaker's workshop contrasts with modern manufacturing methods. The steam engine is featured as the symbol of the industrial revolution and also exhibited are present-day micro-electronics.

FOR CHILDREN

4 Every Saturday and Sunday from June to September a **steam train** takes passengers for an hour's ride from Steyr to Grünburg and back. The line is one of the oldest narrow-gauge railways in Austria and runs through pleasant countryside, always along the Steyr river.

down at source and Steyr became a trading and manufacturing centre for the metal, bringing wealth to its inhabitants. The **Stadtplatz** (town square) bears witness to a great past which is reflected in the beautifully preserved old houses around it. The square itself is really an extension of the old trading route on the left bank of the Enns River. The **Rathaus** (Town Hall) is one of the newer 18th-century buildings and is decorated with a rococo-style façade. One of the best examples of late Gothic style is the so-called **Bummerlhaus**, formerly an inn displaying a lion on its sign. As people felt the lion looked more like a pet dog, they gave it the nickname *Bummerl* (tame dog). Other old houses can be found on the shoreline of the river. Although Steyr is traditionally associated with the iron and steel industry, factories have been kept away from the town centre and thus the medieval core has been preserved.

ⓘ Fremdenverkehrsverband, Rathaus

From Steyr take the 115 south along the Enns river to Weyer Markt and a left turn on the 121 to Waidhofen.

Enns, which shares its name with the river, is thought to be the oldest town in Upper Austria

Seitenstetten Markt, Niederösterreich

6 Seitenstetten is another town which owes its popularity to an abbey. The Benedictine **abbey**, founded here in 1112, was later destroyed by fire and rebuilt in the 13th and 14th centuries in early Gothic style. From another devastating fire in 1250 only the Ritterkapelle (knight's chapel) survived in its early Romanesque style. It was later called the Marienkapelle, the Chapel of Our Lady. The extensive abbey buildings, as they appear today, were completed in 1747 – there is a worthwhile art gallery inside. An imposing library is decorated with frescos, while colourful tapestries with biblical motifs adorn the interior of the abbey church.

ⓘ Fremdenverkehrsamt

Take the 122 west to St Peter and after 3km (2 miles) take a right turn on the LH85 to Haag and turn right on the 42 to join the A1 for Enns.

Enns, Oberösterreich

7 The town of Enns is the last bastion on the river before the Enns joins the Danube at Mauthausen, and its important strategic position was recognised early on. The Celtic *Lorch* became Roman *Lauriacum* and remains of a small but fortified settlement from AD50 can be seen west of

BACK TO NATURE

5 In Waidhofen, a 10-minute walk leads to the **Wildgatter am Fuchsbichl**, a game enclosure on the Buchenberg, south of the town. Deer and moufflon can be seen here all year round.

FOR HISTORY BUFFS

8 Markt St Florian devotes much attention to preserving its past and the **Historisches Feuerwehrzeughaus** exhibits firefighting equipment, from horse-drawn carriages to modern fire engines. Also on view is a partly restored electric tram which used to run between the town and Linz.

Waidhofen an der Ybbs, Niederösterreich

5 A trade agreement brought Styrian iron to Waidhofen, which specialised in the manufacture of swords, knives and scythes. In 1532 an attack by the Turks was repulsed and the hands of the town clock on the **Stadtturm** were permanently set at 11.45, the hour when victory was confirmed. In 1875 Baron Rothschild bought the **town castle** and had it rebuilt by Friedrich von Schmidt in neo-Gothic style. Well preserved houses from the 15th and 16th centuries, with their romantic arcades inside, give a clue to the medieval appearance of the town.

ⓘ Fremdenverkehrsverein

Drive north on 121. At Böhlerwerk take the road to Seitenstetten Markt.

town. After AD18 the **Limes** (wall), which was the northern frontier of the Roman Empire, was erected here together with a fort for 6,000 soldiers of the 2nd Legion. Around AD900 the name Anesapurch – *anesa* (Enns), *purch* (castle) – appears, and Enns became the centre of operations against the Ottoman invaders from the east. The **Stadtturm** was erected between 1565 and 1568 as a watch- and clocktower. There is now a gallery on the fourth floor with good views over the town and surrounding countryside. Enns was again important after World War II, when people from the Soviet-occupied territory of Austria crossed the Iron Curtain here on their way to freedom.

ⓘ Fremdenverkehrsamt

Take the 1 west. Past Asten take a left turn to Markt St Florian.

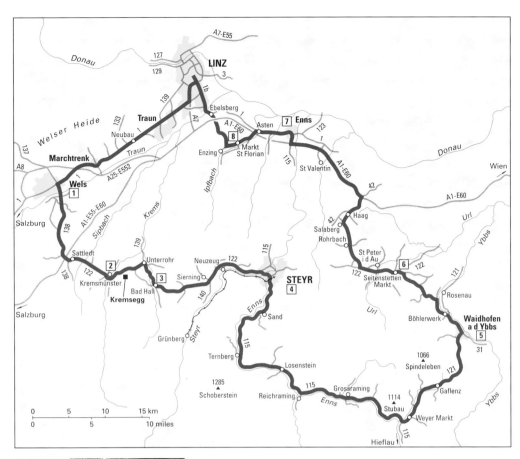

choir. A guided tour through the halls reveals many historically interesting features including the precious painting collection.

ℹ️ Gemeindeamt, Tannstrasse 2

From Markt St Florian take the local road north to Ebelsberg and the 16 to Linz.

Linz – Wels 29 (18)
Wels – Kremsmünster 18 (11)
Kremsmünster – Bad Hall 10 (6)
Bad Hall – Steyr 18 (11)
Steyr – Waidhofen an der Ybbs 62 (39)
Waidhofen an der Ybbs – Seitenstetten Markt 14 (8½)
Seitenstetten Markt – Enns 33 (21)
Enns – Markt St Florian 8 (5)
Markt St Florian – Linz 19 (12)

RECOMMENDED WALKS

6 *En route* from Seitenstetten to Enns a stop at **Haag** is recommended. Just south of the town, in the park of **Schloss Salaberg**, 8km (5-mile) long paths lead past game enclosures with animals from the region and other countries.

Markt St Florian, Oberösterreich

8 The building of the present **abbey**, on a much older site, supposedly where St Florian was martyred, began in 1686. Three great architects, Carlo Antonio Carlone, Jakob Prandtauer and Johann Gotthard Hayberger, created one of the finest sacred buildings in Europe. Albrecht Altdorfer's masterpiece, the Sebastian Altar, dates from 1518 and is now in the gallery. Anton Bruckner, the composer, was appointed organist here in 1845. The organ in the abbey church was named the Brucknerorgel after the composer, and the musical tradition lives on through organ recitals, concerts and the choir of the Florianer Sängerknaben, St Florian's boys'

Bruckner was organist at St Florian Abbey for 10 years

3 days – 359km (223 miles)

SOUTH OF THE DANUBE

Linz • Wilhering • Eferding • Engelhartszell
Schärding • Reichersberg • Braunau am Inn
Ried im Innkreis • Lambach • Linz

Linz is packed with reminiscences of the past. Emperor Friedrich III died in 1493 at the Imperial Stadtpalais and Mozart stayed here from time to time. Between 1762 and 1790 he wrote his *Linzer Symphonie* at Altstadt 17, and was a visitor at Hofgasse 14. Beethoven often stayed with his brother in the house of the Wasser Apotheke and the Zur Stadt Frankfurt inn. Franz Schubert was an honorary member of the Linz Society of Friends of Music and his portrait hangs in Landstrasse 15. Anton Bruckner had an even closer association with Linz – he was cathedral organist from 1856 to 1868.

SCENIC ROUTES

2 Soon after leaving Eferding the road turns towards the Danube and the scenery becomes very attractive, all the way past Engelhartszell towards Passau. A highlight is provided at Schlögen, just where the road reaches the shoreline of the Danube and the river is forced into a U-turn by the surrounding countryside.

i Pfarrgasse 9

From Linz take the 129 west to Wilhering.

Wilhering, Oberösterreich

1 A Cistercian abbey was founded here in 1146. The original building burnt down in 1733 and rebuilding started a year later. The design of the interior makes great use of natural light, and was the combined effort of the Altomonte family. Andreas was responsible for the high altar, Martino for the paintings on the side altars and Bartolomeo created the lavish ceiling fresco. The organ was designed by Nikolaus

Schärding's main square is lined with its distinctive multi-coloured gabled buildings

Rummel and received high praise from Anton Bruckner.

i Fremdenverkehrsamt

Continue on the 129 west to Eferding.

Eferding, Oberösterreich

2 Eferding can trace its origins back to a Celtic settlement and a Roman cavalry camp. **Schloss Eferding** has been kept very much in its 16th-century style: the museum inside is worth seeing.

i Fremdenverkehrsamt

Take the 130 north to Engelhartszell.

Engelhartszell, Oberösterreich

3 Engelhartszell was founded in 1293 by the Bishop of Passau and called *cella angelica* (the angel's cell). It became a Cistercian abbey, and the monks produce their own brand of liqueur made from herbs. Visitors can take boat trips on the Danube and even go fishing. Of interest is the massive **power station** at nearby **Jochenstein**, 1km (½ mile) north of town.

i Fremdenverkehrsamt

Continue on the 130 northwest to Innstadt on the right riverbank and take the road due south to Schärding.

Schärding, Oberösterreich

4 Schärding was first mentioned in AD804 as *Scardinga*, and later became a fortress. Only a few remnants of the former buildings still stand; the most interesting is the **Wasser**tor (water gate) with its pillory. The town's major attraction is its main square. The row of houses on its northern flank is called the **Silberzeile** (Silver Lane) – each house is different from the others, though all have curved gables on top.

i Fremdenverkehrsamt

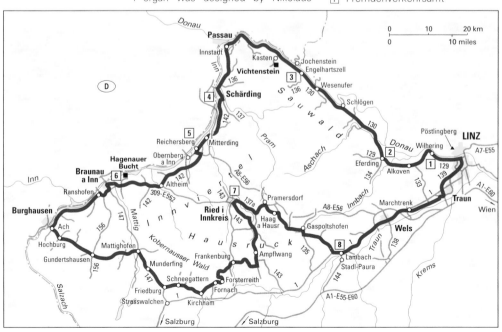

BACK TO NATURE

6 The nature reserve **Hagenauer Bucht** lies 4km (2½ miles) northeast of Braunau. In the **Vogelparadies** (bird's paradise) 172 kinds of birds breed and the whole reserve can be crossed on well laid-out paths for walking or cycling. The reservoir near by provides facilities for paddling and sailing.

FOR CHILDREN

An excursion for the whole family is suggested from Linz-Urfahr up to the **Pöstlingberg**. A historical tramline was inaugurated on 28 May 1898. The track is 2.9km (almost 2 miles) long and the tram travels at an average speed of 12kph (7½mph) to the top. In summer the highlight is a ride in the open summer coach. Small children will be delighted to see fairy tales come true on a ride on the **Grottenbahn** (grotto railway), near the top terminus of the tram line.

SPECIAL TO...

6 On 25 November 1787, Franz Xaver Gruber, the composer of the well known Christmas carol, *Silent Night*, was born in **Hochburg**, south of Braunau. The text of his hymn has been translated into 50 different languages and an organ was donated to the church in his honour.

FOR HISTORY BUFFS

3 A short but steep road leads up from the Danube valley about 7km (4 miles) northeast from Engelhartszell to the **castle of Vichtenstein**. A road existed in the 11th century – even then, its strategic importance was realised. The mighty keep dates back to the 12th century and the chapel of St Hippolyt was added in the 14th century. The castle is well preserved and affords wide views over the Bavarian and Bohemian forests and the Danube valley below.

RECOMMENDED WALKS

7 A stop at **Haag am Hausruck** *en route* from Ried to Lambach is suggested. From here a chairlift takes you to the **Luisenhöhe** and the **Hausruckwarte** viewpoint. A 4km (2½-mile) trail called **Waldlehrpfad Symbrunn** leads through old forest and provides a guide to the different kinds of trees. A fast return downhill is an option provided by the **Sommerrodelbahn** (summer tobogganing run).

Take the 142 south to Reichersberg.

Reichersberg, Oberösterreich

5 The **abbey** stands on a high terrace above the Inn river. It was founded in 1084 by the last members of the noble family of the Reichersbergs. Both church and abbey were rebuilt in the 17th century after a fire. The abbey has now become a cultural centre – concerts are performed in the church and the festival hall.

ℹ️ Fremdenverkehrsamt

Rejoin and continue west on the 142 to Altheim, then turn right on the 309 west to Braunau.

Braunau am Inn, Oberösterreich

6 In spite of a devastating fire in 1874 many old buildings have survived, so that the general view of Braunau, birthplace of Adolf Hitler, is that of a Gothic town, enhanced by its narrow streets and squares. The main square, the **Stadtplatz**, used to be the centre of flourishing trades and crafts; fully-laden salt wagons came through the Inn gate direct on to the square.

ℹ️ Fremdenverkehrsamt, Stadtplatz 9

Drive southwest along the Inn on the L501 to Ach, turn left and continue on the L503 to Mattighofen. Take the 147 to Friedburg and continue east to Schneegattern. Take a right turn southeast to Kirchham and sharp left there to Fornach and Forsterreith. Then drive north around a bend to Frankenburg, east to Ampflwang and north on the 143 to Ried.

Ried im Innkreis, Oberösterreich

7 Ried lies in the centre of the Innviertel and the Hausruck mountains. The **parish church** was erect-

Quiet, unassuming Braunau am Inn

ed between 1721 and 1732 in baroque style and its 73m (240-foot) tower is visible from afar. The **regional museum** provides information on the local Schwanthaler family – they had their studio in Ried from 1632 to 1838 and specialised in sculpture. Other exhibits include rural furniture and local costumes.

ℹ️ Tourismusregion Innviertel, Bayrhammergasse

Take the 137a east to Pramerdorf, turn right and continue from Haag am Hausruck on the L520 southeast to Lambach.

Lambach, Oberösterreich

8 Lambach abbey was founded in the 11th century by the Benedictines. Notable are the frescos in the abbey church, which were painted in 1080. The abbey also contains a well-preserved baroque theatre.

Only 1km (½ mile) south, in **Stadl-Paura**, there is an intriguing 18th-century **church** built in honour of the Holy Trinity at a time of plague. Everything about the church is in threes: towers, altars – it even has three organs.

ℹ️ Fremdenverkehrsverband, Marktplatz 8

Take the 1 northeast towards Traun, then take a left fork and continue on the 139 to Linz.

Linz – Wilhering	9 (5½)
Wilhering – Eferding	17 (10½)
Eferding – Engelhartszell	34 (21)
Engelhartszell – Schärding	43 (27)
Schärding – Reichersberg	20 (12½)
Reichersberg – Braunau am Inn	30 (18½)
Braunau am Inn – Ried im Innkreis	119 (74)
Ried im Innkreis – Lambach	38 (24)
Lambach – Linz	49 (30)

LOWER AUSTRIA & THE BURGENLAND

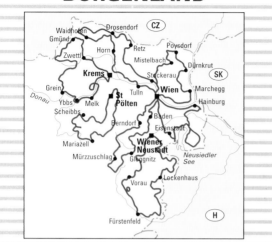

Lower Austria and the Burgenland cover the area around Vienna and the influence of the former imperial capital is felt everywhere. Both have only acquired their own capitals fairly recently. Lower Austria was always ruled from Vienna and its newly chosen capital of St Pölten is scheduled to operate as from the year 2000, when its extensive building programme will be complete. The Burgenland, although part of the Austrian Empire, was actually administered by Hungary until 1919, which did not matter as the two countries were then allied. The former capital of the Burgenland, Ödenburg, was sliced off the province and became a Hungarian enclave following dubious elections after World War I. Eisenstadt was then chosen as the new provincial capital.

The province borders the wide Hungarian plain in the east and also shares its steppe climate around the Neusiedler See (lake), which disappeared for some time during the last century when its water supplies dried up. The area around the lake has been developed over recent decades to cater for visitors because of its rare fauna and flora. The experience of sunrise and sunset on the shores of the lake, teeming with wildlife, is a unique spectacle.

The final ranges of the Eastern Alps lie across the province of Lower Austria and two of the peaks, the Rax and Schneeberg, are by tradition popular excursion centres for the Viennese. Two pipelines draw drinking water from several springs in the area right to the capital's doorstep. The area north of the Danube is called the Waldviertel, the woodlands, which reach right up to the Czech border. Apart from the Danube valley, the area is not as developed as the western parts of Austria and still hides many of its treasured spots from the main tourist routes. The Kamp valley used to be a favourite summer holiday area for the Viennese, before the motor car and air travel encouraged people to travel to more distant destinations. The Kamp river and the charming villages alongside offer very attractive stopping places *en route,* blissfully away from the main roads.

East of the woodlands lies the Weinviertel. As the name implies, this is an area of vineyards where the connoisseur can drop in on one of the many wine cellars dotted about the landscape. An open cellar door signifies an invitation, but the expedition should be made on foot, leaving the car well behind!

Tour 18
This tour starts from the recently appointed capital of St Pölten and turns in a southerly direction through wooded hills and mountains to a large nature park. A visit to a cave is included in the itinerary and the tour then continues past lakes and a reservoir to Mariazell, one of Austria's best-known pilgrim centres and a summer and winter resort.

Tour 19
From the wine area of Krems this tour leads through the woodlands of the province of Lower Austria. It then passes a large reservoir and leisure area and later turns south to visit a fortified medieval castle *en route* to the Danube. Both sides of the river are visited and one of the country's best known baroque abbeys, Stift Melk, stands in a commanding position above the Danube. The most attractive part of the Danube valley, the Wachau, leads gracefully back to Krems, with a visit to another famous abbey standing on its own on the south side of the river.

Tour 20
Vienna is the start of this tour which leads on a gentle drive along the Kamp river, through another part of the Waldviertel, the woodlands district. Ruins and

The Pallas Athene Fountain, designed by Hansen, stands in front of the Parlament in Vienna

the castle of Rosenburg provide rewarding viewpoints along the route, which continues in a northerly direction, passing small lesser known towns and villages.

Tour 21

This tour follows a route through the Weinviertel, the Austrian winelands north of Vienna. On the way you will see oil pumps and derricks shooting out of the fields, but the oil boom, if ever there was one in the area, is nearly over.

Tour 22

A totally different landscape and climate confronts you on this tour. Roman excavations and ruins are encountered on the southern shore of the Danube at the beginning of the tour, but lead on to the Hungarian steppe. Neusiedler See provides the habitat for a great variety of wildlife, rarely seen elsewhere in central Europe, while the surrounding vineyards offer refreshments.

Tour 23

Associations with the former ruling Habsburg family can be seen in this southern part of the Vienna Woods. Heiligenkreuz and nearby Mayerling are visited, then the route continues through attractive mountain landscapes past the two peaks of Rax and Schneeberg, to the Semmering pass and the spas of Bad Vöslau and Baden.

Tour 24

Formidable castles feature on this tour, all built to defend the land against the threatening menace from the east. There are villages where Hungarian, Croat and Slovene are spoken, all reminders of the former multi-national Austrian empire. The final stage leads through a hilly area called the Wechsel (the 'change'), so named as its hills and valleys continually alter the landscape.

Tour 25

Vienna is sheltered by mountains to the north and west. The mighty river running by it forms a border to the east. New development was started across the Danube after World War II, now called the Vienna International Centre. Flooding by the river caused much damage in earlier years, and it has had to be forced into a well defined stretch bypassing the city. The wide mountain range of the Alps peters out to north and west of Vienna and this part is the famous Wiener Wald, the Vienna Woods. Vineyards sprawl down to the villages on the outskirts of the city.

3 days – 289km (179½ miles)

NATURE PARKS & CAVES

St Pölten • Lilienfeld • Frankenfels • Scheibbs
Gaming • Lunz am See • Mariazell
Herzogenburg • St Pölten

The centre of St Pölten, around the Domplatz (cathedral square), was the site of a Roman settlement, *Aelium Cetium*. The monastery of St Hippolyt was founded in AD760 and the name St Pölten is derived from it. Two great architects and builders helped to make St Pölten the centre of baroque in the early 18th century – Jakob Prandtauer and Josef Munggenast. Their chief task was to convert the Romanesque cathedral into the contemporary style of that time, baroque. Prandtauer was involved in the creation of the convent of the Englische Fräulein (English ladies) and Munggenast was responsible for decorating many of the façades, notably that of the Rathaus (town hall). The Rathausplatz and adjoining Riemer- and Herrenplatz form the centre of town, together with the Kremsergasse shopping street, which runs from north to south. In 1968 St Pölten was declared the new provincial capital and is now a growing town with elaborate plans for future development as a centre for conferences and tourism.

The old Gaming-Kompass in Gaming's parish church

ⓘ Tourismusverband, Rathausplatz 1

From St Pölten drive due south on the 20 to Lilienfeld.

Lilienfeld, Niederösterreich

1 Lilienfeld lies in an idyllic position in the valley of the Traisen river, surrounded by hills, meadows and forests. The Cistercian **abbey**, a late Romanesque basilica which stands right in the centre, was founded by Duke Leopold VI of Brandenburg in 1202. Inside, a magnificent painting by Daniel Gran decorates the high altar. Exotic trees have been planted in the adjoining **Stiftspark** and the abbey cellar is a favourite spot for those wanting to try the wines from the abbey's own vineyards. A chair-lift leads up to the **Muckenkogel** from where you get pleasant views: it is also a starting point for many hikes and walks.

ⓘ Tourismusverband, Babenbergerstrasse 10

From Lilienfeld continue on the 20 to Türnitz, then take a right fork for the LH102 to Weissenburg and turn left to Frankenfels.

Frankenfels, Niederösterreich

2 Frankenfels is known for its attractive cave near by, the **Nixhöhle**. A path leads from the main road to the entrance. The cave is 1,400m (4,593 feet) long and is the largest in the province. Well-secured walkways lead visitors past fascinating rock and sediment formations and illuminations enhance the sights. Bones of bears dating from the Ice Age have been found here.

The ruin of **Weissenburg**, 3km (2 miles) north of Frankenfels, dates

SCENIC ROUTES

5 The drive from Lunz am See to Mariazell leads first along the valley of the River Ois, a tributary of the larger Ybbs river. Near Mariazell the two Erlauf lakes, one natural and the other man-made, complete a picture typical of alpine scenery.

SPECIAL TO...

The picturesque, moated castle of Pottenbrunn lies 6km (4 miles) northeast of St Pölten. It houses the Austrian Zinnfiguren-museum (tin figure museum). Over 10,000 figures are used to explain the history of Austria. Two important events, the Siege of Vienna by the Turks in 1683 and the Battle of the Nations against Napoleon near Leipzig in 1813, are featured. The exhibition is open from the end of March to the end of October.

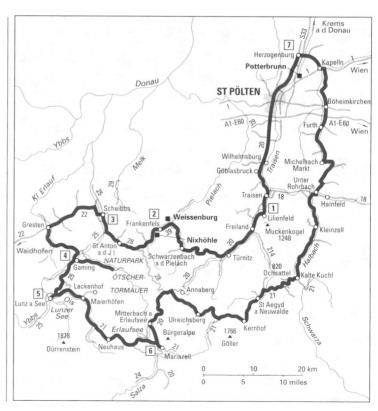

back to the 13th century and provides a good stop-off point *en route*.

ⓘ Tourismusverband

Continue on the 39 southwest until it merges with the 28 and drive west, then northwest to Scheibbs.

1322. Although the Reformation, Turkish attacks and secularisation under Josef II all caused enormous damage, its unique original Gothic design has inspired an extensive restoration programme. The high and narrow church, together with the arcades on the first floor, create

View over the town of Gaming

Scheibbs, Niederösterreich

3 The oldest part of town is the elevated church square with the castle, which was built by Otto von Seibes around 1150. The castle is a square building with an unpretentious exterior – inside it has an attractive courtyard with arcades, a fountain and decorative window boxes. The town was fortified in 1350 and enlarged in the 15th century. The interior of the **parish church of St Magdalena** shows imposing round red pillars with golden baroque-style tops, which support the ceiling. The **Rathaus** and **burghers' houses** all have charming courtyards dating from the 15th and 16th centuries.

ⓘ Rathaus

From Scheibbs continue 2km (1 mile) north, then turn left on the 22 to Gresten and left again on the LH92 to Kienberg and south to Gaming.

Gaming, Niederösterreich

4 At the entrance to the **Naturpark Ötscher-Tormäuer** lies Gaming and a stop here is advised to visit the **Karthause Marienthron**, a secluded monastery founded in

an atmosphere of tranquil seclusion (open daily from May to October).

The Ötscher Nature Park and cave are reached over a 14km (9-mile) drive to the parking area. From here, numerous walks and hikes are available through forests.

ⓘ Gemeindeamt

From Gaming continue on the 25 south to Lunz.

Lunz am See, Niederösterreich

5 The village of Lunz is enclosed by mountains and has a reputation as being the coldest spot in the country in winter. Appropriately it's called the **Kälteloch** (the freezing hole)! The lake is flanked by meadows which, during the second half of May and beginning of June, are white with the blossoms of narcissus flowers. The **Amonhaus**, with its 16th-century sgraffito façade, now houses the village council and a **museum** with geological and zoological collections. Also notable are the exhibits relating to anthropology.

ⓘ Gemeindeamt

FOR HISTORY BUFFS

1 The later **abbey of Lilienfeld** was first planned as a monastery by the founder, Leopold VI, who wanted it called 'Marienthal'. At the end of June 1217 it was the site of an important meeting between the armies of two crusaders, who joined forces here, the armies of Leopold VI and of Ulrich von Passau. Two years later Leopold donated a small piece of the True Cross to the abbey and the relic is still sometimes on display.

BACK TO NATURE

4 The trip to the **Ötscher Nature Park** will be much appreciated by visitors who enjoy unspoilt natural landscapes. Narrow valleys abound and are flanked by limestone rocks with wild, crystal clear streams flowing between them. This natural beauty is enhanced by many gorges and waterfalls.

FOR CHILDREN

6 From Mariazell children will enjoy the six-minute ride by cableway to the **Bürgeralpe**. A special viewing tower up here offers remarkable views over the mountains of Styria and Lower Austria. A two-hour walk down is suggested as an alternative to the cable-way. It leads past the **Höhlenstein**, a small cave.

RECOMMENDED WALKS

5 *En route* from Lunz to Mariazell you can branch off at the hamlet of Maierhöfen for Lackenhof. A chairlift from here takes visitors up to the top terminus at the **Ötscher-haus**. This is the starting point for many walks. Mountaineers might consider a hike to the top of the Ötscher mountain, the high-est in the area, and therefore providing extensive panoram-ic views.

Mariazell, the most popular of all Austrian pilgrimage centres

Drive 4km (2½ miles) northeast on the local road and turn right on the 71 for Mariazell.

Mariazell, Steiermark

6 Mariazell is probably one of the best-known and popular of all pilgrims' destinations in Austria. It was founded in 1157 by the Benedictine monks of St Lambrech and received its charter as a market place in 1342, but it was only in 1948 that it was declared a town. The Romanesque **church** of 1200 was followed by a new building in Gothic style in the second half of the 14th century, and was later convert-ed to baroque. Fischer von Erlach and his son were given the task of transforming the interior. The focal point of the church is the **Gnadenkapelle** (Chapel of Mercy), which is enclosed by a silver grille, a donation from Empress Maria Theresia. The altar in the chapel was executed in silver and surrounds an Austrian national treasure, the *Magna Mater Austriae*, the 'great mother of the country'. It is a late Romanesque stylised picture of Our Lady with the infant Jesus in her arms. Over the years the town of Mariazell has developed into a sum-mer and winter resort and its equal popularity as a pilgrim destination has led to the building of a special narrow-gauge railway line from St Pölten, the **Mariazellerbahn**.

ℹ Verkehrsverein, Hauptplatz 13

*Take the 20 north towards Annaberg, turn right before the village on the **LH101** until it reaches the 21. Take the 21 northeast to Kernhof and Kalte Kuchl. Take a sharp left turn north and continue on the **LH133** to Unter Rohrbach, turn north on the **LH132** to Furth, then contin-ue north on the **LH110** via Böheimkirchen to Herzogenburg.*

Herzogenburg, Niederösterreich

7 The tower of the **abbey church** reaches high above the houses of the town. It was rebuilt in 1714 and chief among the architects was Jakob Prandtauer, who died in 1726 and was succeeded by his pupil, Josef Munggenast, who finally com-pleted the building. The main church hall was designed by Fischer von Erlach, and Daniel Gran painted the picture on the high altar. Bartolomeo Altomonte created several other altar paintings and the magnificent ceiling fresco in 1722. The **Stiftsmuseum** contains an interest-ing collection of Gothic winged altars and other sacral church relics.

ℹ Tourismusverband

*From Herzogenburg take the **LH113** south to St Pölten.*

The baroque tower of Dürnstein's church. There is a good view of the river from the terrace below

ⓘ Fremdenverkehrsbüro, Undstrasse

Take the 37 northwest to Rastenfeld, then a right turn to Peigarten/ Ottenstein.

Ottenstein, Niederösterreich

1 Ottenstein lies on the southern shores of the large Ottenstein reservoir, where the Kamp river produces electric power. About 2km (1¼ miles) north lies 12th-century **Burg Ottenstein**. Three small bridges have to be crossed to get from the entrance along the outer courtyard to the inner, which is adorned with a central fountain. The keep and the square-shaped chapel with wall frescos date from about 1200.

ⓘ Fremdenverkehrsamt Ottenstein/Rastenfeld

From Ottenstein drive back to Rastenfeld and continue west on the 38 to Zwettl.

Zwettl, Niederösterreich

2 Zwettl is an old town at the confluence of the Kamp and Zwettl rivers. Having received its town charter around 1200, the town wall was erected soon afterwards and the towers are well preserved in parts. The **museum** is housed in the **Rathaus** (town hall), which was erected in 1307 and bears the Habsburg Eagle on the top of its tower. The Cistercian **abbey** is notable for its mixture of three building styles – Romanesque, Gothic and baroque. The **Brunnenhaus** (house of the fountain) is 13th-century and still in its original state.

ⓘ Tourist Office, Gartenstrasse 32

Take the 36 north to Vitis, turn left and continue west on the 303 towards Schrems, then turn southwest on 41 to Gmünd.

Gmünd, Niederösterreich

3 Gmünd is an old frontier town – the **Stein und Glasmuseum** on the Stadtplatz describes the 2,000-year-old tradition of stone working in the area, including finds from the early Stone Age. The **glass museum** gives an insight into another famous local industry. **Naturpark Blockheide**, north of town, is known for its peculiarly shaped granite rocks which rise from the heathland and have been given legendary names. There is an open-air **geology museum**.

ⓘ Fremdenverkehrsamt

Continue on the 41 southwest to Weitra.

Weitra, Niederösterreich

4 Weitra has a friendly atmosphere. It has a small **brewery**, a **railway station** on the local line and a **castle**, built between 1590 and 1606. After a fire in 1757 the castle was rebuilt in its present design and the inside of the courtyard reveals attractive arcades on all three floors.

Medieval illustrations in a manuscript in Zwettl abbey

NORTH OF THE DANUBE

Krems an der Donau• Ottenstein • Zwettl Gmünd • Weitra • Rappottenstein • Grein • Ybbs an der Donau • Pöchlarn • Melk • Maria Laach am Jauerling • Weissenkirchen in der Wachau Dürnstein • Göttweig • Krems an der Donau

Krems lies at the entrance to the Wachau, a stretch of the Donau (Danube) where the river pushes through a valley with mountains on either side. The oldest Austrian coin, the *Kremser Pfennig*, was minted here between 1130 and 1190. The town's most famous son was Martin Johann Schmidt, known as 'Kremser' Schmidt, who died in 1801 and was noted for his baroque altar paintings. Krems is the centre for the production of superior Austrian wines, an industry that goes back many years. The old town is reached through the imposing Steiner Tor, a fortified town gate with a centre tower, flanked by two smaller ones on either side. Although the town was bombed during World War II, then plundered by Soviet soldiers, about 400 of its old buildings have been preserved and restored.

SPECIAL TO...

9 A stop at **Aggstein** is suggested *en route* from Melk to Spitz, to visit the ruin of a once-dreaded castle. This belonged to a family of medieval knights who made it their profession to rob everybody passing their way and then withdraw into the safety of their fortress. The ruin provides a very pleasant viewpoint over the Danube valley.

---

i Fremdenverkehrsamt

Continue on the 41 southwest to Karlstift, turn left on the 38 east via Gross Gerungs to Merzenstein, then turn right and continue south on the 124 to Rappottenstein.

Rappottenstein, Niederösterreich

5 Burg Rappottenstein stands about 1km (½ mile) south of the village. It was built in the 12th century and in 1664 became the property of the Counts of Abensperg and Traun whose descendants still own it. An extensive defence system with six gates and five courtyards surrounded by walls and tower, all built of solid rock, made the fortress impregnable. Restoration work in 1947 revealed wall frescos from the 16th century and a slab of a medieval altar.

i Fremdenverkehrsamt

Take the 124 southwest to Arbesbach and Königswiesen, then turn sharp left on the 119a to Linden and continue south on the 119 to Grein.

Grein, Oberösterreich

6 Grein is a small attractive town in an idyllic setting on the Danube. Of particular note is the oldest the-atre in Austria, a small and intimate building, still in its original design, capable of seating only 163 persons. **Schloss Greinburg** stands on a rock just outside the centre of the town and houses a shipping museum. **Burg Clam** lies 7km (4 miles) west of Grein and has belonged to the Counts of Clam since 1454. It is beautifully located above a gorge and has a free-standing keep. The castle and the count's art collection can be visited by prior arrangement.

i Fremdenverkehrsamt

From Grein take the 3 along the Danube to Persenbeug and cross the river to Ybbs.

Ybbs an der Donau, Niederösterreich

7 The Romans built a small harbour on the spot where the Danube bends. Remnants of the **town wall**, **moat** and **burghers' houses** of the 16th century bring alive the historic background of Ybbs. A **park** along the shores of the Danube provides a good opportunity for relaxing strolls. The large complex of the hydroelectric scheme of **Ybbs-Persenbeug** on the Danube is open to visitors and guided tours are free of charge.

i Fremdenverkehrsamt

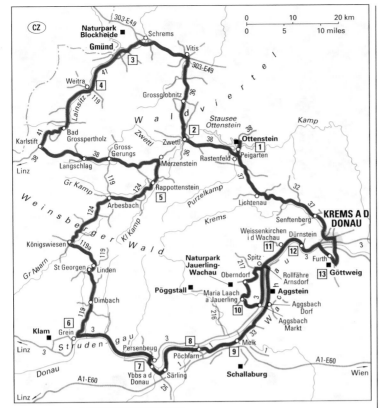

SCENIC ROUTES

9 The part of the Danube valley called the Wachau is only 32km (20 miles) long but it is unquestionably one of the loveliest parts of Austria. On both sides of the Danube, castles, abbeys and ruins crown the hills and many vineyards provide enchanting scenery and views. In spring the blossom of fruit trees transforms the landscape into a sea of colour and in autumn the red leaves announce the gathering of the fruit.

From Ybbs drive southeast to Sarling and continue along the south shore to Pöchlarn.

Pöchlarn, Niederösterreich

8 Pöchlarn dates back to a Roman fort – *Arelape* – which belonged to the Limes line of fortifications along the Danube. Parts of the medieval town wall are still standing and the **Welserturm** (tower), built in 1484, houses the local **museum**. The **parish church** contains three altar paintings by Kremser Schmidt.

[i] Fremdenverkehrsamt

Drive 3km (2 miles) southeast to the junction with the 1 and continue east to Melk.

Melk, Niederösterreich

9 A visit to the **abbey** of Melk is recommended. Built on a solid granite base, its architecture is widely admired. The Emperor's staircase, the Emperor's rooms and the library are not to be missed. The beautiful Library Hall contains 16,000 volumes, but the abbeys' library itself comprises a total of 100,000 books, including 1,800 manuscripts. The **abbey church of St Peter and St Paul** houses three highly treasured objects: the Melker Kreuz is a crucifix in gilded silver with jewels, pearls and a Roman cameo. It was a present from Rudolf IV, the abbey's founder, and contains a piece of the True Cross, which can be seen if you detach the front cover of the crucifix. The portable altar of Swanhild, the first wife of Margrave Ernst, is the second treasure, made of ivory and the third is a reliquary dating from the 13th century. The inside of the abbey church is a masterpiece of baroque

Dürnstein and the Danube. Richard the Lionheart was held in the ruined castle set above them

FOR HISTORY BUFFS

12 One episode in the history of Dürnstein is known both in Austria and Britain. King Richard the Lionheart was imprisoned in the castle here when he was captured in Vienna on his return from the Crusades with Duke Leopold V of Austria. After the conquest of Akkon he tore down the Austrian insignia and refused to share the booty – Duke Leopold informed Emperor Heinrich VI, who later released Richard only on the payment of a large ransom, which was then shared between the Emperor and the Duke.

BACK TO NATURE

2 A Waldlehrpfad (forest lecture trail) leads from Zwettl over 3km (2 miles) and explains nature by living examples, such as trees and other objects to be found in the woods. The trail leads along the Zwettl river, past two quarries.

FOR CHILDREN

9 Across the Danube from Melk the **216** road leads 16km (10 miles) north to **Pöggstall**. The castle keep contains the only medieval torture chamber in Austria, which is kept in its original state.

RECOMMENDED WALKS

10 Naturpark Jauerling-Wachau provides many walking tours and a road leads to the top with far-ranging views over the surrounding area. A special **Naturlehrpfad** (nature trail) and **Kräutermuseum** (herbs museum) should prove interesting and entertaining.

architecture and its highlight is the 18th-century high altar in marble by Antonio Beduzzi. About 7km (4 miles) southeast of Melk lies **Schloss Schallaburg**. The castle is well preserved and the courtyard reveals attractive arcades on two floors, decorated with terracotta figures on the first floor and classified as one of the most significant buildings of Renaissance style in the province.

[i] Fremdenverkehrsstelle, Rathaus

Continue on the 33 north to the Rollfähre Arnsdorf (car ferry) and cross over to Spitz. Take the 217 west and the first turning left up the mountain road to Oberndorf. Turn left to Maria Laach.

Maria Laach am Jauerling, Niederösterreich

10 Maria Laach lies in the hills above the Danube and is known

The incomparable baroque abbey at Melk; inside is equally splendid

for its **pilgrim church**. An overwhelming variety of works of art decorates the interior. The high altar with its double wings is one of the greatest works of Gothic woodcarving. The sarcophagus of Georg III of Kuefstein, who died in 1603, was sculpted in coloured marble by Alexander Colin in the same year. The focus of attention is the painting of *Our Lady with the boy Jesus*, which was brought from the Rhineland by Count Hans von Kuefstein. It is called the Rosary Madonna, as Mary is holding a rosary in her hand and showing six fingers.

[i] Fremdenverkehrsamt

Take the local road to Aggsbach Markt, turn left and continue on the 3 to Weissenkirchen.

Weissenkirchen in der Wachau, Nieder Österreich

11 Exactly 76 steps must be climbed to see the view from the **church tower**, over the enchanting village of Weissenkirchen below. The 54m (177 feet) high tower was fortified in 1531 against the threat of Turkish assault. The **Teisenhofer**

Hof on the market square is a fascinating building, close to the **church**. It was built like a fortified castle with arcades inside the courtyard and a wall with battlements on the top.

[i] Fremdenverkehrsamt

Continue on the 3 to Dürnstein.

Dürnstein, Niederösterreich

12 Romantic Dürnstein grew from a toll station on the shores of the Danube. Jakob Prandtauer and Josef Munggenast, were commissioned to create an eminent church building: its baroque tower is a dominant feature of the town. The interior makes good use of daylight and soft colours have been used for the decorations. The two side altars contain paintings by Kremser Schmidt. Near by, there is a good view from the famous ruins of the 12th-century castle.

[i] Stadtgemeinde, Rathaus

Continue on the 3 to Stein, take a right turn and cross the river to Mautern and then drive southeast to Furth and Göttweig.

Göttweig, Niederösterreich

13 The real development of the abbey of Göttweig began in the 18th century when architect Lucas von Hildebrandt was commissioned to rebuild it. His plans were drawn up in 1719 but could not be fully carried out because they exceeded available funds. Paul Troger and Kremser Schmidt were responsible for the interiors. Most remarkable is the Göttweiger Kaiserstiege, a staircase leading up three floors. It was finished in 1739 and is one of the most elegant staircases to be seen in any Austrian abbey. Four Kaiserzimmer (Emperor's rooms) follow, one of which is called the Napoleon Room, as a reminder of his stay here in 1809. Part of the picture gallery, with works by Altomonte and Kremser Schmidt, is housed in the Cäciliensaal. Further collections of antiques, coins, musical instruments and arms can be seen, together with the Brunnenpyramide (pyramid fountain) in the courtyard, which was designed by the great Fischer von Erlach. The **parish and abbey church of the Assumption of Our Lady** retain past splendour. Considering the size of the abbey, ample time should be allowed for a visit.

[i] Stiftverwaltung

Take the LH100 north to Krems.

Krems an der Donau – Ottenstein 39 (24)
Ottenstein – Zwettl 17 (10½)
Zwettl – Gmünd 37 (23)
Gmünd – Weitra 16 (10)
Weitra – Rappottenstein 56 (35)
Rappottenstein – Grein 58 (36)
Grein – Ybbs an der Donau 22 (13½)
Ybbs an der Donau – Pöchlarn 17 (10½)
Pöchlarn – Melk 11 (7)
Melk – Maria Laach am Jauerling 38 (24)
Maria Laach am Jauerling – Weissenkirchen in der Wachau 21 (13)
Weissenkirchen in der Wachau – Dürnstein 6 (4)
Dürnstein – Göttweig 10 (6)
Göttweig – Krems an der Donau 8 (5)

4 days – 368km (227½ miles)

Fortified Burg Rosenburg

From the centre of Vienna, stay on the west side of the Donaukanal and drive north via Nussdorf and Kahlenbergerdorf, past the foothills of the Leopoldsberg along the Danube on the 14 to Klosterneuburg.

Klosterneuburg, Niederösterreich

1 Klosterneuburg developed around its famous **abbey**, founded in 1106 by Margrave Leopold III. Emperor Karl VI, influenced by the Escorial near Madrid, gave orders to build a new and grander abbey in baroque style, but his plans were thwarted by the sheer size of his project. Ten years after the Emperor's death the architect Josef Kornhäusl completed the work. The focal point inside is the Verdun Altar, finished in 1181 in gilded copper on an enamel base. This masterpiece of medieval art consists of 51 panels depicting the history of humanity in a biblical presentation. The Kaiserzimmer (Imperial Rooms) testify to imperial power and beauty, while the Stiftsmuseum (Abbey Museum) exhibits Karl VI's rich collection of paintings.

ⓘ Fremdenverkehrsverein, Niedermarkt

Take the 14 west to Tulln.

Tulln, Niederösterreich

2 A Danube flotilla was anchored here during Roman times. The **parish church of St Stephen** is a good example of a Romanesque basilica built of stone. The entrance portal remains as one of the few truly Romanesque church entrances in Austria.

ⓘ Tourismusverband, Albrechtsgasse 32

Klosterneuburg abbey and town

THE WOODLANDS

Wien (Vienna) • Klosterneuburg • Tulln Langenlois • Gars am Kamp • Rosenburg am Kamp • Altenburg • Horn • Geras • Raabs an der Thaya • Waidhofen an der Thaya Heidenreichstein • Hardegg • Retz • Pulkau Eggenburg • Wien

This tour leaves Vienna heading north, passing through a narrow part of the Donau (Danube) valley and the eastern end of the mighty Alps. Klosterneuburg offers the chance to see unique historical art treasures. Passing castles, ruins and the abbey of Altenburg, the route continues north to another river valley, the Thayatal, before returning to Vienna via the town of Eggenburg.

SCENIC ROUTES

3 The drive from Langenlois along the Kamp valley to Rosenburg provides photogenic scenery. A wide valley at the start of the journey reveals hills on either side covered with vineyards. Then the mountains come closer to the road and river, and here and there a castle or ruin above the villages completes the view.

Drive due north and cross the Danube, continue to the junction with the 3 and turn left to Kollersdorf. Turn right on the 34 to Hadersdorf am Kamp and then take the local road west to Langenlois.

Langenlois, Niederösterreich

3 Langenlois lies at the end of the Kamp valley, with a large central square where the market used to be held. The baroque-style façades of the houses and their picturesque arcades inside exude a relaxing atmosphere. Langenlois is one of the Austrian centres for wine production and here and on the hills of Zöbing a fruity dry white wine is made.

From Langenlois rejoin and continue north on the 34 to Gars.

Rosenburg am Kamp, Niederösterreich

5 Fortified medieval Burg Rosenburg dominates the valley below from an excellent strategic position, about 100m (328 feet) above the river. Fortunately it was spared from destruction by invading forces, but had to be rebuilt after a fire in 1809, following as closely as possible its original Renaissance style. A visit to the castle provides a good insight into life in the Middle Ages. Entry is through a gate into the **Turnierhof** where tournaments took place. Painted arcades surround the courtyard. The tour continues through the massive, octagonal **Torturm** (gate tower) which has two galleries and where the watch was posted.

ⓘ Burgverwaltung

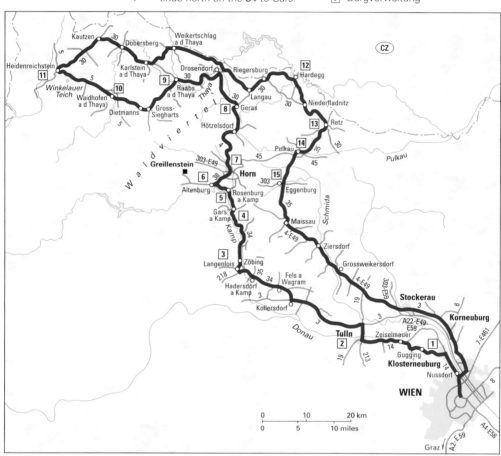

SPECIAL TO...

7 The Höbarthmuseum in Horn has information about Johann Georg Grasel, the infamous robber who terrorised the area as far north as his native Moravia. He sometimes lived in caves to avoid detection and some of these can still be seen around the countryside. He was executed in Vienna in 1818.

Gars am Kamp, Niederösterreich

4 A local exhibition shows finds dating back 5,000 years which have been unearthed in the district. Ruins on the hills above the Kamp valley are proof of a turbulent past. The **castle** stands 120m (394 feet) above the river. The extensions covered three levels of terraces, with the **parish church of St Gertrud** on the lowest level. The basilica was started in 1250 and completed in six stages, and today shows features from the late Romanesque through to baroque style. Notable inside is a window from 1300, a Romanesque font, a pietà from 1420 and many frescos and old gravestones.

ⓘ Tourismusverband Gemeindeamt, Hauptplatz 82

From Gars continue on the 34 north to Rosenburg.

Take the LH53 northwest to Altenburg.

Altenburg, Niederösterreich

6 The **abbey** of Altenburg had humble beginnings in the 12th century, with only 12 monks and an abbot maintaining the small monastery. In the 16th century taxation, the peasant revolt and aggressive Protestant aristocrats from Horn and Rosenburg devastated the abbey. When the abbot built a tower incorporating the treasury and other fortifications it was plundered again and 25 years later its destruction was complete. But between 1645 and 1740 it was finally rebuilt in glorious baroque style. The architect was Josef Munggenast, and the interior reveals a wealth of marble and stucco. The library, with frescos by Paul Troger, is a masterpiece of baroque

Flamboyant baroque architectural detail is one of Altenburg's glories

style. During and after World War II the abbey was damaged but has now been successfully restored.

i Gemeindeamt

Take the 38 east to Horn.

Horn, Niederösterreich

7 Horn lies in the centre of the eastern part of the Waldviertel, an area of wooded countryside. Its inhabitants were heavily involved in the 30 years' war between Catholics and Protestants. In 1539 they supported the Protestant faith, but in 1652 the town was readmitted to the Catholic church. The **parish church of St George** was renovated in 1880 and has an interesting main spire, which is surrounded by a smaller one on each corner of the square-shaped tower. The **Höbarthmuseum** exhibits wideranging prehistoric collections, while the **Mader Museum** is dedicated to the history of agriculture from the simple tools of earlier generations right up to present-day machinery.

i Fremdenverkehrsamt

Take the 4 north to Geras.

Geras, Niederösterreich

8 Like Altenburg, Geras was fortunate enough to employ experts in church building and restoration, Josef Munggenast and Paul Troger. The **abbey** had fallen victim to a fire in 1730 and Munggenast created its present appearance in five years from 1736. The **Marienhof** (Yard of Our Lady) is an outstanding piece of architecture. It consists of three surrounding wings with a central column. Paul Troger painted the ceiling fresco in the Marble Hall, which is used for concerts and receptions.

i Fremdenverkehrsamt

Take the 30 north to Drosendorf and continue west to Raabs.

Raabs an der Thaya, Niederösterreich

9 Raabs lies at the confluence of two rivers, both called Thaya: one comes from Moravia in the north and the other, called the Deutsche Thaya, enters from the western parts of the province. This confluence marked the bridgehead of **Schloss Raabs**, formerly a fortress under the Austrian Babenberg dynasty and later belonging to the Puchheimers, who owned it from 1358 to 1702. They gave the castle its present appearance. The Rittersaal (Hall of the Knights) is now used for concerts.

i Tourismusverband, Hauptstrasse 25

From Raabs take the local road southwest to Gross-Siegharts and continue west on the LH60 to Waidhofen.

Waidhofen an der Thaya, Niederösterreich

10 Waidhofen was founded in the Middle Ages. One tower and large parts of the town wall are still standing. The core of the town is marked by the 16th-century **Rathaus** (town hall) in Renaissance style with an interesting gable.

i Fremdenverkehrsamt

Take the 5 northwest to Heidenreichstein.

Heidenreichstein, Niederösterreich

11 Heidenreichstein has one of the most impressive castles in Austria, surrounded by a moat. Founded by the rulers of Gars and Eggenburg, **Burg Heidenreichstein**

FOR HISTORY BUFFS

6 About 8km (5 miles) northwest of Altenburg stands the imposing Renaissance and baroque-style **castle of Greillenstein**. Exhibits in the museum include medieval torture instruments, apparatus for executions and documents concerning witch hunts and subsequent trials. The 400-year-old courtroom, with its friendly atmosphere, makes it difficult to imagine all the dreadful verdicts the courts must have heard in ancient times.

BACK TO NATURE

8 The **game park** in Geras lies adjacent to the village and is home to deer, moufflon and wild boar. A specially constructed observation tower enables visitors to watch the animals from a distance without disturbing them.

FOR CHILDREN

2 If you stop at Tulln a visit to the **Tullner Aubad** complex is suggested. Here the whole family will enjoy the activities offered by the waters off the main Danube river. Apart from bathing, sailing, waterskiing and rides in motorboats, many other leisure facilities are on offer.

RECOMMENDED WALKS

10 A popular walk leads from Waidhofen to the nearby **chapel in Vestennötting** along the Thaya river.

11 South of Heidenreichstein lies a **nature park** around the Winkelauer Teich (pond). There is a circular trail on offer which also provides information about the forest and the moors, which are being used to make peat moss. A special **museum** in Heidenreichstein supplies more details about the growth and manufacture of peat moss.

was probably built before 1180. It was never conquered or destroyed and is now owned by Count Kinsky.

ⓘ Fremdenverkehrsamt

Take the 30 northeast to Kautzen and continue east via Dobersberg to Karlstein an der Thaya. Take a left turn to Weikertschlag an der Thaya and continue southeast to Drosendorf and on the LH41 to Langau, then join the 30 northeast to Riegersburg and the LH38 to Hardegg.

Hardegg, Niederösterreich

12 A mighty stone-built watchtower guards the entrance to **Burg Hardegg**, which stands high above the town, the smallest in Austria. A fire in the 16th century started the

Heidenreichstein has one of Lower Austria's finest moated castles

gradual decay of the castle, but part restoration saved the complex from becoming a ruin. It now incorporates a museum dedicated to the tragic Emperor Maximilian of Mexico, an armoury and a local museum.

ⓘ Fremdenverkehrsverband

From Hardegg continue on the LH38 southeast to Niederfladnitz and join the 30 to Retz.

Retz, Niederösterreich

13 Retz is well known as an old capital in the vine-growing district of the province. Deep cellars were laid to store the wine and guided tours are available daily. The **town hall** on the large Hauptplatz (main square) contains portraits of Habsburg emperors in the **Ratssaal** (council hall) – the first works of Kremser Schmidt, painted when he was only 18. The **town museum** contains exhibits from the former trade guilds and the sword of the local executioner. Near the calvary stands one of the last Austrian **windmills**, which has become the landmark of Retz.

ⓘ Fremdenverkehrsamt

Take the 35 southwest to Pulkau.

Pulkau, Niederösterreich

14 Pulkau is a lesser known town and seems to wish to hide its treasures from the assault of publicity. It was first mentioned in 1135 as a parish of the Babenbergs and later donated to the Schottenstift (abbey of the Scots) in Vienna. The **parish church of St Michael** stands on an elevated position in the town and was built in the 12th century in Romanesque style. Gothic extensions were added later. Of interest is the 13th-century **Karner** (charnel house), a massive Romanesque tower with a Gothic gable, dedicated to St Bartholomew. Also notable is the **Blutkirche**, church of the Holy Blood, whose building was beset with problems and never completed. The winged altar of 1515, however, became famous, along with its creator who was subsequently called the *Pulkauer Meister* (Masterbuilder of Pulkau). His style of woodcarving belongs to a trend later called the *Donauschule*. Also interesting is the Rathaus (town hall) with its open-air staircase and the pillory on the same square.

ⓘ Fremdenverkehrsamt

From Pulkau continue on the 35 southwest to Eggenburg.

Eggenburg, Niederösterreich

15 Eggenburg is a charming town, enclosed in a medieval wall, with a wide open central square. The surrounding burghers' houses of the 16th to 18th century harmonise with the general appearance of the town and one house, **Das Gemalte Haus** (the Painted House), has attractive sgraffito paintings of 1547. The outside appearance of the mighty **parish church** shows true Romanesque features in the tall, imposing towers of different heights. These are capped by tentshaped roofs, a style typical of the area. Inside the pulpit intricate Gothic stone carvings can be seen, with the side altars showing the influence of Viennese baroque. The **Krahuletz Museum** is well known for its prehistoric finds and collections. It exhibits finds from sediments of former seas estimated to be 20 million years old. Also on show are finds from the Ice and Bronze Age.

ⓘ Fremdenverkehrsamt

Continue on the 35 south to Maissau, take a left turn for the 4 southeast to Stockerau and the 3 via Korneuburg to Vienna.

Bringing in the harvest

From the centre of Vienna head northeast. Cross the Donau (Danube) to take the 3 at Floridsdorf, then north to Korneuburg.

Korneuburg, Niederösterreich

1 Korneuburg lies in the foothills of the **Bisamberg**, a mountain which forms the eastern end of the Alps. The **Rathaus (town hall)** is a 19th-century neo-Gothic building into which the architects incorporated the 1440 **Stadtturm (town tower)**. The **church of St Augustin** was built in late baroque style and has a noteworthy altar painting of *The Last Supper* by Franz Anton Maulbertsch.

ⓘ Tourismusverband

From Korneuburg continue on the 3 northwest to Burg Kreuzenstein, turning right off the 3 to reach the castle.

Burg Kreuzenstein, Niederösterreich

2 When you leave Korneuburg the silhouette of **Burg Kreuzenstein** looms into view. At the turn of the century Count Wilczek needed a location for his Gothic art collection and rebuilt the castle in medieval style. There is a **museum** too.

ⓘ Burgverwaltung

From Burg Kreuzenstein take the LH25 northwest to Leitzersdorf, then turn right for the LH26 to Ernstbrunn.

Ernstbrunn, Niederösterreich

3 The vast **castle complex** stands on a wooded hill in extensive grounds. The **parish church of St Martin** was

THE WINE DISTRICT

Wien (Vienna) • Korneuburg • Burg Kreuzenstein • Ernstbrunn • Mistelbach Asparn an der Zaya • Zistersdorf • Gänserndorf Marchegg • Orth an der Donau • Wien

Soon after this tour crosses the Danube the view is dominated by the imposing form of Burg Kreuzenstein, then it's on through charming, sleepy villages and towns. Among the meadows and fields oil pumps and derricks suddenly appear before the tour continues along the March river, which forms the border with the Slovak republic. Finally, there is a visit to Schloss Eckartsau where the great Habsburg empire came to an end.

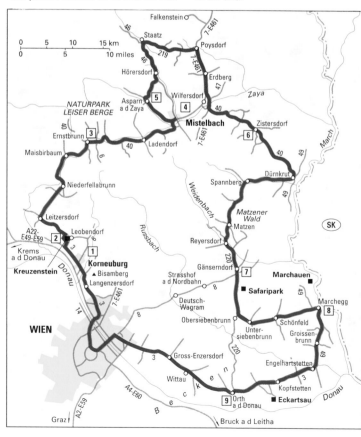

SCENIC ROUTES

4 A detour from Mistelbach north to Poysdorf and Falkenstein leads through one of the main vine-growing districts in the area. The landscape is covered with vineyards with little lanes running across to house the wine cellars, which should make a drive around very enjoyable.

8 The stretch from Marchegg to Engelhartsstetten and further down to the Danube runs through pleasant countryside and good views are offered from the riverbanks.

BACK TO NATURE

3 The area north of Ernstbrunn is a designated **nature park** and includes a small hilly range, the Leiser Berge. Part of it has been set aside for a game park, which is home for deer, wild boar, moufflon, mountain goats and ibex. The park is open from Easter to November.

The vineyards of Lower Austria are renowned for their fine wines

Zistersdorf, Niederösterreich

6 Zistersdorf has a surprise in store: derricks and oil pumps amid agricultural land. Oil was discovered here in 1930 and daily production was then a bare five litres. Over-exploitation during World War II has decimated the supplies. The **pilgrim church of Maria Moos** was erected on top of a spring, which is now in the cellar below the sacristy. The altar painting and the picture in the Annenchapel are works by Paul Troger from 1753 and 1758.

i Gemeindeamt

From Zistersdorf continue on the 40 southeast to Dürnkrut, turn west on the LH11/17 to Spannberg, take the LH18 south to Matzen and the junction with the 220, then turn left to Gänserndorf.

Gänserndorf, Niederösterreich

7 Gänserndorf prides itself on a large **safari park**, where more than 500 different species roam. The park can be crossed by a narrow-gauge railway or by car, taking the usual precautions. The Acapulco death jumpers and other shows provide entertainment!

i Fremdenverkehrsamt

From Gänserndorf take the LH9 south to Obersiebenbrunn and turn east on the LH2 to Marchegg.

Marchegg, Niederösterreich

8 Ottokar II, the King of Bohemia, built himself a **castle** at Marchegg in 1268 and the wall with its two gates is still intact. Following the first siege of Vienna by the Turks in 1529 the castle became the property of Count Niklas Salm, the heroic defender of the city. After several modifications the castle deteriorated and was taken over by the provincial government who converted it into a hunting museum.

i Fremdenverkehrsverband

From Marchegg take the 49 south to Engelhartsstetten, turn right and continue on the 3 west to Orth.

Orth an der Donau, Niederösterreich

9 Schloss Orth, once a moated castle, is now a **fishing museum**. Eight kilometres (five miles) east stands the former hunting lodge of **Schloss Eckartsau**. History was made here on 11 November 1918, when the last Habsburg emperor was forced to abdicate.

i Fremdenverkehrsamt

From Orth take the 3 northwest via Gross-Enzersdorf to Vienna.

SPECIAL TO...

7 Between Gänserndorf and Deutsch Wagram at **Strasshof an der Nordbahn**, fans have erected a **museum** preserving old steam engines, using a former railway workshop. The museum arranges many trips – it also demonstrates the amount of work necessary to get one of these old steam engines going, and the difficulties facing someone who wants to make dreams come true and become an engine driver!

RECOMMENDED WALKS

8 The **nature reserve** of **Marchauen**, north of Marchegg, offers two marked paths with observation towers to watch the only cormorant colony in Austria, and other animals in their natural habitat. It is open all year round.

FOR HISTORY BUFFS

7 Twelve kilometres (7 miles) southwest from Gänserndorf on the **8** lies the village of **Deutsch-Wagram**. Here in July 1809 a great battle was fought between an Austrian army of 120,000 men and Napoleon, who had 180,000 soldiers. Two months earlier the Austrians had defeated Napoleon at Aspern, but this time luck was on Napoleon's side and he won, costing a total of 100,000 lives. The **museum** provides interesting details in the Napoleonzimmer, a hall dedicated to the battle.

---

first mentioned in 1250, but the present structure dates from 1700. The painting on the altar is by Kremser Schmidt.

i Gemeindeamt

From Ernstbrunn take the 40 east to Mistelbach.

Mistelbach, Niederösterreich

4 A charming little **castle** stands near the main square of Mistelbach, called the **Baroqueschlössl**. It was built in baroque style, as its name implies, and dates from 1728. It houses the **Heimatmuseum (local museum)** which is open from April to October.

i Stadtgemeinde, Hauptplatz 6

From Mistelbach take the LH35 northwest to Asparn.

Asparn an der Zaya, Niederösterreich

5 Asparn's **museum** houses a fascinating exhibition of the history of primeval cultures of the province of Lower Austria. The museum is suitably situated in the imposing **Schloss Asparn**, a building which has its origins in a moated castle dating from 1421. In the adjacent park an **open-air museum** exhibits the living and working quarters of settlers from the Ice Age to the Celtic period. The museums are open from April to October.

i Tourismusverband

Take the local road north to Hörersdorf and continue on the 46 northwest to Staatz. Turn right and take the 219 to Poysdorf. Take the 7 south to Wilfersdorf and turn left on the 40 to Zistersdorf.

2 days – 281km (174½ miles)

As well as being a popular lake for water sports, Neusiedler See is also a favoured haunt of birds

From the centre of Vienna head southeast along the Donaukanal and the oil refinery of Schwechat and Vienna airport. From here you join the **9** along the Danube river at the Fischamend exit of the motorway and continue due east to Petronell.

Petronell, Niederösterreich

1 Emperor Tiberius concentrated his army here in AD6 for his battles against the north. *Carnuntum*, as it was then called, was a provincial capital. Excavations provide a good insight into life in a Roman city and show remains of Roman baths, heating and sewage systems.

ℹ Gemeindeamt, Kirchengasse 57

*Continue on the **9** for 4km (2½ miles) to Bad Deutsch-Altenburg.*

Bad Deutsch-Altenburg, Niederösterreich

2 Bad Deutsch-Altenburg is a market town and spa, known for its sulphurous springs. The **parish church** and **charnel house** both stand within the cemetery and show interesting features of 13th-century Romanesque architecture.

ℹ Hauptplatz

Continue for 3km (2 miles) east to Hainburg.

Hainburg an der Donau, Niederösterreich

3 Hainburg was once a fortified town. The fortress ruins dominate this medieval town which went through turbulent times in the 16th and 17th centuries due to Turkish assaults.

ℹ Hauptplatz 23

*Continue on the **9** and turn right after Wolfsthal to Kittsee.*

ALONG THE DANUBE & THE NEUSIEDLER SEE

Wien (Vienna) • Petronell • Bad Deutsch-Altenburg • Hainburg an der Donau • Kittsee Rohrau • Neusiedl am See • Rust • Eisenstadt Laxenburg • Wien

Roman history features at the beginning of this tour, which then makes its way to the Neusiedler See, a superb habitat for birds and insects. Another well-known wine-producing area, the Burgenland, is passed through before returning to Vienna.

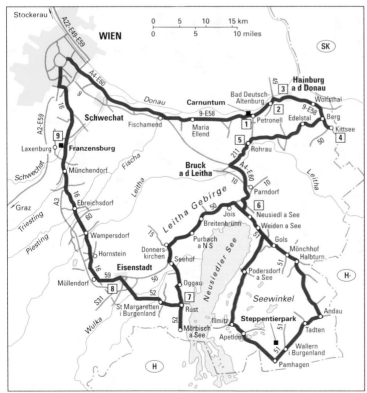

SCENIC ROUTES

6 The circular route on the east side of the Neusiedler See reveals a scenery and climate quite unlike anywhere else in Austria. A steppe-like landscape, the Puszta, starts here and stretches eastwards into Hungary. Flat plains with many small shallow lakes and the larger Neusiedler See – surrounded by reeds – provide memorable scenery, best enjoyed at dawn and sunset.

SPECIAL TO...

7 A short detour to Mörbisch am See enables you to enjoy this attractive village on the Hungarian border. Watch out for operettas at the Mörbisch Seespiele, performed on a floating stage during July and August. A mineral spring can be found near the Seehotel.

FOR HISTORY BUFFS

4 Near Edelstal, about 8km (5 miles) west of Kittsee lies the Römerquelle (Roman spring) which was supposedly used by Emperor Marcus Aurelius for healing purposes. The spring fell into disuse but its radioactive waters are now being used again for cures or as mineral water.

BACK TO NATURE

6 The area around the Neusiedler See is noted for its flora and fauna and counted as a paradise for nature lovers. Northwest of the lake lies the Breitenbrunn nature reserve, which is covered with reeds and can be crossed by artificially laid-out trails. About 250 different species of bird nest here, amongst them herons, ibis, marsh harriers, bee-eaters, wild duck, geese and waders. South of Andau a bird sanctuary has been established. Silence, binoculars and patience are needed to observe them.

FOR CHILDREN

6 A circular trip on the flat-bottomed boats from Neusiedl am See to Podersdorf and across to Rust and back will delight children and adults alike. The lake has a maximum depth of about 2m (6 feet).

RECOMMENDED WALKS

6 The Seewinkel is an area southeast of the lake. Leave the car at Illmitz or Apleton and explore the many small lakes and the countryside. Between Apleton and Wallern lies the entrance to the Steppentierpark, a game reserve where wolves, wild horses, wild boar and birds of prey are kept, mostly in open enclosures. All are natives of the steppe climate.

Schloss Esterházy in Eisenstadt

Kittsee, Burgenland

4 The castle once had a Hungarian name, Schloss Batthyany, but is now Schloss Kittsee. It was rebuilt between 1730 and 1740 in Viennese baroque style. A decorative balustrade was transported from nearby Pressburg – now Bratislava – and was added on to the front. The castle now houses a **museum**.

[i] Gemeindeamt

Turn back north to Berg and take the LH165 west to Rohrau.

Rohrau, Niederösterreich

5 The castle has belonged to the Counts of Harrach since 1524 and has the largest private picture gallery in Austria. It contains about 200 paintings by acclaimed masters such as van Dyck and Rubens. In the village is the birthplace of the composer Joseph Haydn, born here on 31 March 1732, one of 12 children. The house is now a museum.

[i] Fremdenverkehrsamt

Take the 211 southwest to the A4 and drive south to Neusiedl.

Neusiedl am See, Burgenland

6 Neusiedl is a tourist resort on the northern shore of a large and shallow lake, the **Neusiedler See**. The reeds surrounding the lake – which reportedly dried out between 1866 and 1869 – attract many rare birds and over 200 different species breed here, favoured by the steppe climate unique in Austria.

[i] Fremdenverkehrsbüro

Take the 51 southeast to Weiden am See, take a right fork to Podersdorf am See and continue on the L205 to Illmitz and southeast to Pamhagen. Turn northeast on the 51 to Wallern im Burgenland and the L206 to Andau and north to Halbturn. Take a left turn on the L211 via Gols back to Neusiedl and northwest to the 50, turn left via Jols and Purbach am Neusiedler See

until Seehof and take a left fork to Oggau and Rust.

Rust, Burgenland

7 Rust is called the town of storks and wine. Many stork nests can be seen on the chimneys here and in other villages around the lake. Whole streets in the old town of Rust have kept their historic appearance and in 1975 the town was honoured for this during the 'Year of Architectural Heritage'.

[i] Fremdenverkehrsamt

Take the 52 south to Mörbisch am See and return, then take the 52 west to Eisenstadt.

Eisenstadt, Burgenland

8 Until 1918, Eisenstadt was administered by Hungary. The baroque palace was the home of the ruling Esterhazy dynasty. The composer Haydn worked here, and concerts of his music are performed every year from May to October. The **Haydn Museum** is at Haydngasse 21. The town contains other mementoes of Haydn, notably his tomb in the baroque Bergkirche.

[i] Hauptstrasse 35

Take the 59 west to Müllendorf, turn right and continue north on the 16 to Laxenburg.

Laxenburg, Niederösterreich

9 Schloss Franzensburg has recently been transformed into a leisure area. The castle park with its many pavilions provides a romantic location: the focal point is the pond.

[i] Fremdenverkehrsamt

Return north on the 16 to Vienna.

Wien – Petronell 41 (25)
Petronell – Bad Deutsch-Altenburg 4 (2½)
Bad Deutsch-Altenburg – Hainburg an der Donau 3 (2)
Hainburg an der Donau – Kittsee 12 (7½)
Kittsee – Rohrau 19 (12)
Rohrau – Neusiedl am See 18 (11)
Neusiedl am See – Rust 105 (65)
Rust – Eisenstadt 28 (17½)
Eisenstadt – Laxenburg 35 (22)
Laxenburg – Wien 16 (10)

Carved wine barrels such as this can be seen in a number of taverns around Gumpoldskirchen

From the centre of Vienna drive to the ring road, the Gürtel. Take the 12 to Liesing and turn right via Rodaun to Perchtoldsdorf.

Perchtoldsdorf, Niederösterreich

1 On the market square stands the imposing medieval keep and the parish church of St Augustin. The keep now houses a **museum** of local history.

ⓘ Fremdenverkehrsamt

Drive west on the LH127 to Sulz im Wienerwald and continue southeast to Sittendorf. Take a right fork due south to the 11 and turn right to Heiligenkreuz.

Heiligenkreuz, Niederösterreich

2 This Cistercian **abbey** was founded in 1135 and is one of the oldest of this order in Austria. Its name derives from a relic of the True Cross, presented to the monks by Duke Leopold V on his return from the Third Crusade. The interior of the Stiftskirche shows interesting contrasts in style, the dark Romanesque nave and heavy pillars against the bright Gothic choir section. Both Franz Schubert and Anton Bruckner played the organ here.

ⓘ Fremdenverkehrsamt

Take the LH130 south to Sattelbach and turn sharp right on the 210 northwest to Mayerling.

Mayerling, Niederösterreich

3 The tragic story of Mayerling unfolded in a lonely hunting lodge on 29 January 1899. The Crown Prince of Austria, only son of Emperor Franz Josef, first shot his mistress Baroness Vetsera, who was only 17 years old, then killed himself. The Emperor gave orders for the lodge to be converted into a Carmelite convent, to try and atone for the sins of the Prince.

ⓘ Kloster

From Mayerling continue on the 210 northwest to Alland.

Alland, Niederösterreich

4 Alland lies only 2km (1 mile) from Mayerling. It is known for its long cave with stalagmites and stalactites and is a good stopping place. The cave is open from Easter to the autumn: guided tours last about 25 minutes.

Drive on the 11 southwest, then southeast to Weissenbach an der Triesting, continue on the 18 to Berndorf and south to Markt Piesting. Take a right turn and continue on the 21 west to Pernitz and Gutenstein.

Gutenstein, Niederösterreich

5 The **castle** is now a ruin, but there are fascinating views down to the gorges. The **Waldbauernmuseum** (Museum of Hill Farmers) gives an insight into local lives. From Gutenstein, a winding road leads 3km (2 miles) up to the

THE SOUTHERN VIENNA WOODS

Wien (Vienna) • Perchtoldsdorf • Heiligenkreuz
Mayerling • Alland • Gutenstein • Voismaut
Semmering • Hohe Wand • Bad Vöslau • Baden
Gumpoldskirchen • Mödling • Wien

Few will not be stirred by the sight of the magnificent 12th-century Cistercian abbey of Heiligenkreuz, or moved by the tragic events at Mayerling, while the spa towns of Bad Vöslau and Baden offer a glimpse of a former glory and elegance.

Mariahilferberg (mountain), which is 708m (2,323 feet) high. On the peak stands a baroque pilgrim church with excellent views.

From Gutenstein drive 3km (2 miles) west on the 21 and turn left and continue on the LH134 to Voismaut.

Voismaut, Niederösterreich

6 The Falkenstein nature park is only a short distance north from Voismaut, at Schwarzau im Gebirge. Here you can get close to nature and enjoy picnics and barbecues.

ⓘ Schwarzau Naturpark

Take the 27 south to Hirschwang and the first turning right to the LH135 southwest via Prein an der Rax to Kapellen. Turn sharp left on the 23 southeast to Mürzzuschlag. Take the S6 southwest to Krieglach and turn

SCENIC ROUTES

6 The drive from Voismaut to Hirschwang leads through the Höllental (Valley of Hell). It represents a fascinating route through a valley between high peaks on either side, the Rax and the Schneeberg, both more than 2,000m (6,561 feet) above sea level. The detour from Mürzzuschlag via Krieglach to the Semmering is also highly recommended. It leads through an area called the Waldheimat, where the Austrian poet Peter Rosegger was born and found the inspiration for his work in its romantic and unspoilt forests.

SPECIAL TO...

6 A stop at the Wasserleitungsmuseum at **Kaiserbrunn** in the Höllental is suggested. Seven springs from the nearby Schneealpe mountain provide part of the drinking water supply for Vienna. After the end of World War II and the following occupation the safety of the water could no longer be guaranteed. It is now filtered and cleaned before reaching the taps.

FOR HISTORY BUFFS

7 On the top of the Semmering Pass is a memorial to Emperor Karl VI, the builder of the road over the pass. Another monument commemorates the first flight over the pass in 1912 by Eduard Nittner. In 1848 Carl Ritter von Ghega built the first mountain railway in Europe to cross the pass which runs through 17 tunnels and over several attractive viaducts. Recently the Austrian government decided to build a tunnel here in spite of local protests.

BACK TO NATURE

8 The nature park of the Hohe Wand covers the whole area of this elevated plateau. The forests of beech, fir and oak are home to deer, mountain goats and marmots, capercaillie and grouse. At the Bromberg enclave, moufflon and ibex can be seen in open enclosures and additional information is provided about the manufacture of charcoal, which is also sold in the car park.

FOR CHILDREN

6 Just before reaching Hirschwang in the Höllental stands the terminus of the **Raxbahn**, one of the oldest cableways in Austria. It leads up to the high plateau of the Rax mountain. An Alpenlehrpfad (alpine lecture trail) is marked and plaques along the way provide information about the mountains.

7 En route from Semmering to the Hohe Wand stop at **Puchberg am Schneeberg** to take a ride on the old cogwheel railway up to the Schneeberg mountain. The journey takes a little over one hour for the 9km (6 miles) and the track rises gently through extensive forests and pastures.

left on the **72** southeast to St Kathrein am Hauenstein, then take the first turning left on the **L117** via Ratten, Rettenegg and the Pfaffensattel to Steinhaus am Semmering and turn right on the **306** to Semmering.

Semmering, Niederösterreich

7 The Semmering Pass forms the border between the provinces of Styria and Lower Austria. Once a fashionable resort for the elegant Viennese, visitors tend to come now out of nostalgia for the good old days. Plenty of modern facilities aid your enjoyment of restful days in good mountain air.

ⓘ Kurverwaltung

Drive via Maria Schütz to Schottwien and Gloggnitz. Take the **17** to Wimpassing and turn left via Ternitz on the **26** to Puchberg am Schneeberg. Continue on the **26** east to Unterhöflein, turn left to Maisersdorf and left up the mountain road to the Hohe Wand.

Hohe Wand, Niederösterreich

8 The nature park of the Hohe Wand plateau lies on top of a limestone mountain range, which can be reached by driving over a mountain road. The area is a favourite spot for rock climbers.

ⓘ Grünbach am Schneeberg, Gemeindeamt

From Maisersdorf drive east to

Weikersdorf am Steinfelde, turn left and continue on the **LH137** to Bad Fischau. Take the **21** north past Steinabrückl, then turn north via Matzendorf to Bad Vöslau.

Bad Vöslau, Niederösterreich

9 As the name implies, Bad Vöslau is a spa which is fed by a thermal spring producing water at a constant temperature of 24°C. Its heyday was in the 19th century, but visitors are still welcome.

ⓘ Kurdirektion

Take the **212** north to Baden.

Baden, Niederösterreich

10 The thermal springs of Baden bei Wien were known to the Romans. About 4½ million litres of hot water with a high sulphur content are produced daily by 15 springs. The temperature in the large outdoor pools is about 33°C, but it takes some time to get used to the smell of sulphur. At Rathausgasse 10 stands a memorial to the composer Ludwig van Beethoven, who spent the summers of 1821 and 1823 here and composed most of his 9th Symphony in this house. Baden was a popular summer residence for Austrian emperors. The Helenental valley to the west is a popular spot for romantic walks.

ⓘ Kurdirektion

From Baden take the **LH151** north to Gumpoldskirchen.

*An 18th-century Plague Tower
in Baden's town centre*

Gumpoldskirchen, Niederösterreich

11 Gumpoldskirchen lies in the foothills of the Anninger mountain. Its sheltered position is favourable for growing vines. It is best visited in the daytime as it gets very crowded in the summer evenings when the thirsty Viennese frequent the *Heurigen* (taverns).

⌶ Gemeindeamt

Continue north to Mödling.

Mödling, Niederösterreich

12 Mödling became famous in the 19th century when artists discoverd the beauty of the surrounding area. Composers Beethoven and Schubert, among others, stayed here during the summer months. You can hardly miss the aqueduct, which carried fresh mountain water across the valley of the Mödling river to Vienna. The **Freskohaus** in Rathausgasse 6 has sgraffito ornaments on its façade. The **charnel house** in the Kirchenplatz is a 12th-century Romanesque building with an impressive portal. Perhaps the oldest house in Mödling is the **Herzoghof**, Herzogstrasse 4. It was the residence of the Duke of Troppau, who was also the town priest.

Three kilometres (2 miles) north of Mödling stands **Burg Liechtenstein**. The Hinterbrühl area west of Mödling offers a trip on the largest subterranean lake in Europe, by

electric motorboat. The cave was discovered by accident in 1912 and guided tours take place all year round. They also include a visit to a shaft which was artificially dried out and where the Germans produced the first jet fighter at the end of World War II.

⌶ Fremdenverkehrsamt

Drive west to Hinterbrühl and join the A21 at Giesshübl. Continue northeast to the junction with the A2 and drive north to Vienna.

The Vienna Woods, near Baden

Wien – Perchtoldsdorf 10 (6)
Perchtoldsdorf – Heiligenkreuz 30 (18½)
Heiligenkreuz – Mayerling 9 (5½)
Mayerling – Alland 2 (1)
Alland – Gutenstein 56 (35)
Gutenstein – Voismaut 21 (13)
Voismaut – Semmering 104 (65)
Semmering – Hohe Wand 68 (42)
Hohe Wand – Bad Vöslau 39 (24)
Bad Vöslau – Baden 5 (3)
Baden – Gumpoldskirchen 7 (4½)
Gumpoldskirchen – Mödling 5 (3)
Mödling – Wien 26 (16)

RECOMMENDED WALKS

11 In Gumpoldskirchen don't miss a walk among the vineyards in the foothills of the Anninger mountain. You can walk up to one of the two observation towers, the Jubiläums- and the Wilhelmswarte, from where you have wide panoramic views over the Danube plains in the east and also to the higher peaks in the south.

4 days – 433km (269 miles)

FORTRESSES & CASTLES

Wiener Neustadt • Forchtenstein • Kobersdorf
Raiding • Lockenhaus • Stadtschlaining
Güssing • Heiligenkreuz • Vorau
Kirchberg am Wechsel • Wiener Neustadt

Wiener Neustadt was founded by the Babenberg dynasty in 1194 and later fortified, partly with the ransom money obtained from the release of England's Richard the Lionheart. During the 19th century it became an important base for the Habsburg monarchy. The Stadtmuseum exhibits prehistoric and Roman finds, but its most precious object is the Corvinusbecher, a gilt goblet supposed to have been given to the citizens as a gift from the Hungarian King Mathias Corvinus in the 15th century.

Red deer, one of the inhabitants of the nature park near Güssing

Take the 53 towards Neudörfl. Turn right to Bad Sauerbrunn and Mattersburg. Continue southwest to Forchtenstein.

Forchtenstein, Burgenland

1 Forchtenstein's fortress was rebuilt in 1635, just before the Turkish siege of 1683. It withstood all attacks and is still only accessible by a bridge over a dried-out moat. Inside, fascinating collections portray its past.

ℹ Fremdenverkehrsamt

Continue on the local road southwest to Hochwolkersdorf, turn southeast on the LH148 and later the LH103 to Kobersdorf.

Kobersdorf, Burgenland

2 Heavily damaged during the last war, Kobersdorf's castle has been saved from decay. Inside, the courtyard provides a backdrop for open-air theatre performances in July.

ℹ Fremdenverkehrsamt

Take a left fork to Weppersdorf and the 50. Turn sharp left again and take the 62 east for 4km (2½ miles). Then take a right fork on the local road to Raiding.

Raiding, Burgenland

3 Franz Liszt was born here on 22 October 1811. The house is now a memorial to the great composer.

ℹ Fremdenverkehrsamt

SCENIC ROUTES

7 The section from Kaindorf to Pöllau and Vorau leads through the nature park called the Pöllauer Tal, and the circular tour around the Pöllauberg to the pilgrim church is especially attractive.

SPECIAL TO...

8 In Vorau a visit to the Museumsdorf (Museum Village), near the abbey, is suggested. Thirteen old farmhouses are on show here with a notable collection of original furnishings.

FOR HISTORY BUFFS

2 Southwest of Kobersdorf stands the ruin of the castle of Landsee, which was once one of the most powerful fortresses in central Europe. It was erected in the 12th century but totally destroyed by fire in 1772. The inner castle was protected by five rows of walls. The oldest part is the donjon (living quarters). Although the whole complex is now is a state of decay, it is still an attractive site.

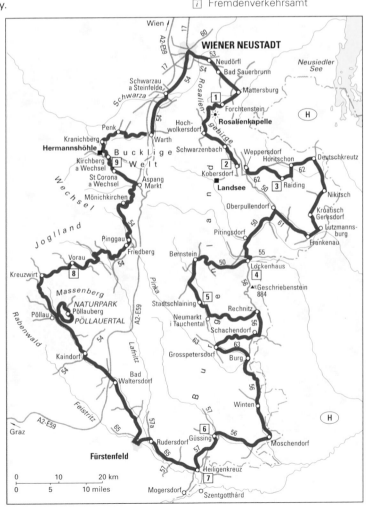

Drive 2km (1 mile) east, then turn sharp left to Horitschon and continue east to Deutschkreutz. Take the *L228* southeast to Lutzmannsburg, then turn right to Frankenau and right again on the *L225* to Oberpullendorf. Take the *50* southwest and turn off to Lockenhaus.

Lockenhaus, Burgenland

4 The **castle** has a mysterious sub-terranean room, the Kultraum (cult room) which gets its daylight only through a circle-shaped opening in the ceiling. Guided tours are available daily.

ⓘ Fremdenverkehrsamt

Join the 50 west to Bernstein and continue south for 7km (4 miles), then take a left fork for the L105 to Stadtschlaining.

Stadtschlaining, Burgenland

5 The medieval **castle** is overshad-owed by its Romanesque keep. A lifesize relief of the knight Andreas Baumkirchner in full armour was erected at his own instigation on the outer wall.

ⓘ Burgerwaltung

Continue on the L105 for 3km (2 miles) south, then turn left and drive east to Rechnitz. Turn south on the 56 to Schachendorf, turn right and follow the 63 west to Grosspetersdorf. Drive east on the local road to Burg and contin-ue south on the 56 to Moschen-dorf and west to Güssing.

Güssing, Burgenland

6 The present **castle** dates from the 16th and 17th centuries and was fortified as a defence against the Turks. The armoury contains many Turkish souvenirs.

ⓘ Fremdenverkehrsamt

Take the 57 to Heiligenkreuz.

Lockenhaus's 13th-century castle

Heiligenkreuz, Burgenland

7 The town of Heiligenkreuz, on the border with Hungary, has become a holiday resort. Eight kilometres (5 miles) south lies **Mogersdorf** and **St Gotthard**, now Hungarian Szent-gotthard. Here in 1664 the Austrian army finally defeated the Turks.

ⓘ Fremdenverkehrsamt

Take the 65 northwest to Fürstenfeld, and the L401 to Bad Waltersdorf, Pöllau and Pöllauberg. Continue northwest from Pöllau, turn right to Kreuzwirt and northeast to Vorau.

Vorau, Steiermark

8 The Augustinian **abbey** is worth a visit and houses a famous collec-tion of medieval handwriting.

ⓘ Fremdenverkehrsamt

Continue west to Friedberg, take the 54 north to Aspang Markt, then turn left on the LH137 via St Corona am Wechsel to Kirchberg.

Kirchberg am Wechsel, Nieder Österreich

9 Kirchberg lies in the Bucklige Welt (World of Hills). A cave near by, the **Hermannshöhle**, has been open to the public since 1869.

Continue north to Kranichberg, turn right to Penk and continue east to Warth. Take the 54 back to Wiener Neustadt.

BACK TO NATURE

6 Not far northeast from Güssing, a **nature park** lies in extensive grounds. The breeding of rare and endan-gered species is protected. There are aurochs (the prede-cessors of the domesticated oxen), wild horses, red deer, Hungarian steppe cattle, black water bison, Dybovsky stags from Korea, Macedonian dwarf donkeys, moufflon and many others. You can also see American bison and 'Beefalos', a crossbreed between bison and cattle. Observation towers are avail-able for visitors and the best time for watching is just before sunset.

FOR CHILDREN

8 St Corona am Wechsel has one of the longest sum-mer tobogganing runs in the province, 8km (5 miles) from top to bottom. It is in opera-tion from May to October. There is also a chairlift which takes visitors up to the Kampstein mountain at 1,249m (4,078 feet) above sea level.

RECOMMENDED WALKS

5 A pleasant walk through shaded paths leads up to the Geschriebenstein, about 7km (4 miles) from Rechnitz. A rewarding view towards the Hungarian plain is provided from the platform of the observation tower and the Austrian–Hungarian border runs right on top of the mountains.

WIEN
– THE IMPERIAL CITY

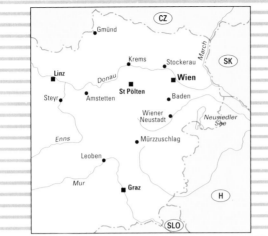

Vienna was the focal point for outside aggressors. From the east and southeast it was the Huns, Magyars and Turks; from the north the Swedes; and from the west Napoleon's troops. Aerial bombardments and the Soviet army inflicted heavy damage during World War II, but all this has now been cleared and rebuilt.

Vienna Centre, southeast

1 The old city wall, the *glacis*, was demolished in the last century under orders from Emperor Franz Josef I, to enable Vienna to expand. The **Ringstrasse** (ring road) more or less confirms the former location of the wall. It is within the Ringstrasse and in the area just outside it that most of the capital's important buildings stand. The impressive **Stephansdom** (St Stephen's Cathedral) marks the heart of the city and has become the unchallenged symbol of Vienna.

The Viennese are very attached to their cathedral, which they affectionately call 'Steffl'. When it was heavily damaged by cannon fire at the end of World War II, the church was one of the first buildings to be repaired, with contributions coming in from all the Austrian provinces. Vienna repaired the 230,000 coloured roof tiles while Tirol supplied the windows with bright new panels which let in more light, but the old stained-glass windows with their beautiful colours could not be replaced. A few of these can still be seen behind the high altar and in more sheltered parts of the cathedral.

From the eastern part of the

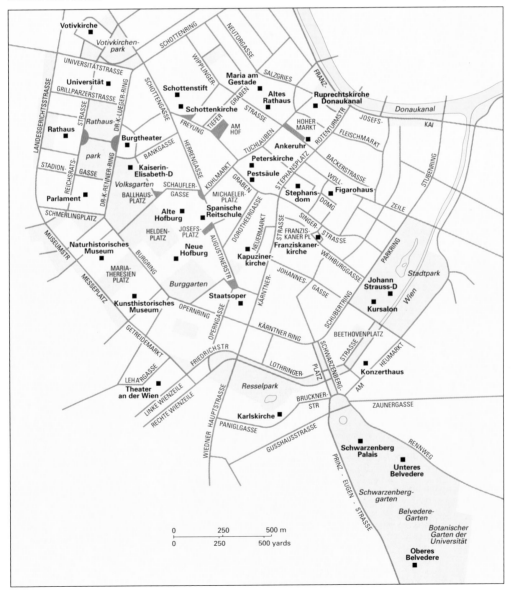

St Stephen's Cathedral with its dazzling yellow, green and black tiled roof – Vienna's landmark

6 A scenic round trip through the Vienna Woods is suggested, starting on the outskirts at the village of Neuwaldegg, northwest of the centre. The route leads uphill past the Exelberg and Scheiblingstein. About 2km (1 mile) later a left turn takes you to the popular Tulbingerkogel. The return route passes through the village of Mauerbach to Hadersdorf and along the River Wien back to the centre. Avoid weekends, if possible.

3 The **Spanische Reitschule** (Spanish Riding School) is internationally famous and is housed in the centre of Vienna at the Josefsplatz. It was founded in 1572 and its name comes from the Spanish horses which were brought to Vienna in 1562. The building was erected between 1729 and 1735 by Josef Fischer von Erlach in baroque style. Morning training can normally be watched between 10am and noon, from February to June and September to mid-December. Performances have to be booked in advance.

square a passage leads to Domgasse and the house where Mozart lived from 1784 to 1787. The house is called the **Figarohaus** after his opera, which was composed here. It houses a museum dedicated to Mozart, and manuscripts, pictures and views of Vienna in his time are exhibited.

At the other end of the Domgasse a right turn into Singerstrasse, then into Weihburggasse leads to the Franziskanerplatz and its church, the **Franziskanerkirche**. The former convent was handed over to the Franciscan monks in 1589. At the beginning of the 17th century the church was rebuilt in Renaissance style and of note inside is the painting by Johann Georg Schmidt which depicts Leopold I with his wife, and a view of Vienna before the second siege by the Turks.

Following the Weihburggasse towards the Ringstrasse takes you to the **Stadtpark**, which was planned in 1860 along the lines of an English park and resembles St James's Park in London. Many monuments are dotted about the park, amongst them one of Johann Strauss, the 'king of waltzes', playing his favourite violin. Other famous composers like Schubert and Bruckner and, on the lighter side, Franz Lehar and Robert Stolz, are remembered here, as well as the Austrian

painters Ferdinand Waldmüller and Hans Makart.

Leaving the Stadtpark through the gate near the Kursalon, a coffee and dance hall, you reach the nearby Beethovenplatz, a square with a monument showing the master of music sitting on a throne. Turning past the Konzerthaus brings you to the Schwarzenbergplatz, with its Soviet monument commemorating their dead in the battle for Vienna in 1945. The Viennese call it the monument of the unknown plunderer, referring to the days of rape and plundering by the Soviet soldiers after their victory. Behind the monument stands the **Schwarzenberg Palais**, part of it now a luxury hotel, leading up to the **Unteres** (Lower) and **Oberes** (Upper) **Belvedere Palaces**, which are separated from each other by a well laid out French-style garden. Both palaces belonged to its founder, Prince Eugene of Savoy, who earned the gratitude of the Viennese and the whole of western Europe for finally defeating the Ottoman Turks after their second assault in the 17th century. He drove them right back through Hungary and the Balkans to the east.

The Upper Belvedere is considered to be one of the finest examples of Austrian baroque style at its peak and was designed by the master architect, Lucas von Hildebrandt.

From the Belvedere you can turn back on the Prinz-Eugen-Strasse towards the centre and turn left to

---

BACK TO NATURE

Southeast of the centre, on the side of the Danube, lies the nature park Lobau. It is one of the rare places near the capital still left in its original state. Small patches of water, fed by the Danube, are intermingled with trees creating a marshlike landscape. The Lobau is an ideal retreat from the bustling capital.

the **Karlskirche**, the second most favoured church in Vienna. When the plague erupted in Vienna for the seventh time, Emperor Karl VI vowed to build a church and commissioned the great Austrian architect Fischer von Erlach to design the building. After St Stephen's it has become the most important church in Vienna and also the most renowned edifice in baroque style. All countries under the Habsburg Crown were asked to contribute to the building fund and various artists were commissioned for the interior, which is maintained in a stylish combination of colours: gold, white and red-brown.

Return to Stephansplatz via the Kärntnerstrasse.

Vienna Centre, northwest

2 The square around St Stephen's Cathedral is now pedestrianised, apart from the eastern section, where a rank for the fiakers – the traditional Viennese horsedrawn carriages – has been established.

Unfortunately one of Vienna's recently created black spots can also be seen on the northern part of St Stephen's Square – a modern glass pavilion which jars with the surrounding atmosphere. Many traditionally minded Viennese dislike the new **Haas Haus** intensely, although it looks quite different when illuminated at night and much more acceptable.

The **Graben** ('ditch') leads away from St Stephen's Square. It was originally designed by the Romans

---

The Plague Tower in the Graben, one of the city's sights

to protect the settlement of *Vindobona*, as Vienna was then called. In the Middle Ages it was filled in and later became a market place. When the priests of nearby St Stephen's complained about the noise they forced the market to change its location. Together with the adjoining Kärntnerstrasse and the Kohlmarkt, the Graben constitutes the finest parade of shops in Vienna. Turning right at the northern end of the Graben and then left leads past a square called Am Hof. A museum at no 9 shows remains of the Roman camp which was situated here. Further north leads to the Freyung, another square surrounded by elegant town houses of the aristocracy.

The **Schottenkirche** on the northern end of the square is part of the **Schottenstift**, the abbey. In 1150 Heinrich II invited Irish monks to Vienna – in the Middle Ages Ireland was known here as New Scotland, hence the name Schottenstift (Abbey of the Scots). When the Irish monks left, the abbey was taken over by the order of St Benedict. Since 1807 a gymnasium (public school) has been incorporated and it is now one of the best-known schools in Vienna.

Vienna Centre, south and southwest

3 From St Stephen's Square (Stephansplatz) Vienna's main up-market shopping street, Kärntnerstrasse, leads to the **Staatsoper** (Opera House), an impressive building counted among the leading opera houses of the world. The auditorium can accommodate more than 2,200 people.

From the Opera House walk in a northerly direction on the Ringstrasse towards the imposing looking museum buildings, erected under Emperor Franz Josef I in a typically heavy neo-classical style. Facing each other, the one on the left is the **Kunsthistorisches Museum** (Museum of Art Hostory) and opposite the **Naturhistorisches Museum** (Natural History Museum). The Kunsthistorisches Museum is one of the few great museums of the world: it houses many art treasures collected by the Habsburgs and others. It is at present undergoing refurbishment. The magnificent entrance hall and staircase to the first floor have been restored to their original glory.

The Natural History Museum is concerned with the laws and wonders of nature. In the middle, between the museums, stands an imposing monument to Empress Maria Theresia, the only woman ever to rule the empire. It shows the Empress sitting on a throne, surrounded by her loyal generals. Apart from her duties as ruler, she gave birth to 16 children.

Returning to the centre you cross the Ringstrasse and enter the Heldenplatz, square of the heroes, a large open space cornered on two sides by the mighty palace of the **Neue Hofburg**. Two equestrian statues adorn the square: Archduke Karl, the victor over Napoleon in the battle of Aspern and opposite,

*There is much to marvel at in the
Kunsthistorisches Museum*

Prince Eugene of Savoy, the victor against the Turks. The main entrance to the Neue Hofburg is truly imperial. The interior now houses museums, amongst them a collection from the excavations in Ephesus in Asia Minor, a gift from the Sultan to Emperor Franz Josef I. From the Neue Hofburg a passage leads to the castle courtyard, surrounded by buildings of the **Alte Hofburg** (the old imperial castle). The yard used to be the spot where the Imperial Guard was changed. The reddish-brown **Schweizertor** (Swiss Gate) now leads to the treasury and the Imperial Chapel, where on Sunday mornings the Wiener Sängerknaben (Vienna Boys' Choir) accompanies mass. The treasury houses priceless antiques including the crown of the Holy Roman Empire, the Austrian Imperial Crown and many other insignia of royal and imperial power through the centuries. The living quarters of the last Austrian Emperors, Franz Josef I and Karl I, can also be visited in the Reichskanzlei and Amalienburg wings of the castle. They have changed little and offer a good insight into their lives. A domed passage leads from the Alte Hofburg to the Michaelerplatz, where recent excavations have revealed remains from Roman times and 19th-century cellars. The Michaeler square was created only in the last century. The Kohlmarkt, on the other side of the square, is now pedestrianised and ideal for strolling about or taking a break at the famous Demel's patisserie for a coffee and Sachertorte (Viennese chocolate cake).

Vienna Centre, west

4 A turn west from Michaelerplatz through Schauflergasse leads to the Ballhausplatz, the seat of the Austrian Chancellor. Opposite, in a wing of the Hofburg, is the office and residence of the Austrian President. The Ballhausplatz achieved notoriety when it was the scene of a *putsch* in 1934 by the Austrian Nazis under the direction of their German masters. They attacked the Austrian Chancellor, Engelbert Dollfuss, and left him to bleed to death.

The **Volksgarten** is another park in the centre of Vienna, and contains a very fine monument to Empress Elisabeth, the wife of Emperor Franz

FOR HISTORY BUFFS

3 For historical interest a visit to the **Kaisergruft** (Imperial Tomb) in the Kapuzinerkirche at the Neuer Markt is recommended. The burial place was for members of the ruling Austrian Habsburg dynasty, with one exception: the Countess Fuchs-Mollardt, the governess and tutor of Empress Maria Theresia. The church and monastery were built between 1622 and 1632 and the tomb was completed in 1633. The most elaborate sarcophagus is that of Maria Theresia and her husband, Franz I. Also notable are those of Emperor Franz Josef I and his wife Elisabeth, Maximilian of Mexico and Crown Prince Rudolf. The most recent burial was that in 1989 of the last Empress, Zita. The deposed Emperor Karl I was buried in Madeira. Altogether about 138 Habsburgs are interred in the Kaisergruft.

RECOMMENDED WALKS

6 The outskirts of Vienna offer innumerable walks, especially the Vienna Woods in the west and north of the city. A very pleasant walk starts in the village of Grinzing and leads after a right turn into the Krapfenwaldlgasse along vineyards, to a little hamlet, called the Krapfenwaldl, which also has an open-air swimming pool with panoramic views over the city. You can either turn left, back to Grinzing, or continue up to the Cobenzl, also offering superb views of the Danube and the city. From here another route leads back to Grinzing.

FOR CHILDREN

The Prater was first mentioned in 1162 and the name is of Spanish origin, (*prado* means meadow). During the Middle Ages it was a hunting ground for the aristocracy and closed to the public. Emperor Josef II declared it open to everybody and it has since become an area of festivities and enjoyment. The old buildings were totally destroyed when Vienna was occupied by the Soviet army, but new ones have sprung up and the Riesenrad, the Giant Wheel, turns around like before. The fun fair, the Wurstelprater, offers many rides and entertainments. A special treat for children and adults is a ride on the Liliputbahn, a narrow-gauge line running right through the Prater landscape and the amusement area.

All the fun of the fair at the Prater, Vienna's major amusement park

Josef I, who was assassinated at Lake Geneva. The monument is in a remote corner of the park, away from crowds, and exudes the noble image of this beautiful and unhappy Empress. Through the Volksgarten park towards the Ringstrasse you can see the **Parlament** (Houses of Parliament), built in neo-classical Greek style, adjoined on the right by the **Rathauspark**. This is flanked on one side by the **Burgtheater,** one of the foremost classical theatres in the German-speaking world. On the other side stands the **Rathaus**, the town hall, an imposing neo-Gothic building.

The **Universität** (Vienna University) comes next as you walk along the Ringstrasse in a northerly direction. It was built in the latter half of the 19th century in neo-classical 'Ringstrasse style', a name given to the many buildings which were erected after Franz Josef gave the order to raze the town wall. Next to the university, standing on its own square, is the **Votivkirche**, a church in neo-Gothic style erected in the reign of Emperor Franz Josef in memory of a failed assassination attempt.

Vienna Centre, north

5The Rotenturmstrasse leads north from St Stephen's Square; take a left turning to a historically interesting square, the Hoher Markt. The Bauernmarkt, a narrow road, has been bridged by an intricate lifesize clock, the **Ankeruhr**. It was erected in 1911 by the painter and sculptor Franz Von Matsch in art-nouveau style. At noon, all the figures on the

clock parade to music appropriate to the period they represent. A plaque on the house next to the bridge provides further information. On the other side of the square is a museum displaying finds from the Roman ruins of *Vindobona*, revealed during building operations.

A short walk towards the Danube canal leads to the **Ruprechtskirche**, a Romanesque-style church and the oldest in Vienna. A walk along the Salzgries leads to another interesting church, **Maria am Gestade**, which has a unique top to its spire. Turning towards Wipplingerstrasse you come to no 8, the **Altes Rathaus**. In 1309, after the assassination of Emperor Albrecht I, a plot by influential Viennese against the new Habsburg rulers was discovered. The house of one of the rebels, Otto Heino, was given to the council of Vienna by Duke Friedrich in 1316. The town hall fulfilled its function until 1885, and has a façade decorated in baroque style, which was added in 1699.

Turning south through the Tuchlauben you come to the **Peterskirche**, which was started in 1702 by Gabriel Montani. It was completed in 1733 and displays elaborate baroque ornaments inside.

Return to St Stephen's Square via the Graben.

Vienna and the Wiener Wald (Vienna Woods)

6A tour of Vienna would not be complete without a drive through its outskirts and the famous Vienna Woods (51km/32 miles – see chart at end of tour). Driving north along the Danube the road leads to Klosterneuburg-Weidling and on a left turn you reach the Höhenstrasse. A few bends lead up to the Leopoldsberg, the last but one elevation of the Alps before the Danube cuts through the foothills of the mountains and leaves the Bisamberg on the other side of the river to mark the Alps' last peak.

From the Leopoldsberg there are fine views over the city and the River Danube. The road then continues to the neighbouring hill, the Kahlenberg, the best known of all the hills surrounding Vienna and a popular spot with the Viennese. At the beginning of the century a cogwheel railway from Grinzing linked the town with one its favourite peaks, but with the arrival of the motor car the railway had outlived its usefulness. Part of the tracks can still be seen amongst the vineyards.

From Kahlenberg the drive continues gently up and down to the Cobenzl, another popular spot with a good view of Vienna lying beneath. The Höhenstrasse continues towards the city borders and the Rohrerwiese, a well-known destination of the many Viennese who indulge in their Sunday passion, an excursion into the Wiener Wald, followed by a walk and usually ending with some refreshments at one of the many tantalising Heurigen. The Höhenstrasse now changes direction from the Rohrerwiese and leads southwest towards the valley of the Wien river at Hütteldorf. Turn right and proceed west, then turn left to the Auhof car

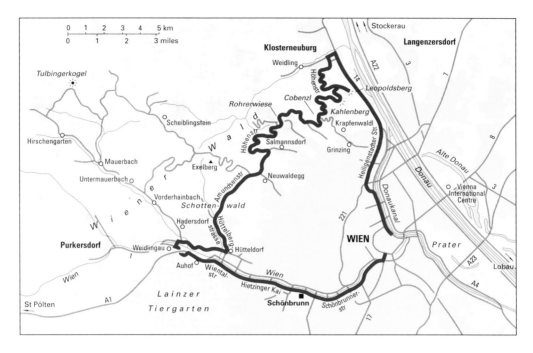

park. This is a good starting point for a walk through the **Lainzer Tiergarten**, a nature park originally laid out for the imperial summer residence of Schönbrunn, which is not far away.

Before returning to the city a visit to **Schloss Schönbrunn** is one of Vienna's great attractions and should not be missed. The forerunner of the present palace was a hunting lodge, established by Maximilian II in 1559. He also planned the Lainzer Tiergarten. In 1619 he discovered a well, which gave its name to the palace and supplied its water until the late 18th century. Fires during the Turkish siege of 1683 destroyed the buildings and the task of rebuilding was given to Fischer von Erlach. The exte-

rior is breathtaking, but Schönbrunn must also be seen from the inside to appreciate the magnificent rooms of the castle. Outside, strolls through the geometrically laid-out paths provide plenty of distractions, such as an obelisk, fountains, a Roman ruin, the Gloriette, the Palmenhaus (conservatory) and many others.

Return to the centre driving east along the Wien river.

Wien – Klosterneuburg 11 (7)
Klosterneuburg – Leopoldsburg 5 (3)
Leopoldsburg – Kahlenberg 2 (1)
Kahlenberg – Cobenzl 4 (2½)
Cobenzl – Rohrerweise 3 (2)
Rohrerweise – Hütteldorf 11 (7)
Hütteldorf – Auhof 4 (2½)
Auhof – Schloss Schönbrunn 6 (4)
Schloss Schönbrunn – Wien 5 (3)

Schloss Schönbrunn

INDEX

ACKNOWLEDGEMENTS

The Automobile Association would like to thank the following photographers, libraries and associations for their assistance in the preparation of this book.

J ALLAN CASH PHOTOLIBRARY 43, 86/7, 95a, 109a
AUSTRIAN NATIONAL TOURIST OFFICE 14, 15, 16/17, 18, 19, 22, 63a, 63b, 83, 85a, 85b, 87b, 88, 92, 93a, 93b, 94, 95b, 96/7, 98, 99b, 101, 102, 103, 104, 105, 106, 111
KÄRNTNER TOURISMUS GESELLSCHAFT m.b.H 46
ADI KRAUS 31, 32a, 51
MATREI IN OSTTIROL 26
NATURE PHOTOGRAPHERS LTD 110 (W S Paton)
SPECTRUM COLOUR LIBRARY 7, 25, 42, 56, 69, 72b, 89
ZEFA PICTURES LTD cover, 4/5
The remaining photographs are held in the Automobile Association's own library (AA PHOTO LIBRARY) and were taken by Adrian Baker with the exception of pages 10b, 13b, 82 and 84 which were taken by Martin Adelman; pages 3, 4, 9, 38/9, 70/1, 72a, 81 and 113 taken by Peter Baker, pages 2, 90/1, 109b, 114 and 115 taken by David Noble and pages 116 and 117 taken by Michael Siebert.

The author would also like to thank Dr Kurt Broer, Austrian National Tourist Office, Vienna; Dr Evelyn Miksch, Vienna Tourist Board; Horst A Dürnsteiner, ÖAMTC, Touristik, Vienna; Georg Bachleitner, Tourismus Mühlviertel, Linz; Heinrich Kastner, Hotel Kärntnerhof, Vienna; Heiner Kolbe, Salzburg Board for Tourism; Sylvia Frenes, Tirol Werbung, Innsbruck and the Austrian National Tourist Office in London.

Copy editor: Dilys Jones